Stolen Time

Stolen Time

Black Fad Performance and the Calypso Craze

SHANE VOGEL

The University of Chicago Press
Chicago and London

The University of Chicago Press, Chicago 60637
The University of Chicago Press, Ltd., London

Published 2018
Printed in the United States of America

27 26 25 24 23 22 21 20 19 18   1 2 3 4 5

ISBN-13: 978-0-226-56830-0 (cloth)
ISBN-13: 978-0-226-56844-7 (paper)
ISBN-13: 978-0-226-56858-4 (e-book)
DOI: https://doi.org/10.7208/chicago/9780226568584.001.0001

Library of Congress Control Number: 2018936918

♾ This paper meets the requirements of ANSI/NISO Z39.48-1992 (Permanence of Paper).

for Scott

CONTENTS

ACKNOWLEDGMENTS

This book began from an attempt to make sense of the incongruous performance of Lena Horne in a midcentury middlebrow calypso musical as the island girl Savannah, the only stage role in her long and storied career. What was this icon of the civil rights movement, pioneer in black musical performance, and quintessence of elegance and sophistication doing in this kitschy piece of Broadway Caribbeana? The answers to this question brought up still deeper questions about race and mass culture that led me to performance traditions across the West Indies and North America, from the early nineteenth century through the twentieth, and over interrelated forms such as sound recordings, nightclub acts, film, television, literature, modern dance, and musical theater. Eventually I discerned the outlines of historical, formal, and philosophical conditions that made Horne's star turn at once a singular instance of creative integrity and representative of an entire stance toward performance in the Jim Crow era.

In pursuing those questions, this project received generous support from a National Endowment for the Humanities Fellowship, an American Council of Learned Societies Fellowship, and a New Frontiers in Creativity and Scholarship Grant from Indiana University. Also at IU, the Department of English, the Office of the Vice Provost for Research, and the Institute for Advanced Study all provided valuable assistance and encouragement. I wish to thank the guidance of research librarians at a number of archives, including the Schomburg Center for Research in Black Culture; the Billy Rose Theater Division and Jerome Robbins Dance Division at the New York Public Library for the Performing Arts; Yale University's Collection of Historical Sound Recordings; Columbia University's Center for Oral History Archives; the E. Y. Harburg Foundation; the Dance Theatre of Harlem; the Paley Center for Media; University of Southern California's Hugh M. Hefner Moving

Image Archive; the Archives Center at the National Museum of American History, Smithsonian Institution; and Indiana University's Archives of Traditional Music. I am particularly grateful to Ernie Harburg and Anthony Saidy for their assistance with archival materials and their permission to reproduce material related to *Jamaica* as well as Nick Markovich of the Harburg Foundation. All of the songs and most of the performances I describe in this book are available in various forms online and through music streaming services, and I hope that interested readers will seek them out.

Early portions of this book appeared in *Theatre Journal*, *Social Text*, and *The Cine-Files: A Scholarly Journal of Cinema Studies*. Although that material has been substantially revised, I am thankful to those journals for supporting this work. I benefited enormously from generous invitations to present parts of this research at various places, including New York University, Yale, Princeton, Washington University at Saint Louis, Northwestern, Cornell, DePaul, Stanford, Duke, and the University of Texas at Austin. I am indebted to those students and faculty for their comments.

This book was written primarily at Indiana University, and I offer my deepest gratitude to all of my colleagues there, especially the most recent English Department chairpersons, Patty Ingham and Paul Gutjahr, and friends Alberto Varon, Rae Greiner, Adrian Matejka, Steve Watt, Linda Charnes, and especially Judith Brown. With large amounts of patience and humor, Lisa LaPlante and Kate Elliott helped me to navigate grant applications, research leaves, licensing rights, and countless other institutional tasks. It has been a privilege to work again with Doug Mitchell, and I am grateful to him for keeping the beat as I imagined this project from first words to final manuscript. He is the finest of editors. Thank you also to Kyle Wagner and the entire production team at the University of Chicago Press, including Joel Score, Dawn Hall, Isaac Tobin, Levi Stahl, and Marilyn Bliss.

It was a deep honor to spend time discussing the calypso craze and black modern dance with Carmen de Lavallade. Throughout her life, she has been a fierce ambassador for beauty and the arts, and I can only hope that some trace of her grace and determination made its way into these pages. I offer my gratitude as well to her archivist, Lana Turner. Both of them welcomed me into worlds of memory and movement that changed the course of this research.

With characteristic foresight, Daphne Brooks provided both big-picture wisdom and discerning insight into archival details that pushed my thinking beyond itself. She is an inspiring reminder that, when done right, performance history and performance theory are the same thing. Soyica Colbert offered thoughtful feedback on the manuscript that helped me to see anew the performances and history I write about. It is my good fortune to have had the enduring support and seemingly infinite generosity of Joseph Roach, George Hutchinson, and Fred Moten; they have enriched this book, and me, in ways both big and small. Denise Cruz and Kevin Walter both helped me to say better the things I wanted to say here (and elsewhere). Josh Chambers-Letson has been a good friend over the course of this writing. Important encouragement at several key moments came from Sean Metzger, whose vote of confidence counts for a lot. This book is part of an ongoing conversation with Alexandra Vazquez that takes place on the phone, over dinner, on the page, and in my head. Defying physics, she somehow created additional hours in the day in order to read all these words, press me to go further, send me more music, show me the secrets of four-hand playing, and make everything smarter: I am deeply thankful to her. I continue to reach toward the example of my teacher and friend José Muñoz. I am beyond grateful to have had so many smart people offer their thoughts on this book. Any missteps are my own.

Finally, I thank those who have provided me with the holding environment that made the writing of this book possible in the first place: John, Tara, Jason, Kevin; my mom (a hero) and dad; my sisters, Erin and Meghan; and my stepfather Jack. Scott Herring read everything, read it again, and listened to a lot of calypso music—and that really is the least of it. I thank him for having the right questions, the right answers, the right words, and the right stuff.

INTRODUCTION

This and That, or, Swiped Calypsos

The calypso craze begins with a disavowal. In 1956, Harry Belafonte's *Calypso* became the first LP album to sell over a million copies. Almost overnight, calypso became the top-selling music in North America—for a brief time it even threatened to supplant rock and roll, according to *Variety*, *Billboard*, and other trade magazines that tracked its popularity. For a few fleeting months, middle-class US consumers helped turn the novelty of calypso into a mass-culture fad. This national sensation presented a spectacle of midcentury popular Caribbeana, standardized a world region, and transformed Trinidadian folk culture into a commodity. Suddenly calypso was everywhere, and black performers took up the opportunities of the fad with wit, energy, and a weary familiarity. The entertainment world quickly crowned Belafonte the King of Calypso. The second-generation Jamaican American singer, however, renounced the emergent calypso craze and his role in it.[1] Calling the fad a "synthetic" creation, he exasperatedly pointed out that "two of my big records right now are not even calypso even though that's what they are called."[2] The eleven songs on his album represented a range of Caribbean folk music, including traditional ballads and work songs, only two of which were proper calypsos. Objecting to the popular conflation of all types of Caribbean and Latin American music under the label calypso, he warned that "opportunists will cheapen the true calypso form and degenerate the level of Calypso entertainment." With foresight, he predicted the calypso cascade that would wash over postwar middlebrow entertainments including sound recordings, nightclub acts, television broadcasts, Broadway musicals, and films. Belafonte condemned the "imitators and the 'bandwagon' element" that would debase the "real beauty and meaning of the music" and turn calypso in the United States into "a caricature of itself." Declaring, "I want no part of the Calypso craze,"

Figure 1. Harry Belafonte recording *Calypso,* 1955. Photo by Metronome. Getty Images.

he vowed that he would "never sing the phony, cliché Calypso material that is already flooding the market. I won't do it, just as I won't become a banner-bearer for those who are looking to make a killing from the current spiraling craze for this special brand of West Indian music."[3] In response, the press grudgingly rechristened him the Reluctant King of Calypso and continued their coverage unabated.[4]

Like every disavowal, Belafonte's contains within it an avowal. In contrast to this synthetic, mass-culture calypso, Belafonte described what he called true calypso (or *kaiso,* the word used in the Caribbean to distinguish traditional calypso from its commercial variants). "True Calypso," he wrote, "is a living newspaper, with verses telling of events, past and present, that are unique to the Islands . . . it is informative, has a free-swinging style and comments critically upon current events."[5] Belafonte glosses the historical origins of calypso as a largely improvised, topical song that voiced an underclass commentary on local events and issued a surreptitious critique of poverty and colonial rule couched in boasts, sarcasm, and biting wit. If, as Belafonte suggested, calypso is a living newspaper, it is the front page, the editorial page, the sports page, and the gossip column all at once—a pointed take on recent events (from the local to the international) delivered in a context steeped in competition, often commenting on the social mores, sexual landscape, and everyday life of the barrack-yard milieu from which it arose. Above all, calypsonians wrote and performed their own songs, as distinct from mere calypso singers, usually those abroad who sang others' songs.

Calypso's origins in the carnival milieu of Trinidad date back to the nineteenth century. It has traces in plantation *Canboulay* festivals, a harvest ritual in which indentured laborers burned sugarcane, beat drums, and danced (the name is a creolized form of the French *cannes brûlées*: burned cane). Canboulay practices—including *kalinda*, or ritualized stick fighting and its accompanying song, *tamboo bamboo*, or the percussive pounding of bamboo tubes on the ground, *flambeaux*, or the illumination of burning torches, and *mas*, or acts of masquerade—were quickly adapted to European carnival festivities and shaped the development of a distinctly New World carnival. By the early twentieth century, calypso music emerged as carnival songs developed first in street parades (also known as *lavway*) and then in seasonal tent shows. The secular lyric- and melody-based creole music borrowed from French, West African, Spanish, and English influences and expressed the point of view of Trinidad's lower orders. This music made inroads into US recording studios as early as the 1910s, and the end of the US occupation of Trinidad after World War II brought a mini-boom of interest in the sounds and styles of calypso across North America. It was Belafonte's *Calypso*, however, that tipped the interest into a brief but intense mass-culture fad in 1956.

To paraphrase Belafonte: *this* is not *that*. His disavowal reverberated through the calypso craze as performers across North America, England, and the Caribbean repeatedly pointed out the inauthenticity of the culture industry's commercialized calypso. As Michael Eldridge, one of the few scholars to write about the calypso craze *as* a craze, puts it, "the paramount thing was the mere act of *making* the distinction. Declaring one's quasi-ethnographic knowledge of 'the real thing,' asserting one's power to discriminate between the genuine and the phony, clucking your tongue over slick American louts perverting pristine folk traditions—this was finally a way of establishing and defining imperial claims of knowing."[6] *This* is not *that*, in other words, functions as a gesture of imperial distinction in the idiom of cultural taste. Yet even while the calypso craze was an act of cultural imperialism, it was also an opportunity for black performers to expand diasporic culture within and against such imperial claims of knowing. Even as many disavowed the calypso craze in favor of "true calypso," as Belafonte did, many other performers fully and shamelessly embraced the calypso craze's inauthenticity and falseness. *Stolen Time* follows the calypso craze as it moved defiantly away from any attempt at authenticity and instead strategically embraced the inauthenticity of calypso kitsch in mood and style. These performers' avowal of inauthenticity expressed a positive and productive relationship to the calypso craze that destabilized authentic/inauthentic binaries and unsettled the epistemological grounds of colonialism and Jim Crow. In doing so, these performances demonstrate how mass culture could unmake and remake diaspora.

This rhetorical gesture—*this* is not *that*—sums up the structuring principle of what I describe in this book as black fad performance, a particular temporal formation of race and entertainment that recurred throughout the Jim Crow–era United States. Black fad performance emerged through cycles of critical intensity in the production and consumption of blackness in US popular culture. It depended on the material conditions governing black entertainment and racialized spectatorship between 1895 and 1965 and was shaped by transformations in technological reproduction such as sheet music publishing, radio and sound recording, and film and television. Marketed largely to white audiences, mass-culture black fads such as the ragtime craze of the 1890s, the Negro vogue of the 1920s, and the calypso craze of the 1950s all produced compromised conditions of representation and cultural expression. The play between disavowal and avowal was one way that black performers modified their stance toward a fad culture that provided both opportunity and constraint. In embracing and acknowledging the inauthentic, such performances modified inauthenticity itself and allowed for the possibility of an authenticity through inauthenticity. Disclosed in and as performance, this authenticity momentarily shimmers through the vulgar time and idle chatter of mass media and the anxiety of US racial antagonisms.[7] The precarious epistemological and ontological conditions of being a fad, explored in detail in chapter 1 and then throughout this book, enabled black performers in the United States to exploit the distance between the ethnographic and the faddish in order to refigure relations between African America and the Afro-Caribbean, using artifice and performance to challenge fixed notions of blackness within the certain finitude of fad performance.

Thus we should understand the calypso craze not primarily as a musical fad or a recording phenomenon but within a larger field of performance that includes music, theater, dance, film, and television as well as the everyday and everynight practices of the fad's millions of participants. Accounting for these understudied aspects of the calypso craze presents a more complex and contradictory understanding of this cultural phenomenon. Rather than dismiss these performances as acts of imperial appropriation or look "behind the mask" to the authentic identity underneath, *Stolen Time* stays on their surface and asks what kinds of black entanglements were invented, critiqued, and imagined through the inauthentic. Although the calypso craze trafficked in stereotypes and cultural distortions, black performers repeatedly and intentionally revealed the inauthenticity of those stereotypes. Remaining within Belafonte's zone of disavowal, *this* becomes more complex and *that* becomes less stable than it seemed. The very function of *this* turns out to question the grounds on which we might make imperial claims of knowingness about *that* in the first place. The calypso craze's avowed failure to be authentic provides insight into the constitutive failures of authenticity as such.

In this sense, Belafonte's disavowal is not simply descriptive or demonstrative; it is performative. *This is not that* is a speech act that not only gestures toward its referents but also produces them as authentic and inauthentic in the moment of its utterance. Return, for example, to Belafonte's turn away from the calypso craze and toward "true calypso." The philosopher J. L. Austin helps to explain the performativity of Belafonte's distinction in his account of the special status of the word *real*, which he places in a unique class of words that includes *proper*, *genuine*, *live*, *true*, *authentic*, and *natural*, as well as *fake*, *artificial*, *makeshift*, and *synthetic*.[8] Unlike other words, for example *blue* or *pig*, words such as *real* and its kin do not have shared criteria that would define their meaning, nor do they have multiple meanings that might lead to ambiguity; rather, they only take on meaning in the specific context of their use. Austin describes the conditions for determining what is meant when something is described as *real*:

> There are no criteria to be laid down *in general* for distinguishing the real from the not real. How this is to be done must depend on *what* it is with respect to which the problem arises in particular cases. Furthermore, even for particular kinds of things, there may be many different ways in which the distinction may be made (there is not just *one* way of being "not a real pig")—this depends on the number and variety of the surprises and dilemmas nature and our fellow men may spring on us, and on the surprises and dilemmas we have been faced with hitherto. And of course, if there is *never* any dilemma or surprise, the question simply doesn't come up; if we had simply never had occasion to distinguish anything as being in any way like

> a pig but not a *real* pig, then the words "real pig" themselves would have no application.[9]

In other words, we cannot know in advance whether something is real or authentic or true until something appears alongside it and presents some sort of dilemma or surprise to its identity. And as he points out, if this never happens, there is never any reason to distinguish something as real in the first place. For Austin, *real* is not an intrinsic quality or characteristic of something, and there is no pregiven set of rules or criteria by which to determine whether something is real. The meaning of *real* only appears in its use and within the particular context in which the word is uttered or written. The not-real casts the real into relief and makes it real in the first place. Further, one cannot anticipate all of the ways that something might pose a surprise or dilemma to another object's identity; such instances are only as limited as the imagination of man and nature (though they are also shaped by prior instances "we have been faced with hitherto," that is, history). We cannot know if something is real "unless I know *just* what, on that particular occasion, the speaker has it in mind to exclude."[10] Belafonte's "true calypso" in this sense becomes legible and audible only when it is necessary to determine what it is not. The real is an a posteriori solution rather than an a priori given.

This is more than simple relativism, as black fad performers well knew. In avowing its inauthenticity, black fad performance continually highlights what Austin calls "the function of 'real,'" which is "not to contribute positively to the characterization of anything, but to exclude possible ways of being *not* real."[11] Paradoxically, *real* is not a positive sentiment but one that works by exclusion and negation. It is the not-real that bears positive force. The impostor creates its original, and then the original disavows it. In one sense, the existence of the not-real helps to secure the real, at least momentarily. But at the same time, the very surprise or dilemma posed by the not-real causes problems for the identity of the real that did not previously exist and leaves it even less secure than it previously was (one account in *Dance Magazine*, for example, promised readers the "real, real calypso").[12] And even when the real is shored up, its authorities can never rest easy. "The criteria we employ at a given time can't be taken as *final*, not liable to change," Austin concludes, since we never know what new surprises or dilemmas may arise.[13] In imagining new ways to be not-real, the performances I discuss in this book all question the grounding identity of the authentic. When the fad ends, such inauthentic images and sounds become trapped in the amber of their historical moment—a fossil record of that now-preposterous time when everybody was into *that*. But during the unstable and uncertain time of being in the fad, the play between the real and the not-real takes on a number of improvisatory forms. Calypso craze performers took advantage of the nongeneral criteria of the utterance *real* to surprise and to present a dilemma, toggling between such oppositional habits of thought as inauthenticity/authenticity, false/true, improper/proper, ungenuine/genuine, and insincerity/sincerity, and refusing them any certain closure.

Although it contains many new insights, interpretations, and details about the calypso craze, *Stolen Time* does not aim to provide an exhaustive survey of the fad. There are at least two excellent accounts that offer broad appraisals of this cultural phenomenon: Donald Hill's landmark *Calypso Callaloo* (1993), which dedicates extended discussion to the craze within its longer history of Trinidadian calypso, and Ray Funk and Michael Eldridge's *Calypso Craze* (2014), a beautifully illustrated volume that accompanies their CD/DVD box set of performances from the fad.[14] These books join a host of cultural histories and ethnomusicological studies of calypso in Trinidad and in the diaspora; of carnival's musical, kinesthetic, and political practices; and of Caribbean popular performance.[15] Building on these works, I look at specific instances of the calypso craze that illuminate the shape of black fad performance in the United States across a range of overlapping media: nightclub acts and sound recordings (chapter 1), film (chapter 2), television (chapter 3), musical theater (chapter 4), and dance (chapter 5). Rather than a sociological approach that details where and how the calypso craze was consumed, I look instead at the creative and unexpected ways that black performers themselves used the conditions of fad culture to (dis)engage with the entertainment industry, trip the performance circuit between the United States and the Caribbean, and shape the history of performance in the United States and its relationship to the black diaspora. Each chapter takes up performances that productively pose surprises or dilemmas to "true calypso." Collectively, these examples delineate the contours of black fad performance in the Jim Crow era and explicate specific aesthetic conditions and strategies—stolen time (chapter 1), critical solipsism and no-fi aesthetics (chapter 2), radical counterprogramming (chapter 3), mock transnational performance (chapter 4), and the phantom gestures and temporal elsewhen evoked through dance (chapter 5)—that create a positive, inventive black culture through a performative stance that modified its relationship to the inauthentic, hokum, and the fake.

The relationship of the calypso craze to diaspora is, needless to say, complex and contradictory. The craze was a largely North American–based middlebrow, mass-culture event that featured American-born black performers imitating Afro-Caribbean sounds and gestures across the color line. The fad for calypso in the United States was related to but distinct from a similar popularity of calypso in England and a repoliticization of it in Trinidad that occurred at the same time. In England, West Indian migration from the British colonies to the metropole following World War II sparked a parallel interest in calypso. The migration heralded by the passage of the postwar troopship *Empire Windrush* that carried hundreds of Afro-Caribbean migrants to England in 1948 (including calypsonians Lord Kitchener and Lord Beginner) transformed the demographics of London, Tilbury, and other cities.[16] Calypso provided a shared cultural resource for newly formed migrant communities and a crucial link to a home culture and sensibility in a new country. While calypso briefly surged in London in the second half of the 1950s—appearing in nightclubs and on televised variety shows—it developed along different if related periodizations, different patterns of production and consumption, and different histories of colonization and immigration than it did in the United States, where the craze was largely advanced by second- and third-generation Afro-Caribbeans and African Americans who had little national affiliation with the Caribbean.

In midcentury Trinidad, calypso was not only a carnival music but also a form of underclass worldmaking, political critique, and, increasingly, an instrument of decolonization. Calypsonians, Gordon Rohlehr remarks, "had from the turn of the century monitored the movement of the islands away from nominated and towards representative government" through independence in 1962 and the subsequent project of nation making.[17] The performances of calypsonian Mighty Sparrow and the choreography of dancer Beryl McBurnie (discussed in more detail in chapter 5), in particular, built on the African influences of Trinidad's popular culture. Their performances played key roles in the cultural campaign for decolonization following the 1956 election of Eric Williams, the historian and first prime minister of Trinidad and Tobago, and his People's National Movement Party. As C. L. R. James observed during this period, "we are Western, yet have to separate what is ours from what is Western, a very difficult task. Sparrow in the popular sphere is doing that with a dedication, even an obstinacy which is very exciting to see. He found a medium already established. But he is making it a genuinely national expression and possession."[18] Other artists and intellectuals including Edward Kamau Brathwaite, Gordon Rohlehr, Derek Walcott, and Errol Hill similarly invest calypso with deep significance to the decolonizing project of cultural nationalism.[19]

This is not *that*. Rather than a direct cultural retention that arrived in the sounds and movements of Trinidadian migrants or an instrument of anticolonial nationalism, the calypso craze was largely a mass-culture distortion of these traditions, a hiccup in this historical inheritance that was shaped more directly by the traditions of commercial black entertainment in the United States. As such, the calypso craze was not only produced by histories of Jim Crow performance and spectatorship but also by the colonizing clutch of US popular culture. As Stephanie Leigh Batiste shows in her history of black performance in the 1930s, African American performers were all too often willing participants in imperial representational projects that perpetuated tropes such as exoticism, primitivism, expansionism, and militarism. Black performers in the United States took up such poisonous depictions, she writes, "in an imperial manner to establish national belonging, alterity, and representational power," but at the same time they also staked out "a position from which international coalitions of disidentification and dissent could be imagined and forged."[20] This contradiction is part of the paradox of diaspora itself, what Nadia Ellis calls the "quest for affinity and the desire to separate [that] is often marked by frustration," or what Brent Hayes Edwards theorizes as the kernel of diasporic discrepancy, "that which cannot be transferred or exchanged, the received biases that refuse to pass over when one crosses the water."[21] The not-real status of the calypso craze—its "*failed* affinity" (Ellis) and "points of misunderstanding, bad faith, unhappy translation" (Edwards)—was its positive condition for the making of black culture and, in marking the mistranslations and misrecognitions of Trinidadian calypso, was a productive engagement with the ontological conditions of diaspora itself.[22]

Swiped Calypsos and Stolen Time

In the calypso craze performances of African American and second-generation Caribbean American artists, a complex politics of entanglement and appropriation surfaces. The calypso craze from this perspective was not a white minstrel escape into blackness or a tourist production of a languid tropic, but a (black) reaching across black difference. Thus while white calypso craze performers such as the Andrews Sisters or the Kingston Trio were complicit with a kind of imperialist theft of Trinidadian culture, the black calypso craze performers I write about enacted a theft of the US culture industry; they appropriated not Caribbean culture but the fad itself and in doing so mocked American epistemologies of racial authenticity. Rather than racial appropriation, the calypso craze offers blackness as change and exchange. It is a copy that displaces the very question of the original. *This* is not *that*.

Langston Hughes, who knew a thing or two about vogues and fads, diagnosed this situation with precision. Writing in 1955, Hughes noticed the growing number of white singers who were copyrighting and recording calypso music, often without crediting their original source. Among others, he had in mind the infamous lawsuit ten years earlier over the provenance of "Rum and Coca-Cola."[23] This calypso voiced a critique of the US occupation of Trinidad and of the local women who sought the sexual attention of US soldiers. In 1944, the Andrews Sisters recorded this song for Decca Records and, despite a radio ban on morality grounds, it emerged as the best-selling single of 1945; sales of the sheet music alone (by then a fading industry) exceeded 300,000 copies. The calypsonian Lord Invader had composed "Rum and Coca-Cola" for carnival competitions the previous year and sang it in calypso tents across Port of Spain, where US comedian Morey Amsterdam heard it while performing for soldiers on a USO tour. On his return to the United States, Amsterdam registered the song with the US Copyright Office. When Lord Invader heard of its success, he traveled to the United States and sued Amsterdam and Decca Records for copyright infringement (according to one account, "after he heard the Andrews Sisters' recording he remarked caustically, 'We don't speak like that'").[24] Composer and impresario Lionel Belasco joined with a second lawsuit claiming property rights over the music. With the same tone that Hughes would later sound, the *Baltimore Afro-American* placed Invader within a genealogy of black fad performance, wryly noting that he would "find himself in the same boat in which W. C. Handy, the late Will M. Cook and other colored composers, who on awakening, found that somebody else had eloped with their brainchild."[25] The attorney for Decca Records argued that as folklore, calypso was not copyrightable, but the judge was unconvinced.[26] After the two-day trial, Invader won his case; the following year, Belasco won his as well.

But by the mid-1950s, it was no longer clear who was stealing what from whom. Hughes observed that, as in previous eras, there was an interesting reaction to such theft. "Curiously enough," he writes, "some Negro singers are now turning around and imitating white singers who are imitating them. Just as Negro actors and singers did back in the minstrel days before 1900, today some young colored performers are copying the styles of white performers who have copied older colored performers."[27] Such "swiped calypsos," as he called them, twisted claims of ownership and possession in unexpected ways. The precedent of the Lord Invader and Lionel Belasco verdicts was rendered carnivalesque by a calypso craze that turned the question of origins on its head. A decade after Invader and Belasco won their lawsuits, for example, *Variety* reported that "one [music] publisher visited the Bahamas and picked up a flock of 'authentic' calypso tunes for possible publication here. He called in a professional writer to dress them up. The latter discovered that one of the 'authentic' numbers was a note-for-note copy of a calypso tune he had copyrighted several years back."[28] This is one example of a more general aspect of black fad performance that I call stolen time or time stolen (back). Following Hughes's lead, I trace in chapter 1 the deep history of black performers copying the styles of white performers copying the styles of black performers through cycles of black fad performance in the Jim Crow era, and throughout subsequent chapters I show how this practice allowed black performers to shape the narrative of musical time and change the pace of the musical line as they moved through fad culture. Hughes's characterization of swiped calypsos can be understood as a mass-cultural dimension of what Edward Kamau Brathwaite calls the interculturation that occurs in contexts of exploitation and colonization, specifically the "subtle action whereby both cultures—the dominant and the subdominant—set up a symbiotic relationship with each other; so that conquerors are conquered and the colonized colonize."[29] It is in such a gesture that we can find traces of Trinidadian calypso's decolonizing impulse, transformed and reimagined, in the context of the North American calypso craze.

Yet despite these circular impersonations and avowals of inauthenticity, the calypso craze was not and could never be fully self-contained or closed off from Trinidadian calypso. As Belafonte's disavowal makes clear, *this* and *that* are deeply entangled and give meaning to each other. Indeed, as Nadia Ellis suggests, diaspora itself often takes the form of a disavowal, "the coming together of people mutually claiming to have no relation to each other. It is, therefore, the claim of separateness that constitutes the connection."[30] Such a connection-in-separation also characterizes the psychoanalytic concept of disavowal, which marks the splitting of the ego in order to allow for two contradictory experiences simultaneously. The psychoanalytic disavowal is a creative mode of defense that works as a compromise formation. Distinct from repression, which removes an unpleasant thought from consciousness altogether, the disavowal allows two contradictory attitudes to sit side by side in a kind of oscillation (in Freud's words).[31] I turn briefly to psychoanalytic theory here not for a diagnostic explanation of any individual psychic disavowal but for the nuanced vocabulary it offers, with some modification, for understanding the structure of black fad performance's cultural disavowal in the context of the black diaspora. What I find useful in the psychoanalytic formulation is, first, that the disavowal is a *process* that retains an idea even as it rejects it. For our purposes, even though it is a rejection of the calypso craze, Belafonte's disavowal still locates the fad in close, oscillating relation to the Trinidadian tradition, a toggling between the two that connects them in their separation. Second, even as the disavowal denies an idea, its affect or feeling persists. That is, even if Belafonte disavows the idea of the calypso craze and its identity with a true calypso, there is still space to accommodate the affect or feeling of calypso that the calypso craze produces. Without needing to resolve Belafonte's disavowal, or argue whether it is right or wrong, or under which conditions it makes sense, the disavowal holds open space to think of calypso's affect—calypso as feeling—without having to make recourse to a definition of calypso that requires positive and verifiable criteria.[32]

In place of such a definition of "true calypso"—cultural, musicological, historical, legal, or whatever—I understand calypso in this book as affect and ethos: a hermeneutic, an aesthetic, and a mode of being that finds its exemplary expression in song. This calypso ethos is characterized by a (dis)stance toward propriety and the proper; a politics of indirection and masquerade; the embrace of a certain looseness of syntax and grammar (a calypsonian "un-gra-ma-ti-calee-tee"[33]) and the sound of what Brathwaite calls nation language;[34] a ritualized form of conflict and its aesthetic resolution (with traces in the stick fighting of *kalinda* and the word duels of *picong*); gossip as history, history as gossip/rumor as truth, truth as rumor;[35] a melodious extemporaneity; a barrack-yard philosophizing; and a carnivalesque vision of a New World order. This calypso ethos is always-already a multiple rather than a single tradition. Its unfixed meaning and creole transformations are exemplified in the contested origins of the very word *calypso*. Some scholars trace the name back to an African derivation from the Hausa word *kai-so*, an exclamation similar in meaning to "bravo"; others to the transformations of the French adjective *carrouseaux* (having to do with festivity and celebration), to the creole spellings *carisseaux* and *calisseaux*, and finally to the shortened *caiso*, *cayiso*, or *calypso*; and still others to the Spanish-Venezuelan *caliso*, a topical popular song, or the indigenous Carib word *carieto*, or "joyous song."[36] Like the ethos it names, "the derivation of the word Calypso must," according to midcentury Trinidadian writers Charles Espinet and Harry Pitts, "always remain a matter for conjecture and theorizing."[37]

This calypso ethos serves different communities at different times and places, and its anticolonial impulse emerges under different names and sounds as it moves throughout the New World: kaiso, sans humanité, picong, lavway, belé, single tone, double tone, the calypso craze, black British calypso, Manhattan calypso, soca, chutney soca—not to mention calypso's literary permutations in, for example, the poetry of Edward Kamau Brathwaite and Derek Walcott or the novels of Samuel Selvon, Merle Hodge, Earl Lovelace, and Marion Patrick Jones. This calypso ethos is, as Gordon Rohlehr has argued, a secular energy and language machine continuously in search of a (musical, literary, political, choreographic) form.[38] For the performers I examine in this book, calypso's faddification became yet another form for calypso. In the avowal of its inauthenticity the calypso craze locates itself within but not self-identical to the calypso tradition. The calypso craze succeeds at its own failure to perform calypso. Such success—all the ways that not-real calypso posed a dilemma and surprise to the absurdity of New World racial logic—further destabilized the unstable ground of the authentic. Calypso, perhaps even more than other musical genres, lends itself to being taken up in the uncertain space between *this* and *that*, not least because of its investment in irony, indirection, and topicality as well as its history in Trinidadian carnival's practices of self-display, such as the carnival tradition of *ole mas*. Only here, unlike the African American dissembling appropriation of the minstrel mask, Trinidadian carnival *mas* wears its unruly anticolonial, anticapitalist expression on, rather than behind, the surface: masking not as disguise but as revelation.

Performance and the Transmediation of Race Crazes

The calypso craze was one of many, many race crazes to recur throughout the first half of the twentieth century. American consumers dabbled in racial exotica through Hawaiian crazes and Polynesian crazes, Egyptomania and mambo mania, the maxixe and the bossa nova, hillbilly crazes, Tango teas, *Salomé* shows, and countless black dance and musical forms. There was even an earlier, lesser calypso craze (in which the Andrews Sisters played a significant part) that washed over radio stations and New York nightclubs a decade prior to the calypso craze of the 1950s. As an adjunct to the expansion of US empire and the system of Jim Crow laws, the consumption of difference was highly profitable for the emergent culture industries that trafficked in clichéd images and stereotypes of nonwhite cultures. It also provided for many nonwhite performers an avenue for gainful employment and a compromised opportunity for self-expression. This ambivalence has been widely noted by scholars who have thoughtfully traced how performers worked within the representational constraints that brought them quickly to a mass audience and just as quickly washed them away, replaced by the next new thing even as the stereotype itself lingered long past the fad that codified it.

The productive imprecision of these race crazes often mixed and matched sounds, gestures, rhythms, instruments, and histories to create something musically hybrid, ersatz, and not-real. The calypso craze, for example, borrowed unabashedly from the popularity of Latin American sounds such as mambo, merengue, rumba, cha-cha-chá, and other genres that were experiencing their own vogues in the decade. Eldridge and Funk call this the "elasticity" of *calypso* in the 1950s, as the word was stretched to describe a range of musical sounds and movements from Latin America and the Caribbean depending on the context.[39] While the craze for mambo preceded the calypso craze by a couple of years, peaking around 1954, there was much overlap between these two fads. Mambo ballrooms that featured renowned bandleaders such as Tito Rodríguez, Tito Puente, and Machito adapted to the new interest in calypso. Beginning in early 1957, for example, the Palladium, that epicenter of mambo mania in New York City, "set aside Wednesday evening for a special 'Calypso Mambo Spectacular' featuring names in the Trinidad tempo field," including Duke of Iron and others. The celebrated Palladium Ballroom dance master Killer Joe Piro even offered lessons on how to dance to calypso music.[40]

These musics traveled across the hemisphere along distinct geographic and linguistic routes that shaped the arrival of Caribbean performance in the United States. At the beginning of the 1950s, for example, the musical itineraries through different US territories in the Caribbean established paths that would wind through mambo mania and the calypso craze later in the decade. *Variety* estimated that about 80 percent of the music played on the radio in Spanish-speaking Puerto Rico was of Latin American origin, while the English-speaking Virgin Islands' sole radio station took its cue from the US hit parade. Increasingly, "as the trickle of tourists to the new American Mediterranean attain[ed] flood proportions," hotels across the Caribbean began booking US acts to entertain their customers, with Puerto Rican hotels and clubs promoting predominantly Spanish-derived musical trends, and hotels in the Virgin Islands tending more toward US popular music, rhythm and blues, and calypso.[41]

Despite the impossibility of keeping musical influences fully separate, Anglophone West Indian immigrants to the United States found more performance opportunities under the banner of calypso, while Hispanophone Latino/a and Latin American performers found such opportunities under the sign of Spanish-language genres such as the mambo. This was the case not only in theater venues and performance circuits but on record labels as well. For example, two Latin-based record labels entered the British market in 1954: South American and Spanish-language music was promoted on the Fiesta label, while English-language Caribbean music was promoted on the Calypso-Time label.[42] As these migratory musical routes suggest, the logics of territorial ownership deeply inform the logics of cultural ownership, particularly during the Cold War. Yet in its avowal of inauthenticity, the calypso craze often upended the impulse to ownership altogether. These language migrations shaped the perceptions of the calypso craze in the United States, where African American performers found in the English-language tradition a sound and movement thorough which to identify with a diasporic vision of the New World. Yet, as we will see, the calypso craze often blurred with other crazes for Latin music such as mambo and rumba, and blackness and latinidad intersected in a number of new ways in US mass culture. At the levels of sound and embodied performance, the histories of race crazes in the United States continually confounded the easy racial and ethnic simplifications required by mass-culture marketing.

The expansion of Caribbean tourism facilitated even greater circulation of performers between the United States and the Caribbean. Following World War II, US hotels began investing millions of dollars to develop resorts across the Caribbean, including luxury hotels not only in Puerto Rico and the Virgin Islands but also in Cuba, the Dominican Republic, and Jamaica. These resorts offered package airfare with Pan American airlines ($198 round-trip tickets "designed for island hopping").[43] By 1955 a Caribbean nightclub circuit was established between hotels and nightclubs across the archipelago to go after "Yanqui dollars" and recruit US performers.[44] Dubbed the "coconut circuit," the network allowed hotels "to cut down travel costs by routing the same act on stopovers and jumping them across the Caribe sea island checkerboard in the most economical way possible."[45] The circuit moved performers from Miami through Havana, Nassau, Santo Domingo (then Ciudad Trujillo), San Juan, and the

British Virgin Islands.[46] As this travel itinerary suggests, the calypso craze took advantage of the postwar expansion of the middle class in the United States, new tourist markets for leisure and recreation, and new developments in mass media. While such tourist productions distort local culture, they also screen it from investigatory, imperial, or lecherous eyes, distracting the sightseer from other projects that may be going on. And, as I argue throughout *Stolen Time*, sometimes those other projects happen on the surface, hidden in plain sight.

Thus while the calypso craze is colored by more than a little of what Jelly Roll Morton called "the Spanish tinge," it remains an important hinge in the history of US black performance and mass culture in the twentieth century.[47] On the one hand, it looked backward. The calypso craze was haunted by the representational constraints of black entertainment during Jim Crow and its modes of racialized spectatorship, here flavored with an ersatz tropicana. It was background music for an emergent suburbia and dance floor music for West Indian migrants in the metropole, consumed everywhere from high school sock hops to downtown nightclubs to tenement apartments to middle-class living rooms. Like the contemporaneous fad for the hula-hoop, which began in 1958, and a Polynesian craze that scattered Tiki bars across the United States, the calypso craze participated in a middle-class curiosity with island exotica, new kinesthetic movements, and tropical leisure. On the other hand, it looked forward. As an effect/affect of Cold War geopolitics and Afro-Caribbean migrations, it provided opportunities to extend African American culture and its relationship to diasporic consciousness. In the context of the civil rights movement, decolonization, and a reorganization of global geographies, the calypso craze imagined new forms of blackness not limited by the histories, taxonomies, laws, and boundaries of the nation-state.

Like these other race crazes, the calypso craze was a transmedia event that is usefully examined under the rubric of performance. The media used during the calypso craze included the body (on nightclub stages, theaters, concert halls, dance floors, and suburban rec rooms); sound recordings; live and recorded television broadcasts; film and photography; print culture, fanzines, and lifestyle magazines; material culture and collectibles; and word of mouth. Black fad performance describes the whole network of these media as they join together in the ephemeral temporality of the fad. It is a communicative system of meaning (signification), affect (feeling), and power (resistance). This expanded understanding of performance is at odds with the divergent disciplinary histories of media studies and performance studies, which often oppose live performance and mediated performance on phenomenological, ontological, and anthropological grounds. Over three decades ago, acclaimed theater scholar Martin Esslin lamented this opposition and called for an approach to performance that could account for what happens in film and other media. "I have always thought it absurd," he wrote, "that the rigid separation of stage drama from the cinematic media in higher education has led to the creation of separate theater and film departments at most universities and colleges, often hardly communicating with each other when each could greatly profit from sharing their insights into what, basically, are closely related and sometimes identical areas of theory and practice, which could much more effectively be covered in a unified performing arts department."[48] I am less concerned with Esslin's administrative admonishments than his keen grasp of what this segregation of knowledge production prevents. Although I approach the calypso craze from the field of performance studies, I do so with an openness to the interaction between live and mediated performance. This is not so much to ignore the irreducible differences between live and mediated performance as it is to ask what possibilities for thought can occur when such oppositional and exclusive thinking is momentarily suspended.

This question (posed most directly in chapter 2) is especially acute when considering the absence that lies at the center of all performance history: the irrecoverability of the live event presented by the physical presence of animate bodies. In a critique of the critique of mediation in performance historiography, Alexandra Vazquez embraces sound recordings as what she evocatively calls "performance's hereafter."[49] The hereafter is a time simultaneously *here* and *after*. The phrase resonates by capturing the residual element of the performance that has passed and the emergent performance of the recorded event in the current moment. In another sense, *hereafter* also means: starting now. Rather than nostalgically lament the loss of a performance that we did not or could not have seen, Vazquez understands *liveness* to be a sign of "a productive not-being-there, rather than as a term for easy access to bodies on a theatrical stage."[50] This formulation respects the opacity at the center of performance history, recognizes the limits of what we can claim of any performance, and allows the performance an element of freedom from its seeming capture by technologies of mechanical inscription. At the same time, these limits are all productive and involve critical acts of imagination, the "creative and necessary ways that many have had to imagine the live—especially from those who also bear a historical, embodied relationship to its more horrific manifestations."[51]

In a similarly enabling formulation, Fred Moten displaces the opposition between live and mediated performance with a shift to the sensory play of the visual and the aural that also foregrounds the importance of imagination. Moten writes:

> If the sensual dominant of a performance is visual (if you're there, live, at the club), then the aural emerges as that which is given its fullest possibility by the visual: you hear [Ed] Blackwell most clearly in seeing him—the small kit, the softness and slow grace of his movement; or Cecil [Taylor] most clearly in the blur of his hands. Similarly, if the sensual dominant in the performance is aural (if you're at home, in your room, with the recording), then the visual emerges as that which is given its fullest possibility by the aural: you see Blackwell most clearly in hearing the space and silence, the density and sound, that indicate and are generated by his movement; or Cecil most clearly in sound's anticipation of dance at, to, and away from the instrument. These are questions of memory, descent, and projection. The visual and the aural are before one another.[52]

This attention to what Moten calls the "sensual dominant" shifts our focus from the presence or absence of the performer to the sensory attunement of the spectator/listener in the club or in her room. Here live is not the privileged term, nor is mediation seen as derivative; the performance may be live or mediated, and the sensory register of that performance will shift accordingly. The contours of a performance are experienced within a particular activation of the senses rather than in one's presence at an allegedly original event. Performance here is not defined by its liveness but by the new sensory arrangement of the spectator/listener, and it involves the interplay of "memory, descent, and projection," which is another way of describing the work of imagination. In this radical act of nonhierarchization in which the visual and aural are before one another, the interplay of sound and sight activates memories of prior performances as well as personal or collective memories that the performance calls forth; sends one down lines of historical descent; and animates regions of fantasy and desire. As much as any performance, this is the sensory field of black fad performance in the Jim Crow United States.

Throughout *Stolen Time* I describe multifarious enactments of the calypso craze across media as instances of black fad performance. Building on Vazquez and Moten, I invoke another sense of liveness. Liveness can mean not only presence or a fixed space and time (for example, the "here and now") but can also describe a sensation, a charge carried by some recorded sounds and objects, as in a live wire; the activation of imagination; or the fact of necessary chance. The performances of the calypso craze on records, television, film, stage, and in print media conduct a variety of currents. I consider various mediated performances in this book—from Josephine Premice's sound recordings and nightclub acts to Maya Angelou's cinematic turn to Melville and Frances Herskovits's Trinidadian field recordings to Duke Ellington and Billy Strayhorn's televised diasporic fantasia to Lena Horne's stage performance on Broadway to Carmen de Lavallade's and Geoffrey Holder's choreography—and ask what charge they carried not only "then and there" but still carry "here and now." In viewing the calypso craze as a whole performance event that includes both live and mediated performance, new dimensions of black performance history and sensations emerge.

The Belafonte Effect: When Blackness Became Middlebrow

At a time when jazz and existentialism were both modeling new attitudes for the postwar era, the calypso craze appeared as decidedly not cool.[53] As the previous discussion of popular race crazes and transmediated dissemination suggests, it was a mass-produced consumer good that allowed for the marketing of cultural difference within a recognizable taste framework: the postwar middlebrow and the related form of racial kitsch. *Stolen Time* joins a number of books published in the last decade that reexamine how black cultural production in the middle of the twentieth century shaped identity categories, political allegiances, and Cold War domestic and foreign policy, including Farah Jasmine Griffin's *Harlem Nocturne*, Lawrence Jackson's *The Indignant Generation*, Mary Helen Washington's *The Other Blacklist*, and William Maxwell's *F. B. Eyes*.[54] These studies of black creative expression and cultural institutions look at midcentury literature, high cultural performances of concert dance and jazz, and proletarian art and literature. *Stolen Time* complements such work by looking to unmistakably middlebrow cultural forms in the 1950s. Among other things, a turn to middlebrow culture can provide greater specificity and nuance about how taste, as part of but in excess of the cultural politics of respectability, shaped black arts in the twentieth century.

The middlebrow refers to the newly emergent bandwidth on a cultural dial that ranged from lowbrow, popular forms of culture to highbrow, erudite forms. It combined the distributional reach of mass culture with the aspirational grasp of those who would aim for high culture. In doing so, middlebrow aesthetics and institutions sought to democratize high culture and revalue pleasure and enjoyment as modes of cultural improvement. The middlebrow had an explicitly pedagogical element that sought to bring cultural literacy to a greater number of people through institutions such as the Book-of-the-Month Club and mass-circulated paperbacks, musical theater, and corporate-sponsored television broadcasts. As scholars such as Anna McCarthy and Christina Klein demonstrate (and as we will see in chapter 3), this middlebrow mission of edification became instrumentalized in the 1950s as an ideological project that aimed to educate American citizens into a new postwar liberal order that promoted Cold War internationalism, racial integration, and citizenship-through-consumption.[55] Especially as the contradictions of Jim Crowism and democracy became increasingly difficult to maintain on the global stage, blackness became middlebrow as political and cultural leaders made abstract values such as freedom, equality, tolerance, and opportunity central to postwar domestic and foreign policy.

Belafonte's *Calypso*—and the calypso craze more generally—was the culmination of a decades-long middlebrowification of blackness that addressed US race relations through the consumption of sentimentalized forms of leisure. There has always been a black presence in the American middlebrow imagination, back to its prehistory in nineteenth-century sentimental culture that included works such as Harriet Beecher Stowe's *Uncle Tom's Cabin* (which, as the first US novel to sell over a million copies, shares a cultural benchmark with *Calypso*). But following World War II and the rise of the civil rights movement, the middlebrow imagination became a key location for the symbolic engagement of race relations within a new mode of liberal governance, of which the calypso craze was a part. The Book-of-the-Month Club, for example, offered as main selections Richard Wright's *Native Son* (1940) and *Black Boy* (1945) and Ethel Waters's autobiography *His Eye Is on the Sparrow* (1951). The latter two books in particular voiced vivid critiques of the Jim Crow South and absorbed narratives of black struggle and uplift into a national story about liberal democracy. Nonetheless, the artistic concessions necessary to conform to middlebrow tastes often left their political efficacy and aesthetic integrity compromised at best. Richard Wright's biographer Hazel Rowley, for example, details the alterations that Wright made to his novel *American Hunger* in order to make it palatable as a main selection for the Book-of-the-Month Club. The intrusive editorial interferences included changing the title (to *Black Boy*); bowdlerizing passages; and cutting the entire last third of the novel, which described the racism Wright encountered in the North, his disillusionment with the Communist Party, and the overall failure of the American democratic project.[56]

Such compromises structure the calypso craze and were typical of the way blackness appeared in the middlebrow imagination. When the midcentury middlebrow directly engaged with questions of race in domestic or international contexts it was, as Janice Radway puts it, "deeply involved in the ongoing project of reconstructing whiteness in the face of a threat posed by peoples who could no longer be ignored or fully controlled by the apparatuses of colonial administration and domination."[57] The calypso craze culturally displaced and disavowed more radical contemporaneous anticolonial projects—including the Afro-Asian Bandung Conference in 1955; the First Congress of Negro Writers and Artists in 1956 (in Paris); the establishment of the West Indies Federation in 1958; the American Society of African Culture Writers' Conference in 1959 (in New York City); and the ongoing civil rights movement in the United States—that imagined new cultural and political forms for black internationalism in the mid-twentieth century. Belafonte described a crucial element of his success at this moment frankly: "for white audiences, I carried a reassuring presence, enhanced by my Caribbean diction. Black, but . . . not *too* black."[58] *This* is not *that*. Like other prominent black male performers who appeared in middlebrow productions, including Nat King Cole, Sidney Poitier, Sammy Davis Jr., and Duke Ellington (the subject of chapter 3), Belafonte crafted a star image based on a dignified, suave, and—most importantly—unthreatening masculinity that appealed to middle-class white consumers.

This was the Belafonte effect: the management and displacement of domestic and international cultural tensions through the calypso craze; the middlebrow sublimation of interracial sexuality; the cultural passage from de jure Jim Crowism to Cold War liberalism; and the dizzying, prismatic refractions of race, nation, and performance in mass culture. Belafonte was a palimpsest, his effect the simultaneous inscription and erasure of long-standing racial anxieties during the civil rights and decolonization movements of the 1950s—in short, a disavowal. As Belafonte himself noted, for example, his "Caribbean diction" was a crucial element of his appeal. Although he was closely associated with US civil rights activism and viewed as African American within US popular culture, his slight Jamaican cadence in performance permitted white audiences to engage with his blackness one step removed from the representations of African Americans that circulated in the Jim Crow era. Simply being a fan of Belafonte became a kind of political statement. Describing the effect of his popularity in the 1950s, Belafonte explained that when white consumers purchased one of his albums, "you were connecting with your better angels, reaching across the racial divide. Consciously or not, you were casting your vote for equality, and for a phrase about to hit the mainstream: *civil rights*."[59] This white consumption of black culture was not the bohemian slumming or stage-managed transgressions of 1920s nightlife but a more mundane and middlebrow consumption of kitsch that allowed for the affective experience of identifying with the civil rights movement through consumer purchases.

Accordingly, Belafonte appears throughout this book less as a presence than as an effect. His name was (and remains) synonymous in most minds with the calypso fad. At the end of 1956, *Variety* wrote that "although calypso has always had a following in the US, the rapid spread of its popularity recently is held to be chiefly the work of Harry Belafonte. Via his nitery act and, more importantly, his RCA Victor discs, Belafonte has given a tremendous hypo to calypso."[60] There would have been no craze without him, but he refused to participate in it (and in refusing, sold millions of albums). He was attached to the calypso craze in all of its genres. His social significance film *Island in the Sun* (1957) was made and marketed during the calypso craze and set on a Caribbean island, but it was tangential to Hollywood's cinematic calypso craze. He was cast in a calypso musical on Broadway, in a role written specifically for him, but he dropped out of the production at the last minute. He directed his creative energies toward leftist politics, including civil rights activism and the left-populist world folk music revival of the 1950s and 1960s. Even as white Americans were imitating Belafonte's tenor in "Day O (The Banana Boat Song)," the singer himself was helping financially and organizationally to support the Montgomery bus boycott over the fall of 1956, pivoting from mass culture to movement politics. But despite his self-removal from the fad, he haunted every enunciation of it. Performance after performance evokes him, mimics him, sometimes mocks him, and even disavows him. As such, though it begins with him, the rest of *Stolen Time* largely looks beside, behind, and beyond Belafonte to the performances that he eclipsed, especially those by women performers (such as Josephine Premice, Maya Angelou, and Carmen de Lavallade, among others) whose contributions to black performance history are far less recognized.

Unsurprisingly, an interracial sexual fascination and taboo structured the calypso craze's middlebrow consumer politics. Belafonte's midcentury performance worked along a sexual frequency that simultaneously evoked and diffused white interracial desire. As cultural critic Lisa McGill puts it, "Belafonte's performance of a black Caribbean body afforded a sexual freedom not made available to his black American one."[61] A key element of the Belafonte effect was to provide an alibi and outlet for the expression of a sublimated racial erotics—one typically rerouted into a violent antiblackness. James Baldwin offers a firsthand description of this effect in a penetrating account of marching alongside Belafonte during a civil rights protest in the streets of Montgomery, Alabama:

> From upstairs office windows, white American secretaries were leaning out of windows, jeering and mocking, and using the ancient Roman sentence of death: thumbs down. Then they saw Harry, who is my very dear friend and a beautiful cat, and who is also, in this most desperately schizophrenic of republics, a major, a reigning matinee idol. . . . When the girls saw Harry Belafonte, a collision occurred in them so visible as to be at once hilarious and unutterably sad. At one moment, the thumbs were down, they were barricaded within their skins, at the next moment, those down turned thumbs flew to their mouths, their fingers pointed, their faces changed, and exactly like bobby-soxers, they oohed, and aahed and moaned. God knows what was happening in the minds and hearts of those girls. Perhaps they would like to be free.[62]

The Belafonte effect names an affective "collision" within whiteness, a catalyst (or car crash) that instantaneously transmutes racial hatred into racial desire. Baldwin's account reminds us how closely connected these two feelings are in the psychic life of racism, and how one can become the other in an instant. The scene of protest becomes a scene of middlebrow cultural consumption: the office windows holding the secretaries become movie house balconies as the angry lynch mob is transformed into star-struck fans in the presence of the matinee idol. The catharsis of racial violence (the thumbs down death sentence) is transformed into sexual release (the moans and sighs that issue from their mouths). For a brief moment, Baldwin speculates, the young women are seized by the possibility of their own freedom, a crack in the barricade of their whiteness brought about by the sight of Belafonte. We can see in this anecdote how the circulation of blackness in the postwar middlebrow imagination attempted to manage the schizophrenia and pathos of whiteness in the United States through culture (in this case, cinema and celebrity) during the ongoing struggle for desegregation.[63] Throughout the calypso craze, as McGill details, Belafonte's "Caribbean body served as the symbolic means of negotiating integration and even its dangers in American society."[64] To state the obvious, Baldwin, Belafonte, and especially the local black Montgomery residents who joined this march faced enormous risk. And while we are on the topic of risk, we should also not overlook Baldwin's own displaced desire in this description, and the cross-gender, cross-racial identifications that occur when Baldwin describes Belafonte's beauty. Flirting with suspect desire, including queerness and miscegenation, the calypso craze again and again provided middlebrow moments of erotic displacement and desublimation that were, as Baldwin understood, "at once hilarious and unutterably sad." We will see these dynamics recur throughout the chapters that follow.

Such political and sexual displacements locate the calypso craze within the tradition of middlebrow racial kitsch. Racial kitsch displaces political and sexual anxieties onto mass-produced caricatured images and sounds that render blackness harmless to white power. This kitsch participates in representational economies of pleasure and violence that continue the long history of blackness's fungibility in the New World. Like the Jim Crow collectibles and racial memorabilia that emerged in the 1890s and circulated across the United States throughout the twentieth century, the calypso craze cultivated a Caribbean kitsch in a visual culture of palm trees, straw hats, donkey carts, coconuts, voodoo exoticism, and brown-skinned islanders. The craze provided a soundtrack for these images, animating them with musical sounds and patter divorced from the context of their production. In his well-known 1939 *Partisan Review* essay denouncing middlebrow culture, art critic Clement Greenberg described kitsch, as Belafonte described the calypso craze, as "vicarious experience and faked sensations." Kitsch was the inevitable product of a culture industry that sought to commodify difference. "To fill the demand of the new market," Greenberg lamented, "a new commodity was devised: ersatz culture, kitsch, destined for those who, insensible to the values of genuine culture, are hungry nevertheless for the diversion that only culture of some sort can provide."[65] In his lengthy excoriation of kitsch and its flattening, standardizing effects on culture, one element has particular relevance to the calypso craze. Anticipating Belafonte's distinction between the calypso craze and true calypso, Greenberg maintains that kitsch requires a "fully matured cultural tradition, whose discoveries, acquisitions, and perfected self-consciousness kitsch can take advantage of for its own ends." Kitsch absorbs this tradition, drawing "its life blood, so to speak, from this reservoir of accumulated experience."[66] Greenberg and Belafonte both offer us an image of the calypso craze as a cultural vampirism feeding off the folk culture of Trinidad and the greater Caribbean.

Yet, despite this undeadness, the calypso craze also became a positive and living condition for the extension of black culture over and beyond the desiccated cultural husk that kitsch left behind. Black fad performers used the conditions of kitsch to imagine new relationships to blackness in the United States and the diaspora, and they did so primarily by reworking a long history of race, commodification, and the not-real into a condition of creative possibility. As we will see in the pages that follow, such a creative engagement with the calypso craze brought about what cultural historian Tavia Nyong'o describes as a shift "from racist kitsch to racial kitsch" that comes from modifying one's confrontation with the inauthentic racial caricature.[67] Significantly, it is not the kitsch that changes in this shift; it remains an object in the circuit of objectification, dehumanization, and white enjoyment. It is instead *the stance toward* kitsch that the black fad performers I discuss in this book transform. This modified stance toward inauthenticity is one way the racialized performer or spectator might repossess—steal back—her ownmost sense of being.

If the decades after World War II saw blackness become middlebrow as part of Cold War foreign and domestic politics, it also saw the complementary development of a black middlebrow counterpublic that marketed itself toward black consumers and cultivated black advertisers, especially in print culture. Johnson Publishing Company, the Chicago-based African American publishing house, helped to create this counterpublic in these postwar years by launching lifestyle magazines targeting middle-class black audiences, including *Negro Digest* (1942), *Ebony* (1945), *Jet* (1951), and *Hue* (1953).[68] A distinct Caribbean middlebrow, too, developed in the late nineteenth and early twentieth centuries in the British West Indies. Belinda Edmondson explains how a Caribbean literary culture developed for a black and brown middle class that was "dissociated from many of the 'low-brow' cultural traditions of the black peasantry" but "also at odds with the politics and attitudes of the white ruling elite."[69] As in the United States, this was an "aspirational popular culture," but the Caribbean middlebrow differed from the US middlebrow in that it was a continual negotiation between local, popular culture and the colonizer's aesthetic values that signified education and class.[70] This was a middlebrow that developed in Jamaica, Trinidad, and other English-speaking colonies not only in popular novels and serialized stories but also in beauty pageants, cricket matches, music festivals, and dialect fiction.

Each of these middlebrow cultures cast calypso in a different role. The African American middlebrow counterpublic covered celebrities such as Belafonte and commented on his performances and personal life with the same attention as white journals that covered the calypso craze, but they also reembedded his celebrity and matinee star image within the larger civil rights moment. In the black middlebrow counterpublic, the calypso craze did not displace but rather amplified political consciousness. In the Caribbean middlebrow that Edmondson describes, calypso (and carnival culture more broadly) continues to be an ambivalent location of struggle between a radical lower class and an aspirational middle class that aims to reform carnival into a respectable affair, always aware of its global reach and role in tourist economies. Even as we explore throughout this book how the calypso craze functioned in the mainstream US middlebrow imagination, it is important to keep in mind these "other middlebrows" that advanced sometimes complementary, sometimes competing images of the calypso ethos across the diaspora.

The Calypso Craze Funnyhouse

If, now and then, the story of the calypso craze that I tell in *Stolen Time* feels burdened by contradiction, paradox, aporia, disavowal, irony, recursivity, groundlessness, interpretative cul-de-sacs, and representational dead ends, the fault is not entirely mine. It is a fact and reflection of the absurdism and (il)logic of the New World racial order and the machinery of its perpetuation in popular culture. The calypso craze as a cultural phenomenon offers us neither the moral transparency of tragedy nor the tidy resolution of comedy (though at moments it approaches both). It is tempting to dismiss it as farce or travesty, but the theatrical genre to which black fad performance most closely corresponds is the theater of the absurd. Scholar and performance artist Stephanie Batiste generously offers an extended metaphor from her own biography to help visualize this. In the prologue to her history of African American complicity in the production of imperial representations in popular culture, Batiste shares an existentially harrowing memory from her childhood. As an eight-year-old girl she found herself disoriented and rendered immobile when she followed her sister into a county fair funhouse hall of mirrors. Lost in the mise en abyme of the "perplexing, ungraspable infinity," she saw her body suspended and replicated in an endless succession of reflections.[71] Even as she saw herself thrown into an infinite recession of horizon, the two-dimensional surface of the mirrors kept her walled in. The funhouse became a funnyhouse. Slumping to the ground she fantasized that the lights would go out, darkening the mirrors, as she squinted deep into the "most distant image I could perceive in this visual echo of myself, trying to determine if there was ever a point where I disappeared, if at some point deep within that chasm of myself everything went black."[72] With the help of her sister she at last made her way out of the maze.

Batiste (and, before her, playwright Adrienne Kennedy) offers this funnyhouse as a metaphor and conceptual framework for the multiplied reflections that shape and distort black difference in the African diaspora in the twentieth century. "Performative systems," Batiste writes, "act as a house of mirrors, a visual sound chamber, as it were, where bodies, performances, discourses, and the technologies involved volley meaning in endless reverberations of images."[73] As we will continue to see in the chapters to come, the calypso craze is a performative system that suspends performers and audience alike in a similar volley and reverberation of images, sounds, and gestures over an infinite recession of horizon. Even while this abyssal self-reflexivity ultimately causes the calypso craze to collapse on itself, it also turns its inwardness outward and creates passages through which performers might make their way through the wreckage. Concavingly and convexingly, calypso craze performers found their path through the maze of reflections in ways that mirror the performativity of race itself. Manipulating the appearance of surface and depth, black fad performance embraces the inauthentic to push further and farther beyond the funnyhouse mirrors of race and mass culture, where what appears miles away is in reality inches from one's face.

As Batiste's description of being momentarily trapped in this mirrored labyrinth suggests, the concerns of black fad performance with (in)authenticity are not only representational and semiotic but also existential and ontological. How blackness is represented—by whom and to whom—is intimately related to how race is lived and what race *is* and *is not*. As such, her description of being lost in a house of mirrors echoes another well-known moment of looking in postcolonial and black studies that crystallizes the primal scene of New World racialization: that of Martinican philosopher and revolutionary Frantz Fanon's encounter with a young white child in Lyon, France. In this encounter, Fanon is marked and fixed by the repeated exclamations—"Look, a Negro!"—as the child becomes increasingly afraid.[74] The encounter deforms Fanon's being and perception. In this moment, he ceases being-for-himself and can only experience a being-for-others. The child's fear supplants his own perception of bodily experience and replaces it with what he calls a historical-racial bodily schema. This historical-racial bodily schema remaps the spatiotemporal bearings of his body according to the laminations of history and representation that are provided "by the other, the white man, who had woven me out of a thousand details, anecdotes, stories."[75] As if in a house of mirrors, his very body is multiplied and unmoored from its bearings in the World. The annihilating utterance and the racializing look of the other casts Fanon into what he designates a "zone of nonbeing" that leaves him searching for his ownmost self in a dizzying abyss of distorted reflections.[76] In the pages that follow, we will see again and again and again how the calypso craze teases out some of the numerous threads that, as Fanon writes it, knot together cultural (in)authenticity and existential (in)authenticity.

Four years after Fanon, Trinidadian writer Samuel Selvon's novel *The Lonely Londoners* (1956) repeated this primal scene of racialization with a difference. Part of the literature of the mass migration of West Indians to England following World War II, *The Lonely Londoners* depicts a group of young men as they navigate the alienation and solidarity of such colonial movements. The picaresque novel narrates these characters' experiences of work, love, conviviality, isolation, and homesickness in the nation language and cadence of Trinidadian speech and the comic mood of the calypso.[77] One character known by the sobriquet Sir Galahad slowly adjusts to urban life after settling in London's Bayswater neighborhood. Gradually he comes to enjoy the rhythms and sensations of the city. He takes great pleasure in the urban self-fashioning that London allows as he prepares one evening to meet a girl in Piccadilly Circus—dressing in "the smartest and latest cut" and "taking the brush and touching the hair like a tonsorial specialist, here and there, and when he finish, the hair comb well."[78] On his way to his rendezvous, Galahad's evening is briefly halted by a repetition of Fanon's earlier encounter:

> "Mummy, look at that black man!" A little child, holding on to the mother hand, look up at Sir Galahad.
>
> "You mustn't say that, dear!" The mother chide the child.
>
> But Galahad skin like rubber at this stage, he bend down and pat the child cheek, and the child cower and shrink and begin to cry.
>
> "What a sweet child!" Galahad say, putting on the old English accent, "What's your name?"
>
> But the child mother uneasy as they stand up there on the pavement with so many white people around: if they was alone she might have talked a little, and ask Galahad what part of the world he come from, but instead she pull the child along and she look at Galahad and give a sickly sort of smile, and the old Galahad, knowing how it is, smile back and walk on.
>
> If that episode did happen around the first time when he land up in London, oh Lord! he would have run to the boys, telling them he have big ballad. But at this stage Galahad like duck back when rain fall—everything running off.[79]

Unlike Fanon's rendition of this scene, there is no clenched jaw or strained smile here, no quickening of the pulse, no torn sky, no crushing objecthood. If anything, there is a polite boredom, knowing how it is. It is as if Selvon seeks, lovingly, to write for Fanon a different outcome to his famous encounter. Yet Galahad's nonchalance should not be mistaken for indifference. It is a world-weary and hard-earned response that comes from repeated previous encounters of this scene. Galahad achieves his response through the survival of a series of similar incidents, ones that had become so commonplace since his arrival in London that they no longer pose the existential undoing that they do in Fanon's archetypal description. Selvon offers instead a record of how Galahad goes on after such existential undoing, and does not allow it to hinder his own self-fashioning or his pursuit of pleasure. Instead, in the face of Galahad's engagement with the mother and child, it is whiteness that loses ontological security. Galahad speaks to the child: "what's your name?" But the mother becomes uncomfortable. In this moment of address, she herself has no name. Like the young secretaries in Baldwin's scene, she is barricaded within her own skin. Whiteness's own historical-racial schema totters as other white people gaze on her conversation with Galahad and police the cross-racial contact between a white British woman and a black West Indian man. Here, as Baldwin and others would wryly propose, it is so-called white people themselves who are ontologically impoverished by the accumulated histories of racism and colonialism.[80] Whiteness here is exposed in the mise en abyme of reflected looks that multiply the woman and estrange her from herself and others as her child's utterance refracts back toward her.

Galahad, by now unfazed by the commonplace utterance, imagines his reaction if that scene had happened when he had first arrived in London: he'd have "big ballad," a melodramatic, musical, calypso rendering of the encounter that would tell a tale of suffering and despair.[81] It would have been an event worthy of being enshrined in song. But on this particular night, in this particular mood, he pauses just long enough to be polite before continuing in pursuit of his own pleasure. The utterance spills off Galahad like water off a duck's back. The child's words simply splash to the pavement, and his being remains intact—which is not to say that a Fanonian onto-corporeal disintegration may not happen again in the next such encounter, as the pages that follow this scene suggest.[82] Such reflections of reflections, and the ways that performers both volleyed and dodged them within the echo chamber of black fad performance, establish the groundlessness of the calypso craze's not-real. The funnyhouse of black fad performance anticipates and repeats the calypso ethos voiced in Selvon's *The Lonely Londoners*. It reflects the Fanonian moment back on itself and avows the inauthentic in order to puzzle the representational logic of the New World racial order and to risk opportunities for understanding one's authentic being-in-the-world. Galahad's lesson generously offers a dilemma and surprise that is as freeing as it is abyssal: this is not that; that is not me.

ONE

Stolen Time: The Ontology of Black Fad Performance

There's time enough, but none to spare.

—Charles Chesnutt, *The Marrow of Tradition* (1901)

The relationship between African American modernity, black entertainment, and fad cycles was the topic of sharp debate in the late nineteenth century, especially over the rise of sheet-music publishing firms that often drew on long-standing repertoires of racial stereotypes in their products and marketing campaigns. This new corporate music production transformed the minor genre of ragtime music into a national craze that allowed a small but significant number of black performers to take advantage of white desire for this music to reroute the conventions of the minstrel stage toward more formally inventive productions. Writing in the African American newspaper *Indianapolis Freeman* in 1896, theater critic R. W. Thompson meditated on the ragtime craze and its consequences for the black entertainer. "Taste runs in cycles," he wrote. "Everything has its hour, and gives way to the next sensation. The Negro's chance for survival comes in his talent for versatility, to his ready adaption to the duty required. The legitimate outcome of this rise in the profession will be better salaries for the deserving, a higher personal esteem, and an increased dignity to the calling itself."[1] Thompson's call for black performers to be attuned to the timeliness of popular tastes may seem naive or shortsighted, given this craze's (and subsequent vogues') economic exploitations, deformations of blackness, and severe aesthetic restraints. But it is through the temporal paradox of the fad—its claim to the new presented through its cyclical repetition—that Thompson sees a "chance for survival."

Thompson was prescient, and his attention to the cyclical nature of popular sensations and race crazes tells us something about recurrent moments of critical intensity across the Jim Crow era. In this chapter I take up Thompson's cue to examine the structure of the fad cycle that shaped race, entertainment, and mass culture from the ragtime craze (or so-called coon craze) of the 1890s to the Negro vogue of the 1920s to the calypso craze of the 1950s. To better understand the possibilities and the limitations that mass-cultural performance held for black performers, this chapter locates the calypso craze within recurrent cycles of the production, distribution, and consumption of blackness. Such critical intensity was attached to practices and repertoires of performance and was coordinated by the fad logic of cycle/moment. Like all fads, the calypso craze was fleeting, but a careful consideration of its contours *as* a fad can tell us something about the production and consumption of blackness in the Jim Crow era.

Fads are not only a marker of a specific historical time but also a sign for temporality itself.[2] One of the twentieth century's earliest scholars of fads sought to define fads' temporal quality as they became an enduring feature of consumer culture. For several decades beginning in 1914, sociologist Emory Bogardus undertook a longitudinal study that compiled extensive data (primarily through massive surveys) on patterns of mass conformity and the logic of fad cycles. For all their triviality, Bogardus concluded, fads could be seen as emblems of modernity. In his findings, the adoption of new fashions reflected individuality and a will "to differentiate one's self from others," "an impulse to be free," and a "spirit of progress."[3] But amid this celebration of consumer culture, Bogardus also sounded a warning: the new thing can generate a mass excitement that "paralyzes one's critical powers and releases the native impulse to act irrationally."[4] When a new fashion becomes an unthinking fad, it dulls one's ability to discern between the dazzling latest thing and "sensible and enduring values."[5] Voicing a common anxiety in response to the standardizations of mass culture, Bogardus cautioned against indulging too enthusiastically in the "superficially new and that designed to be glamorous rather than real contributions to progress."[6] Fads cans belie the economic rationality of their production and, in an ominous reversal, "may actually defeat progress."[7]

Bogardus's concerns over mass excitement reflect the scientific progressivism that literary theorist James Snead diagnosed as an effect of Western cultures' active struggle to repress or disavow cyclical notions of time in favor of linear progress. In his influential essay, "On Repetition in Black Culture," Snead explains that, to the extent that Western cultures recognize repetition, they nonetheless insist on a logic of linearity and accumulation, as in the patterns of economic growth and financial crisis intrinsic to capitalism's business cycles. For Snead, black culture (specifically the musical traditions of jazz and the blues) counters this accumulative logic of progressive time with a cyclical and circulatory temporality that is nonprogressive and discontinuous.[8] In such a formulation, African American modernity is shaped by a recursivity that renders it nonsynchronous to itself. The experience of a moment nonsynchronous to itself is often worked through formally, for example in the *tempo rubato* (literally: stolen time) of ragtime as it varied the time signature of the march.

Such movement without movement, perhaps, is how Thompson can find "a chance for survival" for black performers within the very cycles that Bogardus worries "may defeat progress" itself. The chance for survival might even, it turns out, depend on such defeat. This is the central paradox of the fad as a cultural phenomenon: a fad is predicated on the new object or activity, yet each fad's appearance follows the same strict and unvarying pattern of rapid adoption, wide circulation, and precipitous abandonment—what one sociologist characterizes as the cycle of "emerging, surging, and purging."[9] Even as a fad promises something new (its content) the fad cycle itself (its structure) renders each fad interchangeable with the ones that came before it. In a fad, everything new is old again, and the sense of progress or forward motion it implies is underwritten by a structural repetition of the same.

This formal stance toward repetition (which Snead calls black culture) as it intersects with the structural repetitions of consumer capitalism and fad culture is the subject of this chapter. Specifically, I pursue the insights into time and history disclosed by black fad performance's repetitions. As Snead suggests, where we find repetition in cultural forms such as the fad we often find "the willed grafting onto culture of an essentially philosophical insight about the shape of time and history."[10] I thus approach black fad performance not through a representational or semiotic analysis of signs and signifiers but as a historical-ontological situation. In doing so, I ask how the ontology of black fad performance—the existential condition of racialized performance when a performer knows she is performing her own obsolescence—both constrained and unlocked possibilities for black performers.[11]

Or to put this more simply: What does it mean to be a fad? In this chapter, I outline a historically specific ontology that unfolds within the political economy of race and entertainment between the 1890s and the 1960s. I argue that the special temporality of fad culture creates perilous conditions for black fad performers that corroborate black social and political life under Jim Crow. Within this horizon of (im)possibility, the repetition of fad cycles over time are a kind of eternal return of the same that trapped performers in cycles of racialized consumption. But they also allowed some fad performances to co-opt this co-opted time, even if only momentarily. My argument advances in three stages: first historically, then politico-economically, and finally ontologically. I begin with an account of the three major black fad cycles of the Jim Crow era: the ragtime craze, the Negro vogue, and the calypso craze. What makes these three moments of critical intensity distinct from numerous other surges of blackness within popular culture is, as we will see, their distinct self-reflexivity and their density of creative innovation. While attending to their specific contexts, I focus on the structural repetitions that shape these fad cycles and allow us to see the ragtime craze and the Negro vogue not only as antecedents to the calypso craze but also in anticipation of it and as prior iterations of it. I then consider the political economy and double temporality of the fad—as both cycle and moment—to explain the unstable life span of amusement: to be a fad is to experience your existence within a circumscribed temporality and to perform your own obsolescence. Finally, I turn to the long-limbed, gravel-voiced calypso chanteuse Josephine Premice who, at the height of the calypso craze, allegorized the ontology of black fad performance—its horizon of (im)possibility—by explicitly thematizing the opportunities to pilfer the time of the fad for oneself.

Jim Crow Fad Cycles

In 1896, black vaudeville star Ernest Hogan wrote the song "All Coons Look Alike to Me" and started a craze. Hogan's composition picked up on a minor genre of popular music known disparagingly as "coon songs" that had been growing in popularity since the early 1880s and trafficked in a deformed representation of African American life. Alain Locke called the coon song a "relic of the worst minstrel days; slap-stick farce about razors, chickens, watermelon, ham-bones, flannel shirts and camp meetings."[12] Hogan's hit drew on the familiar elements of the genre: a travestied black dialect, syncopated ragtime rhythm, and stereotyped imagery and scenarios. Hogan did not invent the coon song, but his hit was the tipping point for what became known as the coon craze. Almost overnight, such songs were everywhere. By most accounts, the next five years saw the publication of over six hundred titles that sold millions of copies.[13] The vast majority of these songs were written, performed, and listened to by white people. It was one of the primary vehicles by which ragtime crossed over from black cultural spaces to mass US culture. New York publishing firms competed fiercely to generate as many variations on the formula as possible. Black dances such as the Cakewalk, the Pas Ma La, and the Bombershay spread across the country along with the songs.[14] White composers learned how to syncopate rhythm and white female vaudeville stars such as May Irwin, Clarice Vance, and Marie Cahill Harris repackaged themselves as "coon shouters" and incorporated these numbers into their acts.

At the same time, a small but significant number of black performers took advantage of white desire for this music to reroute the conventions of the minstrel stage toward more formally inventive productions. In a market saturated with white "coon singers," rising vaudeville stars Bert Williams and George Walker billed themselves as "Two Real Coons" and went on to become acclaimed stars of the era. The craze transformed black musical theater, as Bob Cole and Billy Johnson collaborated on *A Trip to Coontown* (1897), the first prominent black musical to break from the variety format and feature a narrative through line. This musical was followed by Will Marion Cook and Paul Laurence Dunbar's *Clorindy; or, The Origins of the Cakewalk* (1898), their *Senegambian Carnival* (1899), Hogan's *King of Coontown* (1899), and Williams and Walker's *In Dahomey* (1903). Each featured black-authored coon songs and rearticulated its formula within a highly self-reflexive theatrical idiom. This last production, for example, included J. Leubrie Hill's song "That's How the Cakewalk's Done" in a showstopping number that described the dance craze's omnipresence: "Cakewalking craze, it's a fad nowadays / With black folk and white folks too / And I really declare it's done ev'rywhere."[15] As we will see, this knowing self-awareness marks an engagement with the performance's own status as a fad. This is a critical dimension of black fad performance that works "in the service of dismantling a dominant ontological paradigm" and disclosing another, as Daphne Brooks writes about the cakewalk craze.[16]

This ragtime craze, in other words, was the first black fad in the United States and established the dynamic between production and consumption that shaped black fad cycles throughout the Jim Crow era. The concept of a fad as a short-lived enthusiasm and an act of mass participation through consumption emerges in the 1890s as an effect of economic transformations that saw a shift from local to mass consumer cultures. The 1890s, notes literary theorist Jennifer Fleissner, "usher in a fad for fads themselves" as throngs rushed to purchase the latest and newest thing.[17] Chain stores and department stores led to the mass diffusion of commodities, and nascent advertising and branding strategies turned consumption itself into a symbolic system of status and value as the consumer became an identity category and marketing demographic.

Emergent entertainment industries were well poised to take advantage of these transformations. This ragtime craze was driven largely by the standardization of popular musical production that would become known as Tin Pan Alley. Hogan's song was published by Isidore Witmark, one of the pioneers of this new industry whose sheet-music firms published numerous coon songs, including many of those written by black writers. The transformations in the rhythms of consumption were reflected in the rhythms of music itself. It was during the 1890s, Witmark wrote, that "the ballad and the waltz type [of popular song] gradually yielded, often to the accompaniment of stern moral denunciation, to the allurements of ragtime."[18] Tin Pan Alley provided a crucial infrastructure for the distribution of ragtime music, as did the consolidation of theater booking agencies in these years, which helped to ensure that theater circuits would feature increasingly standardized and centrally organized shows. Vaudeville stages, sheet music, and even dance moves amounted to an extensive distribution network that supported the short-lived craze.

To call this precipitous interest in black performance a fad is not to trivialize it; its effects reached far beyond the world of entertainment. The craze was a political technology that aided the implementation of a new racial regime of legislatively sanctioned segregation. With its origins in the North but its reach national, the craze provided a cultural screen that obscured and rationalized the violence of the 1896 *Plessy v. Ferguson* ruling, which declared segregation constitutional and inaugurated the Jim Crow era. As advancements gained during Reconstruction were systematically rolled back, such songs presented a comic image of African Americans that belied active black disenfranchisement across the nation. Even as the musical form of ragtime heralded a black modernism, the themes and staging of coon songs denied that modernism. An extensive visual culture accompanied this craze as illustrations on sheet music presented grotesque caricatures of blackness that were to be enacted in verse.[19] Yet despite these aesthetic constraints, many black performers ambivalently embraced the fad and used irony and parody to challenge its representations and voice black political critique on the variety stage and in musical theater. This was the case, for example, in *A Trip to Coon Town*'s showstopping number, "No Coons Allowed," which was a direct response to the recent *Plessy v. Ferguson* ruling and described the affront to dignity that segregation posed while advocating legal and political mobilization, all in the ragged tempo and debasing faux-dialect of the coon song.[20]

The fad for ragtime did not last much into the twentieth century. By 1905, according to *A Trip to Coontown*'s composer Bob Cole, the craze had "passed with the softly flowing tide of revelations."[21] Its racist iconography persisted, however, and continued to exact damaging and long-lasting consequences on the development of black performance. But the critical intensity of its popularity quickly waned as other entertainments appeared and consumers' attentions drifted toward other amusements. Some of the black performers who became famous during the craze continued to produce music and theater, though many more found work hard to come by. In hindsight, the few advances made by black artists under the auspices of the fad seemed like increasingly insignificant compromises that were obscured by the tide of white attention, imitation, and finally indifference. Ernest Hogan reportedly expressed deep regret for having written "All Coons Look Alike to Me."

About two and a half decades after the ragtime craze, white consumers again rushed to consume black music and dance in the "Negro vogue" of the 1920s. Composer Eubie Blake described this moment as "what we in show business call a 'heat wave.'"[22] White spectators hurried to see black musical revues, buy black recordings, and frequent cabarets in black entertainment districts. This fad cycle was precipitated by two events. The first was the flood of black musical theater and vaudeville shows that followed the success of the musical *Shuffle Along* in 1921. To poet Langston Hughes, *Shuffle Along* "gave just the proper push—a pre-Charleston kick—to that Negro vogue of the 20s."[23] The wildly popular show had a national tour and launched the careers of performers such as Florence Mills, Josephine Baker, and Paul Robeson. Numerous writers and producers sought to exploit its popularity with stage and nightclub imitators such as *Strut Miss Lizzie* (1923), *Runnin' Wild* (1923), *The Chocolate Dandies* (1924), *Blackbirds* (1926), and *Blackbirds of 1928*.

The second catalyst for the Negro vogue was the rapid increase in recordings of commercialized blues and vaudeville music following blues singer Mamie Smith's unexpected hit record "Crazy Blues." Recorded for Okeh Records in 1920, "Crazy Blues" sold thousands of copies in the first week, 75,000 in the first month, and over a million copies in the first six months.[24] Quickly thereafter, other record companies such as Paramount and Victor spun off "race labels" to capitalize on the newly discovered market for black recordings that included African American consumers as well as white ones. Hundreds of recordings were issued in the next several years. By the mid-1920s, live radio broadcasts from the Savoy Ballroom and the Cotton Club ensured that the commercial sounds coming from Harlem were available to a national audience, and extensive theater and vaudeville booking circuits such as the Theatre Owners Booking Association, the

Southern Consolidated Circuit, and the Quality Amusement Corporation slotted acts originating in New York into spaces large and small across the United States.[25] Like the earlier transformations of sheet-music publishing that made the ragtime craze a national fad, the Negro vogue developed through emergent distributional and technological infrastructures that made black sound consumable in new ways.

This Negro vogue was not only a national fad but an international one as well. Paris has its own *vogue nègre* that reached its apotheosis with Josephine Baker's celebrated debut in *La Revue Nègre* in 1925. Baker's success ignited what historian William Shack calls a "cult of Bakerism" that spread across France and spectacularly announced the arrival of US racial amusement in the clubs and theaters of Paris.[26] Prior to the 1920s, musicians like Louis Mitchell, Will Marion Cook, and Eugene Bullard laid the groundwork for later international stars such as Baker, Ada "Bricktop" Smith, Noble Sissle, and other US expatriate jazz musicians to find employment in nightclubs and cabarets. This crest of black American entertainment in France merged with Afro-Caribbean music and dance as colonial Antilleans, many conscripted for fighting in the Great War, set up shop across European metropoles. In such hot spots, new dance steps spread—especially the Charleston from the United States (introduced by the 1923 New York review *Runnin' Wild*) and the Martinican beguine (immortalized later in Cole Porter's 1935 song "Begin the Beguine"). While Harlem and Paris were centers of the Negro vogue, it spread much farther than these cosmopolitan locales through the expansion of new distribution networks such as radio and sound recordings.

The intensity of white interest in black entertainment and the rapid succession of black musicals were self-consciously commented on within the vogue itself. The *Ziegfeld Follies* of 1922, for example, featured a number called "It's Getting Dark on Old Broadway." The lyrics harked back to an earlier moment of Jim Crow fad performance: "Just like an eclipse on the moon / Ev'ry café now has the dancing coon. / Pretty choc'late babies / Shake and shimmie ev'rywhere. / Real darktown entertainers hold the stage, / You must black up to be the latest rage." These by-now outdated references to "coon" and "darktown" drew on the cultural memory of black fad performance and the tradition of blackface. We see in this lyric a return not only of the coon trope but also more significantly of a framework—the earlier craze—for interpreting the popularity of black performance. This lyric suggests that the Negro vogue of the 1920s saw itself from its onset as a return of the 1890s.

And it is not a coincidence that this return of the 1890s occurred at the exact moment that black artists and intellectuals were actively seeking to dispel once and for all its persistent and still potent stereotypes with a New Negro who would reflect black modernity and complexity. The Negro vogue collided with the New Negro Renaissance as black writers and artists struggled to lay claim to something more lasting than mere faddishness. By 1924, Alain Locke felt the need to differentiate artists' turn to the rich resources of racial art from anything "that might be dismissed as a mere contagion of fad or vogue."[27] The New Negro Renaissance, in Locke's turn, would be of permanent and deep consequence, not susceptible to the infectious triviality of mass consumption.[28] Similarly, the easy consumption of blackness in Paris, Berlin, and other continental locales came into conflict with politically committed projects undertaken by black writers and activists fighting for self-determination, especially in response to French colonialism in Africa and the Caribbean. The ragtime craze and the Negro vogue both had a latent Afro-Caribbean element that, until recently, has been overlooked in histories that initially viewed these race crazes through national lenses. Bert Williams, for example, one of the most successful and enduring performers to emerge from the ragtime craze, was born in Antigua.[29] And many of the Parisian clubs in the cosmopolitan *vogue nègre* introduced Caribbean music and dance to the continent.

In 1956 that Caribbean influence itself became the fad when Jamaican American Harry Belafonte's album *Calypso* became the first LP to sell over a million copies. As we saw in this book's introduction, Belafonte began to gain significant popular attention in upscale nightclubs and on Broadway the preceding years, but the success of *Calypso* put him on par with Elvis Presley, and for a few brief months commentators believed that calypso would supersede rock and roll as the lasting musical form. The calypso craze appeared through sound recordings, nightclub acts, television specials, musical theater, film, and dance. Concerts were staged at Carnegie Hall and the Apollo Theater. Nightclubs such as the Village Vanguard in New York City, the Blue Angel in Chicago, and the Carousel in Boston converted themselves into "calypso rooms" that featured elaborate calypso revues. In the summer of 1957, Sarah Vaughan and the Count Basie Orchestra headlined a record-breaking engagement titled "Calypso Carnival" at the Waldorf Astoria's glamorous Starlight Roof Ballroom.[30] Performers from previous generations such as Duke Ellington and Lena Horne dabbled in calypso facades to stay relevant to the changing trends.

Once again transformations in entertainment technologies played a key role in turning calypso into a fad. By the mid-1950s there were over forty million television sets in the United States, and television specials featured calypso singers and Caribbean dancers in prime-time broadcasts.[31] One critic coined the phrase "TV Pan Alley" to describe "television's impact on the music biz, already evident in the medium's ability to make hits with the speed of light."[32] TV became an updated version of the turn-of-the-century song plugger as corporations used television programming to feature the products of their recording subsidiaries. Belafonte's *Calypso*, for example, was partially inspired by his much-heralded appearance in a twenty-minute segment on NBC's *Colgate Comedy Hour* in 1955 titled "Holiday in Trinidad."[33]

The film industry was too rudimentary to play a major part in the Negro vogue, but by the 1950s the Hollywood studio system made producing calypso films fast and inexpensive. Studios rushed films through production to capitalize on the popularity of calypso. By early 1957, at least nine Hollywood films were reportedly in production, though only a portion of these made it to the big screen, including United Artists' *Bop Girl Goes Calypso* (1957), Allied Artists' *Calypso Joe* (1957), Columbia's *Calypso Heat Wave* (1957), and Twentieth Century Fox's *Island in the Sun* (1957), which, though not a calypso film proper, traded on the fame of star Harry Belafonte and its Caribbean setting.[34] These films all featured Trinidadian calypsonians, some internationally renowned, as background musical performers. The presentation of these performers—sometimes identified, sometimes not—was as local color and divorced from the cultural milieu or context from which they came, existing for their audience only in the context of the craze.

The calypso craze drew on a familiar store of devices from earlier black fad performance. The stock figure of Calypso Joe—a shirtless, carefree island native who appeared on stage, in song lyrics, and in the visual culture of the craze—was a new guise for an old character: Jim Crow in a Caribbean mask. The craze had its own fad vernacular, a calypsoizing of language that harked back to the faux-black dialect of the ragtime craze and the "Harlemese" of the Negro vogue. In Boston, *Variety* reported, the "local citizenry are on a calypso dialectic [*sic*] kick . . . as the result of the stint here of Pat Matthews, femme calypso chantoosey at the Hotel Bostonian's Jewel Room. The songstress is practically running a speech school with requests from the local chi-chi set to get calypso talk hip."[35] Overseas, the British Broadcasting Company experimented for a while with delivering the news in a calypso patois.[36] There was even talk of Twentieth Century Fox producing a feature film about the life of Bert Williams, starring Harry Belafonte in the lead role.[37] Although the film never materialized, this proposed reappearance of Williams in the 1950s confirms how earlier moments of black fad performance stubbornly haunted the calypso craze.

As this thumbnail sketch suggests, these iterations of black fad performance in the Jim Crow era share a number of similarities. These historical commonalities indicate the repetition of the fad structure in which the content itself is adapted to new technologies and tastes.[38] Seen as such, a number of recurrent patterns become intelligible. First, black fad performance was materially produced through transformations in media and entertainment technologies: sheet-music publishing, radio transmissions and sound recordings, television and film. And conversely, black fad performance helped to refine and spread such technological innovations. While each of these fads was driven by music, the fads found their fullest expression across a range of performances including theater, dance, literature, visual culture, and, later, film and television. Dance in particular—whether the Cakewalk, the Charleston, or the Limbo—was an important conduit of each fad (as we will see in detail in chapter 5).

Second, each fad supported loose generational networks of collaboration and affiliation between performers who found creative outlets in black fad performance. During the ragtime craze, performers, composers, and dancers including James Weldon Johnson, J. Rosamond Johnson, Bert Williams, George Walker, Aida Overton Walker, and Ernest Hogan worked together, shared tips about new opportunities, promoted each other, and collaborated on new musical and theatrical forms. The Negro vogue found a similar cohort of creative artists who reshaped black culture within the constraints and opportunities of the fad, including Duke Ellington, Ethel Waters, Cab Calloway, Florence Mills, Noble Sissle, Eubie Blake, and Langston Hughes. As we will see throughout this book, the calypso craze did the same for performers such as Josephine Premice, Geoffrey Holder, Carmen de Lavallade, Enid Mosier, Duke of Iron, Maya Angelou, and others. Although the calypso craze has not received as much attention as these earlier two instances of fad performance, it too put artists into contact with each other and created opportunities for each of them to experiment with new diasporic aesthetics in the postwar era.

Third, and relatedly, each fad cycle saw important developments of black entrepreneurship in the entertainment industry. With the enormous revenue and the cultural capital accrued by some, black performers launched black-owned production companies in an attempt to create alternatives to the corporate interests that profited from them. The ragtime craze saw the founding of Gotham-Attucks Publishing Company in 1905, a black-owned sheet-music firm. The Pace Phonographic Corporation, which included the subsidiary Black Swan label, was founded by Harry Pace in 1921 and marketed its jazz, blues, and popular music recordings to black consumers. Black Swan competed with other black-owned firms such as Handy Brothers Music Company and the Perry Bradford Music Company. And in 1956, Harry Belafonte founded Belafonte Enterprises Inc., and its film subsidiary, HarBel Productions. Under these auspices, Belafonte backed Broadway plays, including Lorraine Hansberry's landmark *A Raisin in the Sun* (1959). These business ventures didn't all last—Gotham-Attucks went out of business in 1911 after six years, and Pace Phonographic went out of business in 1923 after two years (Paramount purchased its catalog in 1924)—but they were important moments of self-determination within fad cycles. Related to this economic self-determination, black fad performance was often a means to political advocacy. Successful performers used their public position and visibility in dominant culture in order to advocate for political programs that challenged Jim Crow.

Fourth, each fad maintained but altered the contours of the color line. As mass-produced commodities purchased by national and international audiences, black fad performances reached far across allegedly fixed lines with the putative freedom that consumer capital created, though in doing so they often carried the color line with them. Thus they produced multiple audiences, spatially (in segregated theaters or neighborhoods) as well as in a sensibility of multicoded songs. Black fad performance—as a mode of black performance that relies on multiple meanings, irony, and knowingness—did not simply mediate national anxieties but also constituted new points of anxiety in the Jim Crow regime that were negated or redirected before they could come to fruition.

And fifth, because of this circulation across the color line, each fad cycle became a dense point for discussion about authenticity and hokum, one we will explore throughout this book. As E. Patrick Johnson has argued, it is the "constructing/deconstructing, avowing/disavowing, and expanding/delimiting dynamic that occurs in the production of blackness" that constitutes something like "authenticity" at all.[39] In marking the limits of commercial representations of Africa and the Caribbean and highlighting white provincialism, Jim Crow fad cycles imaginatively engaged to varying degrees with global geographies and black diasporas. While it was the form and not the content of the fads that recurred, each fad cycle was nonetheless predicated on a representational or symbolic violence that was closely linked to sociopolitical, ontological, and oftentimes physical brutality.

Many of these characteristics can be found in black performance throughout the Jim Crow era and beyond. And it goes without saying that not all black performance in these periods was part of the fad that dominated it. But when seen diachronically, these resemblances between the ragtime craze, the Negro vogue, and the calypso craze appear as more than superficial likenesses, and they have consequences for how we understand the history of black performance. These similarities are simultaneously effects of and responses to a deeper structure of repetition within mass culture in the Jim Crow era. Despite its seeming embrace of novelty, black fad cycles in the Jim Crow era more often looked backward than forward. This nonsynchronous temporality of black fad performance renders it always-already outmoded and regressive, even as it emerges as "the latest thing" through the most innovative and modern technological developments. We will see in the final section how this pattern of recurrence—very different from the improvisatory practices of repetition-with-a-difference that have been a resource for African American performance—creates conditions for imagining a future for black performance that is not beholden to a concept of linear time but that emerges from the market's own disavowal of cyclical time.

Performance in the Cascade Regime

While mass-culture industries took up blackness continuously throughout the Jim Crow period, these three flashpoints represent telling moments of critical intensity. Over the last three decades, scholarship in African American studies and theater history has recovered performances of the ragtime craze and the Negro vogue, historicized them, analyzed them, critiqued them, recuperated them, and critiqued them again. Numerous studies have demonstrated how these crazes mediated cultural anxieties and how performers manipulated or parodied the faddish stereotypes that limited black expression. These studies, especially those that have recuperated the resistant agency of black performers, largely approach black entertainment through an analysis of representation and performance semiotics. Some carefully attend to the slippages between signified and signifier that widen the distance between the actor and the character. Others have developed and nuanced the trope of "wearing the mask" to explain the polysemic performances of the Jim Crow period. In this section, I bracket the representational content of these performances in order to approach the fad itself as a communicative form. Doing so foregrounds the production of desire and affect in consumer capitalism and helps us to understand the structural repetition of the three crazes already described. This section thus builds on but augments the frameworks of fetishization, reification, exploitation, and double-consciousness that have structured our understanding of black entertainment in the Jim Crow era.

How did Hogan's "All Coons Look Alike to Me," Sissle and Blake's *Shuffle Along*, and Belafonte's *Calypso* spark fads in black performance? How do we understand the temporal feeling of these fad cycles? In the early 1990s, a trio of political economists developed a theory to explain the conformity of mass behavior and the rapid, seemingly spontaneous adoption of new ideas that is helpful in answering these questions. Sushil Bikhchandani, David Hirshleifer, and Ivo Welch define fad consumption as the effect of an "informational cascade." Cascade theory seeks to describe "the *process* by which society switches from one equilibrium to another."[40] Positing the consumer as a rational agent, informational cascade theory explains how fads gain intensity as individuals make decisions based not on their own observable criteria but by observing the observations of others, resulting in an exponential spread of knowledge. "An informational cascade occurs," they write, "when it is optimal for an individual, having observed the actions of those ahead of him, to follow the behavior of the preceding individual without regard to his own information."[41] An individual adopts certain behaviors based on an evaluation of its payoff or effect, but because direct analyses of the effects of either adoption or nonadoption can be inefficient and time consuming, an individual will often base her decision on the actions—and perceived benefits—of others. Thus, "cascades form when the public information set has become precise enough to outweigh an individual's private signal in determining his action."[42]

We need not uncritically subscribe to informational cascade theory's model of the rational individual in order to recognize its usefulness in explaining how fads spread, how music is consumed, and the role of knowledge and affect in driving fad cycles. Informational cascade theory is helpful as an analytic tool. It importantly locates fad consumption as a political-economic concern, rather than treating the fad as political economy's irrational limit (as Emory Bogardus did in the early part of the century). But even as it does so, it overemphasizes the role of conscious choice and neglects the importance of feeling and mood in its account of fad cycles. The production of consumer desire, excesses of white enjoyment, and the pleasures of consumption, participation, and conformity are more significant to the recurrence of black fad cascades than rational choice. Accordingly, I want to balance the rational calculation of cascade theory's fictive consumer with an attention to the affective dimension of fad cycles that is part of, not foreign to, any fad's political-economic rationality.

Take, for example, that ineffable quality known as "charisma" that attaches to certain black entertainers in the Jim Crow era and quickly becomes naturalized within ascriptive regimes of race. As Erica Edwards has argued, the weight placed on black charisma has oriented black political movements in the twentieth century away from the masses and toward a handful of elite male leaders and individuals.[43] We can also see how charisma has been part of a larger apparatus of subjection in the Jim Crow era predicated on amiability, elevating some cultural workers to high-profile stages and ensuring that white audiences will not have their own sense of self threatened by the performance they consume. Informational cascade theory helps to decenter or displace the emphasis given to personal charisma by locating black fad performance as a larger political economic concern. It is undeniable that Bert Williams, Josephine Baker, and Harry Belafonte had an indefinable quality and personal magnetism that attracted large audiences, but cascade theory does not rely on this personal charisma to explain the reason for their uptake in a particular historical moment. Instead it poses the possibility that their charisma is largely an effect of the fad rather than the cause, a retrospective revision of consumers' relationship to the performer-commodity. Williams, Baker, Belafonte, and others are charismatic because they are fads, rather than the other way around. This is not to minimize their talent or performative genius (testified to by the fact that they exceeded their particular fad moments, though they never fully shed the aura of that particular historicity). It is instead to understand their charisma as inseparable from the way they produced themselves and were produced within the swift currents of the fad cascade.[44]

It may be, then, less the charismatic effect of any performer than the circulation of information about what others are buying, watching, or dancing to that drives a fad cascade. As we have seen, black fad performances cluster around innovations in the entertainment industry's communication systems, information networks, and distributional webs.[45] In the ragtime craze, song-pluggers and vaudeville performers publicized new hit songs that could be purchased as sheet music from firms such as Witmark and Sons. Centralized theater circuits and the marketing of commercialized blues and jazz records in the 1920s propelled the Negro vogue. Similarly, ever more sophisticated demographic research and marketing technologies in the 1950s amplified the postwar calypso craze. *Variety* estimated that about 75 percent of towns in the United States had no record stores, and record companies developed innovative ways to create and then compete for musical consumers. The Columbia Record Club, started in 1955, made albums available through direct mail. RCA Victor (Belafonte's label) launched a "Personal Service" plan, in which "appliance dealers in small towns not serviced by record stores can buy RCA's coupon books. Under this setup, the customer can order from the dealer any one of the 400 LPs which are mailed directly to him from Victor's Indianapolis plant."[46] Companies also began displaying albums in wire record stands in food supermarkets across the United States in a practice known as "rack-jobbing" that "exposed disks to housewives and other shoppers who ordinarily don't go to record stores" (seen more recently in chains such as Starbucks to expose coffee drinkers to commercial jazz and world music).[47] These supermarket racks "typically display[ed] the top hits plus some standard disks," which signaled to consumers what everybody else was listening to and suggests how second-level information can rapidly produce a cascade.[48]

We can see the infrastructure of such fad cascades revealed in an advertisement targeted to retail stores that appeared in the trade magazine *Variety* in 1956. This ad lays bare the distributional and informational infrastructure of the calypso craze. In a marketing scheme that had been used previously for Elvis Presley (resulting in $2 million more in Presley sales), RCA Victor reissued twenty top-selling Belafonte singles and created a colorful merchandise display kit to hold five of each single (for a total of one hundred records), each in a record sleeve adorned with a colorful image of Belafonte (fig. 2).[49] The ad exhorts distributors to "Get in on the Belafonte Boom!" and shows how the display kit will quickly push the commodity as it depicts five different white hands reaching over each other to grab at the recordings. "Don't get caught short," the ad warns. "Call your RCA Victor Record Distributor and place your order today, then stand by to reorder as dividends in sales start rolling in."[50] Such innovations not only promoted a product but also created new markets, new consumers, and new desires. These transformations in commodity distribution are simultaneously transformations in knowledge dissemination and vividly illustrate how the calypso craze and other black performance fads gained momentum.

Once this momentum starts, it increases exponentially. Informational cascade theory calls the conditions governing the rapid adoption and quick conformity of behavior a "cascade regime."[51] A particular epistemological posture that is aware of the second-level analysis by which knowledge is evaluated characterizes a cascade regime. In other words, one knows when one is in a fad cascade, and this *knowingness* of one's limited knowledge (which is also and even primarily a feeling) is a key aspect of the fad. Black

Figure 2. RCA Victor merchandiser display ad. *Variety*, February 13, 1957.

fad performance self-reflexively played with this knowingness to comment on its own status as a fad. Songs were recorded about the fad in the fad's idiom, and then in turn were consumed as part of the fad, such as when the 1922 *Ziegfeld Follies* announced to audiences that now "You must black up to be the latest rage." This knowingness and self-reflexivity occur repeatedly throughout the calypso craze, which constantly (as we will see) named the fad as a fad within the fad. Black fad cultures are, in this way, autogenerating and self-replicating.

A fad cascade's knowingness also guarantees the kind of fatigue that comes with fad consumption. In the late 1890s, for example, the song

"Not Another Coon Song" voiced exhaustion with the whole thing. How does informational cascade theory explain this exhaustion? Or, more to the point, why do cascade regimes fail? How do fads end? One of the consequences of the informational cascade's second-order knowledge is a perpetual state of doubt. In a cascade regime, the consumer knows (or feels) that he or she is operating on very little information, and subsequently her relationship to the fad is shaped by skepticism: "intuitively, and in contrast with a full-information regime, individuals are not very confident that the original cascade was correct."[52] This skepticism makes cascade regimes fundamentally unstable and susceptible to rapid transformations that can reroute consumer choices or behaviors as quickly as they began. Bikhchandani, Hirshleifer, and Welch explain that "several possible kinds of shock could dislodge a cascade: for example, the arrival of better informed individuals, the release of new public information, and shifts in the underlying value of adoption versus rejection. Indeed, when participants know that they are in a cascade, they also know that the cascade is based on little information relative to the information of private individuals. Thus, a key prediction of the theory is that behavior in cascades is *fragile* with respect to small shocks."[53] This precariousness explains the truncated "life cycle" of fads—by the time a fad is recognized as a fad, the clock has already started ticking.

As mass media distribution and marketing research became increasingly sophisticated following World War II, fad cycles became ever more short-lived and fragile. Just a year after declaring rock and roll buried by calypso's ascendance, *Variety* magazine reversed itself and announced in a headline that the calypso craze was "Stone Cold Dead in the Marketplace" (a reference to the popular song of the same name). In early 1957, the trade magazine reported first that calypso recordings had slowed down ("as against 20 or 25 releases four or five weeks ago, during the past week only a couple of struggling calypso tunes were put out"), and then that nightclub bookings were drying up ("there are still several spots in town that are working the calypso displays, but not too many are expected to survive into the fall").[54] By the middle of the year, the autopsy was underway as the magazine asked: "Natural Death or Murder?"[55] The general finding was that the shallow stock of commercial calypso music was not deep enough to last more than a few months and that "the lack of representative performers and paucity of authentic material handicapped the growth of the fad."[56]

Put another way, fads, like people, have life spans. In black entertainment in the Jim Crow era, this sense of commercial life span is not unrelated to the nonmetaphorical sense of social-biological life span. Black fad performance allegorizes the particular racialized condition that Abdul R. JanMohamed calls a "death-bound subjectivity" in order to describe "the subject who is formed, from infancy on, by the imminent and ubiquitous threat of death."[57] For JanMohamed, this death-bound subjectivity is shaped as an effect of a "constant yet unpredictable" threat posed by lynching and state violence in the first half of the twentieth century as well as the "*effects* of that terror on the processes of subject formation."[58] But black fad performance shows us how it is also shaped by more mundane and metaphorical consumptions of blackness. The precarious position of the fad performer allegorizes the more literal threat to black life as a fad's condition of existence is its own imminent obsolescence, and this perilous temporality helps us to understand the aura of deathliness that haunts the compulsory animation of racialized entertainment in the Jim Crow era.

The "death" to which the black fad performer is bound is, of course, a symbolic or representational death, though to the extent that it may imperil the performer's "livelihood" or ability to "make a living" it also has considerable material effects. Clearly, falling out of fashion is nothing like the violence of lynch law. But these scenes of frenzied consumption are not as unrelated as we might wish to think. In his early sociological work on the fad, Bogardus identified similarities between the affective frenzy of commercial crazes and pogroms against stigmatized groups.[59] In the New York City race riot of 1900, the connection between fad performance and the lynch mob became visible as throngs of white men reportedly called out for Ernest Hogan, Bert Williams, George Walker, and other popular ragtime performers as they attacked residents in a black neighborhood; Walker was beaten and narrowly escaped, and Hogan sought refuge from an advancing mob in a black hotel.[60] And as many firsthand accounts throughout the early twentieth century testify, the high visibility of successful black performers traveling to distant towns on vaudeville circuits regularly exposed them to the threat and, often, realization of physical violence. Nathan Huggins relays one example: "the veteran comic Tom Fletcher recalled that many of the small southern towns his company performed in were so hostile to Negroes that violence was always threatening, murder seemed in the shadow of the white men's eyes."[61] In the estimation of calypso craze performer Geoffrey Holder, by the civil rights era white consumption of black entertainment was nothing so much as the sublimation of this violence into tolerance. "Just as lynching is a symbolic sacrificial act, so it is in reverse," he wrote. "The black celebrity is in a noose he never made: a black icon, victimized by the reverence of people in search of instant atonement, absolution, amends."[62] Such histories cast the RCA Victor marketing kit advertisement previously described in a different light. As the five, separate, white hands all grab for the Belafonte sleeve, the records become an effigy of Belafonte, and the fad monger and the lynch mob are brought uncomfortably close together in their shared desire for the consumption of the black body.

It is the fad performer's axiom: this time is not yours. Fads have no future (though they may have an afterlife). To be a fad is to know one is swept up in an informational cascade that more often than not trapped black performers in its representational eddies. Black fad performance is subject to market conditions shaped by a profound skepticism in value and a fragile life span. Although we are accustomed to thinking of Jim Crow mass culture as the representational straitjacket that inhibited black expressive form, R. W. Thompson (and countless others after him) identified a dialectics of blackness and mass culture that also produced new relations and forms. In the rush to profit from a fad's consumer frenzy yet uncertain about where exactly the fad's value laid, entertainment industries quickly marketed timely performances, movements, and sounds. But the fad cascade's very state of insecurity provided performers with opportunities to seize this time and the newly available resources that came with it. Thompson pointed to three likely outcomes of the black performer's relationship to the fad: higher salaries, a kind of self-worth, and "an increased dignity to the calling itself."[63] Or, to parse this surprising claim another way, fad cascades offered opportunities for material, psychic, and formal transformation. These transformations came about not only, or even necessarily, from the representational manipulations of popular performance. Rather, they are immanent to the fad's ontological condition. Indeed, it may be the case that black fad performance was more damaging to black cultural forms *after* a fad cascade receded, leaving stagnant imagery and representational fixity without any of the flux and dizzying uncertainty that characterized the fad itself. The very precariousness of the fad and its epistemological uncertainty is what made this time open to repossession. Always receding, the fad moment briefly interrupts the death-bound trajectory of the black fad performer and allows her to use that time for herself, to repossess a commercial time for financial advancement, collective worth, and the development of a tradition.

The Story of the Lost Watch

> "Behold," I continued, "this moment! From this gateway, Moment, a long, eternal lane leads backward: behind us lies an eternity. Must not whatever can walk

> have walked on this lane before? Must not whatever can happen have happened, have been done, have passed by before?"
>
> —Friedrich Nietzsche

> Supposing Nietzsche to be black—what then?
>
> —Robert Gooding-Williams

Although Thompson's observations were made in the 1890s, at the emergence of black fad performance, they reverberate through subsequent moments across the Jim Crow era. As we saw in the first section of this chapter, the ragtime craze, the Negro vogue, and the calypso craze were racialized fad cascades that moved in eddies, circling back to earlier structures of racialized affect and keeping black performance trapped within patterns of entertainment and enjoyment that reproduced subjection. This repetition is less like the repetition-with-a-difference that has been a crucial resource for black performance than it is a kind of eternal return that ensnares the performer in an endless temporal loop. The notion of an eternal return is associated with the thought of Friedrich Nietzsche, but it is an idea with a long history outside of the West (through Indian, Egyptian, and Persian cosmologies) that often leaves it out of sync with Western logos. In scattered fragments throughout his later writing, Nietzsche reintroduced the idea of the eternal return into Western philosophy: in an infinite universe, everything that has happened has already happened and will happen again. Nietzsche called this his "most abysmal thought": the doctrine of eternal return posits a cyclical concept of time rather than a linear one and recognizes historical and existential repetitions that do not always indicate progress.[64]

How might the doctrine of eternal return help us to understand the negotiation of cycle and moment that structures the repetitions of black fad performance? While some strict adherents to Nietzsche's doctrine see the eternal return as a literal, physics-based return of the same, most interpretations understand it figuratively as what Nietzsche scholar Bernd Magnus calls an "ontology in allegory which is designed to function as an alternative to the dominant tradition."[65] Nietzsche's proposal of the eternal return offers some provisional insight into the ontological horizon of (im)possibility that characterizes Jim Crow fad cycles. In turning to Nietzsche, I follow the lead of both James Snead, whose account of black culture as a particular stance toward repetition draws on Nietzsche, and philosopher Robert Gooding-Williams, who invites us to cautiously and conditionally repurpose Nietzsche's insights toward a critique of white supremacy and antiblack racism. Mindful of the nationalist and supremacist impulses that underlie his philosophy, Gooding-Williams argues nonetheless that Nietzsche's critique of Western culture can be strategically appropriated and rearticulated within the concerns of black study and thought.[66]

With this intervention in mind, I approach the historical-ontological situation of black fad performance in the Jim Crow era as a particular form of eternal return. The historical and political-economic structures that we have seen throughout this chapter have shown fad cycles to be an apparatus of repetition that reproduces relations of performance and racial subordination. This is not a kind of return of the repressed (since these images are never repressed or removed from popular culture as much as they are simply out of style). Nor is it performance as twice-behaved behavior, the changing-same, or repetition-with-a-difference. Rather, it is the recurrence of a particular structure or form of race, affect, and capital in and as Jim Crow performance. It is performance as capture, like a needle stuck on a record wherein every variation is a further instance of stuckness. This form of return across the Jim Crow era—from ragtime craze to Negro vogue to calypso craze—determined the situation of the black fad performer; his or her relationship to cultural production, distribution, and consumption; and the (im)possibilities of agency, resistance, or authenticity. One became a fad within the culturally recursive horizon of Jim Crow, and what returned in this history is the logic, temporality, and ontology of black fad performance itself. As a temporal opening, any particular moment of black fad performance that occurs in the general structure of a fad cycle is not only a passing instance in the flows of mass culture but also a figure for the relation of the past to the future. This sense of return was produced not only (or even primarily) by the drearily familiar recycling of tropes and stereotypes from different eras, but also by the ontological condition of blackness in mass-culture fad cascades.

Approaching black fad performance through this ontological framework turns our attention to something other than the manipulation of signs or representations that scholars such as David Krasner, Houston Baker Jr., and others have identified as strategies of parody and resistance. In addition to such strategies, the possibilities for self-worth and greater integrity for performance that the *Indianapolis Freeman* called for can also be located in black fad performance's encounter with its own temporality. This aspect of black fad performance helps explain how the most inauthentic, commercial, and coerced performances repeatedly disclosed themselves as deeply engaged with inventing black cultures and politics. It is at this ontological level, not only or just its semiotic level, that black fad performance critiques, exploits, modifies, and sometimes transcends its inauthenticity and reclaims time for itself, affirming itself in the face of its obsolescence. In proclaiming its inauthenticity, black fad performance capitalizes on the structural doubt of the cascade regime to imagine a kind of authenticity through authenticity's negation. This is not authenticity as something revealed, already there, behind the inauthentic—behind the mask—but rather the affirmative, performative repossession of fad time and its conditions of skepticism in order to realize a different understanding, value, truth, and world. And yet the fad moment does not make a claim to a fully self-present temporality. Rather, it acknowledges the impossibility of any such self-possessed time. Fad time is only ever borrowed time.

Or stolen. This is the claim made repeatedly, at any rate, by the performances of one of the calypso craze's most discerning and elegant performers, Josephine Premice (fig. 3). In the decade before the calypso craze, Premice perfected the role of the calypso chanteuse. She began performing calypso numbers at the Village Vanguard in New York City in the 1940s and was well positioned to capitalize on the renewed interest in calypso following Belafonte's *Calypso*. She studied dance with Martha Graham and Katherine Dunham, performing in the First African Dance Festival at Carnegie Hall in 1943 and with the Dunham Company in the 1945 Broadway revue *Blue Holiday*. Like Dunham, she studied anthropology, completing an undergraduate degree at Columbia University. She appeared in the two biggest calypso musicals of the 1950s—*House of Flowers* (1954) and *Jamaica* (1957)—but was most successful in her nightclub acts. With supper club sophistication, she belied the island folk stereotype: she took the stage in Dior gowns and high heels rather than the costume peasant clothes and bare feet common for such acts.[67] In addition to Trinidadian calypsos, she performed popular standards in calypso arrangements (such as George Gershwin's "The Man I Love") and often sang French numbers that were more evocative of Edith Piaf than Trinidadian tent music.[68] By 1952 she was earning $1,500 a week for engagements in the United States and across Europe, where she was hailed as "le petite Josephine" (as heir to Josephine Baker) and, more simply, as "La Bombe."[69]

Because of her Caribbean-inflected repertoire and visibility on the nightclub circuit, she invariably drew comparisons to another prominent second-generation Caribbean American fad performer. "If there's an opposite number of Harry Belafonte in the opposite sex," began one review of her act, "it must be Josephine Premice."[70] Yet as will become clear, despite the fact that his album appeared before hers, Premice was not derivative

Figure 3. Josephine Premice, 1956. Photo by Gilles Petard. Referns/Getty Images.

but in advance of Belafonte as the preeminent performer of the calypso craze. Within three months, at the height of the calypso craze, Premice recorded two albums that were in dialogue with Belafonte's rising success and the sudden cascade in commercial calypso: *Calypso* (GNP Crescendo, recorded in December 1956) and *Caribe* (Verve, recorded in March 1957), the former directly signifying on Belafonte's recent breakthrough album (which was recorded in the fall of 1955 and released in May the following year). Premice's albums imagined the popular calypso tradition from a female vantage point. The liner notes to the first album dub her "Calypso Jo," a gender play on the stereotyped figure of calypso masculinity Calypso Joe.[71] In the Trinidadian tradition, female calypsonians were rare in the male-dominated tent shows and carnival milieu before independence.[72] But in the United States, a tradition of black women's nightclub performance paved the way for Premice and others to expand the possibilities of Trinidadian popular song.

Calypso and *Caribe* drew from Premice's nightclub acts and playfully but incisively scrutinized the temporal and ontological aspects of fad performance that I have described. Her songs, that is, stage an encounter with their own temporality and describe and enact the theft of time itself. A close consideration of her recording of the Trinidadian song "The Lost Watch" from *Calypso* will demonstrate what I mean. This song has a short but rich history. It was written and performed by the influential calypsonian Roaring Lion (Rafael de Leon) for the 1948 Calypso King tent competition, where it placed fourth.[73] It had much more success in the US calypso craze eight years later, where it was recorded at least four different times, including versions by Duke of Iron (1956), Robert Mitchum (1957), the Kingston Trio (1959), and Premice herself. It was covered under various titles—"Tick! Tick! (The Story of the Lost Watch)," "The Missing Watch," "Tic Tic Tic," and "The Lost Watch"—but each version told the same story: a young woman pickpocket named Melda lifts a watch from a man at a train station. Although the police can hear the watch ticking, they cannot locate it on the suspect. At the police station, a matron is called in to conduct a more thorough inspection. Finally, the matron finds the watch hidden in the woman's mouth.

"The Lost Watch" is a remarkable song, and Premice's choice to record it as the first cut on her *Calypso* album—an album named after (or stolen from) Belafonte—holds deep significance. This song about the impossibility of possessing one's own time stands as a commentary on the relationship between the calypso craze, gender, and the temporal condition of black fad performance:

> What a confusion!
> A fellow lost his watch in the railway station.
> What a confusion!
> A fellow lost his watch in the railway station.

A saga girl named Melda was accused of being the burglar.
She had no purse, no pocket in her clothes.
Where she hid the watch only goodness knows.
And they were hearing:

Tick! Tick! Tick! Everybody looking!
Tick! Tick! Tick! See them how they're searching!
Tick! Tick! Tick! That's all they're hearing!
But they couldn't find out where the watch was hiding.

The song identifies Melda as a saga girl, locating her within the Trinidadian youth subculture of the 1940s that took its sartorial cue from the Zoot suit–wearing hipsters of Harlem. Historian Harvey Neptune explains that saga was a style and an attitude, and that saga boys "signified an uncompromising gesture of refusal" to the values of middle-class respectability and "embodied the triumph of urban leisure and pleasure."[74] The character in the song comes from this subcultural milieu, and "saga girl" might also gloss as "prostitute," given the association of saga boys with vice and crime in Trinidad's underworld. In the context of the calypso tent competition for which Roaring Lion first wrote the song, "The Lost Watch" invites both identification with the saga girl—who reflects the social world of the audience at the tent competitions—and objectification as the male singer describes the investigation of the woman's body and the probing of her interior:

Under suspicion, they took her down to the police station
And asked for the matron
To examine all the clothes that she had on.
The matron examined with care,
She even made her pull down her long hair.
She searched and she couldn't search no more
But the watch now ticking louder than before.
And they're hearing:

(Chorus)

Confusion now in the station.
They made the searching by inspiration.
The watch ticking louder and louder
And the matron moving up closer.

The matron is convinced, there's no doubt,
She push her hand inside Melda's mouth.
And do you know her idea came true—
When she found the watch it was ten to two.

Still ticking!

(Chorus)

The punch line of the song turns on the double entendre in the final verse. Most male recordings of the song emphasize the sexual connotation of the lyrics by taking an extra beat before the word "mouth," allowing the listener to anticipate and imagine other bodily locations where the watch might be hidden. Here, the premise is different. Double entendre was not Premice's style. One critic even noted that, unlike most calypso-themed shows, Premice's "special material depends more on sharpness than the gray intermediacy of suggestive entendre."[75] This sharpness was a refusal of coyness that made her version more pointed and confrontational. When she reached the most sexually suggestive moment in "The Lost Watch," she did not linger on the double entendre. In passing over the joke, she steals the song back from the pornographic punchline and refuses innuendo. Although the meaning of the lyric is clear, in performance Premice takes away its irony and the song becomes a surface.

The singer's recording of it is thus also a gender theft. Premise gives Melda a different embodiment than when the number is performed by Roaring Lion or Robert Mitchum. At moments in the song, her voice and by implication her body stand in for Melda's voice/body in a way that cannot happen when a male singer performs it. Premice's recording, that is, shifts the song from description to presentation (and we might also detect possibilities for a queer disidentification with the song, given the iconography of the butch police matron in popular and sexological discourses of the first half of the twentieth century, combined with what some might characterize as Premice's faultless performance of femininity). The sharpness and impenetrability of Premice stands in defiant tension with the penetration of Melda. Her version, moreover, omitted an entire verse included by all the male-recorded versions in which the police matron declares Melda "crazy," strips her (in a line that plays on the double meaning of "divest" as stripping her of her rights as well as her clothing) and "turn Melda's inside outside."[76] Leaving out this verse tempers—if only slightly—the violence of police power that the song presents.

Premice transforms the song from a scene of voyeuristic violation into one of savvy virtuosity. Understood as a response to the conditions of the calypso craze, the song functions as an allegory for fad time itself and the black fad performer's relationship to it. This time is hidden away in the mouth—the location from which the song itself originates. When Premice sings the lyrics "Tick! Tick! Tick!" at the chorus, the stolen watch and the very song that Premice sings become one. Premice sings of a stolen time that is simultaneously the time of the song itself as it is sung. But while the song ends with the discovery of the watch and its return to its rightful owner, it nevertheless continues for one more reprise of the chorus that begins with the defiant exclamation: "Still ticking!" Even though the property has been restored, Melda still has some seconds secreted away. The description of the ongoing search, even after the watch has been found, indicates that Melda still ticks, is still subject to detainment and search, and is still rendering great confusion. The song affirms the act of theft and allows for the possibility that Melda/Premice has some element of time that eludes police capture.

If "The Lost Watch" can be understood as a commentary on the performer's relationship to the calypso craze as a craze, a second song by Premice makes this implicit critique explicit and further demonstrates the ontology of black fad performance as stolen time. In "The Thief," from her album *Caribe*, Premice uses calypsonian devices such as irony and inversion to indict the entire calypso craze as a kind of theft. The thief of the title is Premice herself, who decides to engineer a reverse fad by stealing American folk songs and taking them back to Trinidad in imitation of the calypso craze:

In American it is the fad
To sing the songs of Trinidad.
Yankees borrow the melodies
Of calypsos from the West Indies.

So I check into legality
Of borrowing words and the melody.
And then I go up to New York City
And take a great big trunk with me.

I stay a couple of week
And I find the thing I seek.

Then I come back to Trinidad
And now I'm gonna start me own fad.

I bring back: "Way down upon the Swanee River,"
All the words and the melody.
I borrow: "Way down upon the Swanee River,"
And now I make the big money!

Premice as reverse-ethnographer comes from the periphery to the center in order to pack up specimens of local culture and defamiliarize the calypso craze. The phrase "I bring back" functions both geographically and temporally: she brings these songs back to Trinidad and she brings them back into circulation and makes them fashionable again, recycling them in time as well as space. Standing in momentarily as Trinidadian—both in her general recording of calypso and in the particular narrative of this song—the Haitian American Premice describes a reverse musical migration in which she travels to the Caribbean with a trunk overfull of US folk songs, with which she successfully starts her own fad in Trinidad. In taking on a Trinidadian character in this song, Premice enacts a kind of national impersonation that historian Micol Seigel describes as "nation drag."[77] African American popular performers caught up in early twentieth-century race crazes across the Western Hemisphere often playfully stepped into other national traditions and personas. As Seigel shows, this practice was less often an attempt to pass than an avowed and even campy imitation, a performance of a racialized national identity that drew attention to its impersonation with a knowing wink.[78] In performing as Trinidadian in this song, Premice emphasizes the uneven alignments of pan-Caribbean identity, transnational migration, folk tradition, and consumer culture with an ironic return to the island from which she never came in the first place.

The song's refrain repeatedly accuses Premice of cultural theft. In a dialogue sung between the singer and a chorus of male voices, Premice responds with a self-defense that turns attention back onto the calypso craze itself:

MEN: Thief! Thief!
PREMICE: I'm not the thief.
MEN: Oh, yes you are!
PREMICE: I'm not the thief like the Yankees say.
MEN: Thief! Thief!

PREMICE: I'm not the thief.
MEN: Oh, yes you are!
PREMICE: Turnabout is oynly fair play.

The chorus issues a direct critique of the cultural imperialism of the calypso craze, but it remains entertainment rather than indictment precisely because these conditions are already out in the open: nobody believes that the fad is any kind of ethnographically pure calypso anyway. She further insists on the inauthenticity of the calypso craze by noting in a particularly piquant line of verse: "Favorite songs of the community / Never were sung by Harry Belafonte." Here again, in this reference to Belafonte's nonrelation to the folk songs of Trinidad, we find the knowingness of the fad cascade that I previously described. "The Thief" amplifies the message of "The Lost Watch" by reminding us that the stolen time of black fad performance is in fact time stolen (back) under the principle Premice articulates: turnabout is fair play.

The trope of theft in this song is not only thematic but also enacted musically along the melodic line. When Premice unpacks her trunk of stolen songs back in Port of Spain, she makes "big money" off of plantation numbers such as "Old Folks at Home," American folk songs such as "I've Been Working on the Railroad" and "Home on the Range," and, for good Commonwealth measure, the Australian ballad "Waltzing Matilda." As she lists her new catalog, she alters the melodic line of "The Thief" with a sample of each of these familiar songs. The number thus performs Premice's theft as it incorporates, for example, the melody of Stephen Foster's "Old Folks at Home" or Daniel Kelley's "Home on the Range" into its calypso line. For the listener, the effect is momentarily disorienting, not only because of the sudden interruption of West Indian style with these (to a US audience) familiar tunes, but also because it alters the tempo of the song. It is as if hearing a record slowed down from its proper speed for a few bars of music. The inclusion of "Old Folks at Home" among her sheet music doubles the theft in Premice's repertoire, shaped as that song was by the nineteenth-century blackface tradition. The songs that Premice steals are themselves prior thefts of blackness. As in "The Lost Watch," it is the fad itself that is stolen back. This turnabout-is-fair-play principle is further enacted in Premice's calypsoized versions of jazz standards such as "The Man I Love" and "Taking a Chance on Love" and other songs on *Caribe* that she inflects with her own Caribbean idiom. And on *Calypso*, Premice recorded an affectionate version of the popular ballad "Yellow Bird" that she recalled from her childhood. According to her daughter, "if there was any theft [in the calypso craze] in her view, it was of the song 'Yellow Bird,' a Haitian peasant ditty appropriated by unscrupulous songwriters."[79] Premice recorded her version under its French title, "Choucoune," in a tender act of repatriation.

I take Premice's performances on *Calypso* and *Caribe* as exemplary instances of black fad performance and the performer's relationship to knowingness, self-referentiality, precariousness, and recurrence. This stance toward her own performance is something she shared with black fad performers such as Bert Williams, Josephine Baker, and many others. While Premice teaches us how to understand the calypso craze in these songs, these qualities are not unique to her recordings. They are omnipresent throughout calypso craze performances and characterize not only the thematic but also the ontological matter of black fad performance. Black fad performance is predicated on its own symbolic death, but in the face of this precarious temporality fad performers often confront their imminent expiration to produce timeless performances. Not timeless in the nostalgic sense of everlasting, but its opposite: the instant that does not last. This being-without-time is described in the recordings of "The Lost Watch" and "The Thief" and can be heard throughout every song on *Caribe* and *Calypso*. If the performer in a cascade regime is subject to the tempos and tastes of the marketplace—belonging to a time that is not hers—these songs thematize the black fad performer's ability to appropriate fad time in order to carve out a possible temporality for herself, a chance for survival. Premice does not perform the calypso craze but steals it. Or, put another way, in her performance theft itself is stolen (back). Theft is return. It is not the cultural appropriation of a Trinidadian calypso tradition that she makes her own, but the fad itself. In this stance toward the calypso craze, Premice established a relationship of "mine-ness" to the craze that makes this a moment of authenticity in and through the conditions of inauthenticity. Black fad performance's being becomes itself not through disappearance but through theft: theft *of* ontology and theft *as* ontology. Dispossession is possessed, displacement is placed, divestment is vested, and turnabout is fair play. At the end of "The Lost Watch"—and at the end of the calypso craze—Premice and Melda are still ticking, with time enough but none to spare.

TWO

The Calypso Program: Technology, Performance, Cinema

The calypso craze occurred, as it were, twice: first as novelty, then as fad. In the 1940s, during and immediately after the United States' borrowed occupation of Trinidad during World War II, a national curiosity with calypso spread across airwaves and nightclub stages. Unlike the later Belafonte-fueled fad that repeatedly named itself as artifice, this earlier craze relied on concepts of origin and authenticity. The biggest hit of the period, the Andrews Sisters' infamous version of "Rum and Coca-Cola," spent ten weeks as number one on *Billboard*'s top ten and eight weeks on *Variety*'s, even as calypsonians Lord Invader and Lionel Belasco successfully brought a high-profile lawsuit against the songwriter to demonstrate that they were the song's true authors (as we saw in this book's introduction).[1] Trinidadian-born calypsonians Duke of Iron, Macbeth the Great, and Sir Lancelot played nightclubs in New York, Chicago, and across Europe; in 1947 the trio staged a "Monarch Competition" at Harlem's Renaissance Ballroom and Casino to crown an expatriate Calypso King (calypsonians who remained in Trinidad such as Roaring Lion and Atilla the Hun viewed these New York–based performers with remote derision for peddling their culture in the United States).[2] Stages across New York City offered spectacular displays of Trinidadian culture. Choreographer-anthropologists such as Katherine Dunham and Pearl Primus brought their ethnographically informed dance to theaters and concert halls. Elaborate revues presenting Caribbean culture such as Gerald Clark's *Carnival Dance of Trinidad* (1942), Carnegie Hall's *Calypso!* concert (1947; so popular it was revived for a second performance the following month), Sam Manning's *Caribbean Carnival* (1947), and Wilmoth Houdini's *Carnival and Dance* (1947) all featured first- and second-generation Caribbean performers from New York's West Indian communities. With such shows, Donald Hill writes, "a new pan-Caribbean artistic culture was being formed" in the United States.[3] By the end of the 1940s, calypso began to ebb, never fully receding but waning in popular interest until Belafonte interrupted the ascendency of rock and roll and started the second calypso craze with his 1956 album *Calypso*.

Although far removed from the barracks-yards and tent shows of Port of Spain, the performances and recordings of the 1940s professed to present calypso ethnographically. Houdini's *Carnival and Dance*, for example, promised fans "a virtual transplant [of] one of the famous tent carnivals, with all its colorful excitement" and described itself as an "Afro–West Indian Shango Dance Carnival."[4] Clark's *Carnival Dance* promised "an authentic duplication of what transpires at just that Sunday in Trinidad."[5] And Carnegie Hall similarly promoted that "for the first time in history an authentic West Indian Carnival will be presented. . . . All the color of the Caribbean island of Trinidad will be transplanted to the Carnegie stage with a complete reproduction of one of the traditional carnivals that are annual highlights in Trinidad."[6] This was a far cry from the avowals of inauthenticity that underwrote the calypso craze a decade later. The two calypso crazes represent two different ways of thinking about the music of Trinidad as it was marketed and consumed in the United States. The first calypso craze relied on a dominant logic of cultural authenticity and ethnographic authority, the second on a dominant logic of inauthenticity that, in the idiom of black fad performance, called into question the authentic/inauthentic dualism that has shaped race and mass culture throughout the twentieth century.[7]

Despite this fundamental difference, however, both calypso crazes depended on the interplay between race, performance, and mass media such as sound recordings and films. The relationship between live and mediated performance is the focus of this chapter. Like other black fad performances, the calypso craze spread through a combination of live performance events (such as the staged carnivals organized by Manning and Houdini or the nightclub acts of Josephine Premice) and mediated events (including the proliferation of sound recordings, television specials, and films). Neither of these types of performance took precedence over the other in the fad. They worked in tandem to advance the calypso craze. Seen within this transmedia production, we can view the calypso craze as a particular cultural *program*. I adapt the term *program* from media theorist Vilém Flusser, who came to see postwar society as increasingly shaped by technology programmed to generate images and meaning.[8] Writing in the late Cold War, Flusser grappled with the ontological effects of the revolution in information systems brought about by media apparatuses such as photography, film, and computers.

In particular, Flusser was struck by how such apparatuses are both programmed and programmer. The camera, for example, is programmed to take pictures and in turn programs the casual photographer who can manipulate the camera as a device but likely has no understanding of the technical operations that occur inside of it. Every apparatus nests within a larger program, such as "that of the photographic industry that programmed the camera; that of the industrial complex that programmed the photographic industry; that of the socio-economic system that programmed the industrial complex, and so on."[9] The calypso craze, likewise, was programmed by recording apparatuses that were programmed by an entertainment industry that was programmed by a long history of white supremacy, colonialism, and compulsory racial performance, and so on (indeed, at one point Flusser describes the West itself as a program).[10] All fads are programmed, and all fads program. Once the fad cascade begins, all the elements function as if automatically. Program here is both verb and noun; it is at once a doing, a thing done, and a blueprint for a future act. A program is a schedule, an itinerary, a plan to be executed, a sequence of operations, a code, a composition, a score (akin to music), a frequency, a strategy. It is a series of rules or a set of instruction that governs technological apparatuses in the automatic reproduction of information content. In their quasi-automation, however, programs are also vital "challenges to improvise."[11]

As a program and transmedia event, the calypso craze repeatedly brought live performance into contact with apparatuses of technological reproduction. By early 1957, for example, nearly a dozen calypso films were reportedly in production (one report wildly claimed that film studios had registered thirty titles containing the word "calypso"), though only a fraction of these were actually made.[12] Of those, each is notable for its self-reflexivity. They are all products *of* the calypso craze, but they are all also *about* the calypso craze. Unlike the performance spectacles of the 1940s and their ethnographic ambitions, none of these films tell stories of Trinidadian carnival or (with minor exceptions) present scenes of island folk music. Rather, they are backstage stories about record producers or nightclub impresarios trying to capitalize on the calypso craze. Studios made films about the fad in the fad's idiom, and these in turn became part of the fad. In other words, all of these films are films about themselves. Such a dynamic highlights the autogenerating and self-replicating dynamic of black fad performance more generally. This is black fad performance's *critical solipsism*: a solipsism that knowingly uses the fact that there is nothing to know outside of itself in order to gesture toward the conditions that make the fad possible and thus to hold open a space of freedom for that which lies beyond it. In making the fad about itself, this critical solipsism displaced questions of origin and authenticity in order to pose different questions about blackness in the New World. The calypso craze thus remained faithful to the Trinidadian calypso tradition in its betrayal of it.

This chapter draws a line from the theatrical displays of ethnographic calypso of the 1940s to the inauthentic kitsch of the calypso revue of the 1950s to its take-up by Hollywood as part of the cinematic calypso craze. Across this trajectory, I pay close attention to the technological apparatuses of the calypso craze because these are the locations where possibilities for the interruption or malfunction of the calypso program are most likely—and perhaps inevitable. As we saw in chapter 1, black fad performance is structured by an intrinsic epistemic malfunction: the skepticism and paradox that are its conditions of possibility. The calypso craze's knowingness and critical solipsism created incongruous moments that provide insight into the technological (re)production of race and nation. The low-budget musical movies made in time to capitalize on the fad—*Calypso Joe* (Allied Artists, 1957), *Bop Girl Goes Calypso* (United Artists, 1957), and *Calypso Heat Wave* (Columbia, 1957)—all turn the pursuit of authenticity on its head and bring the ethnographic momentum of the craze of the 1940s to a halt. They cause the technologies of authenticity to malfunction. In the universe of technical images, as Flusser describes the postwar world increasingly saturated with mass-produced images, "we can no longer be revolutionaries, which means to be opposed to the operative program through other programs. We can only be saboteurs, which means to throw sand on the apparatus' wheels."[13] While Flusser may overstate the inevitable futility of revolutionary action, his call to sabotage the apparatus reverberates throughout the history of race in the Americas. In its knowingness and self-referentiality, black fad performance routinely draws attention to its program and isolates the apparatuses that help to carry it out.

The films of the calypso craze, at any rate, depict the apparatuses of their own production as machines that can be halted, sped up, or reprogrammed. We might even think of these films' ability to imagine the malfunction of the apparatus as symbolic kin to the time-honored act of workers' struggle that historian Eric J. Hobsbawm called "machine wrecking."[14] These films betray the fundamental role of technological apparatuses in the production of racial meaning. In not disavowing or obscuring the apparatus, the films draw attention to their own program and perform their inauthenticity. Unlike the ethnographic program that informed the calypso boom of the 1940s, where apparatuses produced authenticity-effects through the disavowal of their mediating function, the films of the calypso craze of the 1950s repeatedly draw attention to themselves as apparatuses. Rather than offering an opportunity to *look through* or *past* the film to the calypso performance behind it, they insist that we can only *look at* or *on* the calypso craze as surface. Later in this chapter I will demonstrate this with the example of two films from the cinematic calypso craze: *Bop Girl Goes Calypso,* which dramatizes the malfunction of technologies of racial measurement, and *Calypso Heat Wave,* which disrupts the technologies of racial representation and reproduction. These films throw sand on the fad's wheels and gum up the works of the calypso craze's technological reproduction of blackness.

An underlying argument of this chapter, one whose importance will become increasingly clear, is that our understanding of black performance history is unnecessarily impoverished by theories of performance that insist on liveness or copresence and exclude the mediated fashioning of the body in song, story, and movement—or what we can think of as deferred performance. The calypso craze demands a more capacious understanding of performance. Performance deferred is still performance. Or, put another way, all performance is performance deferred, and coabsence (in Alexandra Vazquez's terms) becomes just as important to understanding performance as copresence.[15] The uneven continuities of history, aesthetics, form, and politics that make up the tradition of black performance in the Americas are arbitrarily interrupted by a performance/media divide that prioritizes the live over the mediated as ontologically prior and primary. Media in the calypso craze is not simply a record of or conduit for performance, but is itself a mode of performance. In the discussion of the cinematic calypso craze that follows, I thus treat recorded performance as coequal to live performance, something different but not derivative. There are at least two important issues at stake in this approach. First, if what we call black performance is limited only to the live and the immediate, then entire domains of embodied black self-fashioning and their effects are barred from consideration for the study of black performance. One consequence of this is that performance scholars are left with an incomplete understanding of racial performativity and the ways that blackness complicates any easy boundary between "live" and "mediated."[16] Second, as I will elaborate, the insistence on presence and liveness reproduces a mode of subjection that Bryan Wagner calls the *principle of live fidelity* and José Esteban Muñoz calls the *burden of liveness*. Among other drawbacks, the view of recording as something-other-than-performance denies the performative excess of the recording itself, erroneously grants ontological priority to live performance over sonic and visual reproduction, and can contribute to the myth that on enough viewings or listenings a recording can render black performance transparent, fixed, or fully knowable. On the contrary, as Vazquez reminds us, "the recording itself demands a kind of running or chase without end as it always avoids capture."[17]

Jumping the Groove

Before turning to the cinematic calypso craze of the 1950s, I first visit some revealing moments that illustrate the ethnographic logic of the first calypso craze (a logic that the second craze will refuse) and shed light on the complex interactions between race, performance, and apparatus. This excursion will highlight some key encounters between the calypso ethos and influential folklore collectors such as Melville Herskovits and Alan Lomax. The first occurs in and around the Trinidad field expedition taken by US anthropologists Melville and Frances Herskovits and the preparatory arrangements, diary, field recordings, and published ethnography that documented their trip. At the height of the postwar calypso boom in 1947, Knopf brought out the Herskovitses' *Trinidad Village*. They based this study on several months of fieldwork they conducted in Toco, a rural village in the far northeast corner of Trinidad, in the summer of 1939. *Trinidad Village* was not part of any calypso craze per se, but the publisher marketed the book toward a general as well as a specialist reader and it appeared in a postwar moment when US culture was increasingly attuned to Trinidadian music and culture.

While family life and religious practices occupy most of *Trinidad Village*, a chapter on "The Avenues of Self-Expression" contains a discussion of recreation and music. By the time of its publication Trinidad was already advertising itself to North Americans as "The Land of Calypso," but the Herskovitses surprisingly downplayed the song in their study.[18] Following a discussion of sacred rituals and communal songs, they conclude that "there is also the calypso, but calypso is a name not often heard in Toco, except when commercial records are being discussed" (it is worth noting that the Herskovitses conducted their fieldwork during the summer months and were not present for carnival season or the preparations leading up to it). They further emphasized that "the calypso has been made famous by the recordings that have come to wide distribution outside Trinidad."[19] The authors disappointedly describe how this foreign incursion makes Trinidadian culture unknown to itself. They recount that many Tocoan youth approached them to perform local folk songs, only to deliver "little changed commercial recordings—Trinidad calypsos, and Harlem blues."[20] Their association of calypso with "Harlem blues" lets slip their anthropological suspicion of technology. In folkloric terms, "Harlem blues" would refer to a commercial urban blues sound developed in the 1920s and seen as a derivative imitation of rural or country blues. For the Herskovitses, the commercial reproduction of calypso renders it alien to the traditions of rural Toco, a cosmopolitan and modern influence that threatens the particularity of Trinidadian folk culture with a mass-produced homogeneity. In this account, calypso music appears as something that enters Toco from outside, arriving in the form of commercial records from North America or radio broadcasts from urban centers such as Port of Spain.

But just as quickly as the US anthropologists draw a boundary around Toco to keep calypso out, they reverse themselves and argue that, in fact, true calypso as an expression of village life has been in Toco all along. "Even in the commercially recorded calypsos," they go on to write, "the same themes we have found in the Toco reel and bele, *bongo* and calenda, are to be constantly encountered."[21] Calypso's popularity abroad, the Herskovitses conclude, does not in the end detract from its "vitality," and has "no special significance for communities such as Toco, where calypso songs of local origin are part of the broader stream of musical self-expression."[22] According to their logic, calypso and its themes persist as part of the everyday fabric of Toco life after all, though this calypso ethos is notably different from the commercial calypso records that separate the song from its origin and return it to the village as something other than when it left, touched by the glitz and polish of the metropole. Careful discernment can identify the vestigial traces and retentions of Caribbean themes in the North American circulation of recorded calypsos, but this is a feeble etiolation of calypso's folk vitality. Isolated from the flows of everyday village life, *that* calypso is of little concern to the villager and of little use to the anthropologist. If Harry Belafonte would later insist during the calypso craze of the 1950s that *this* is not *that*, the Herskovitses insisted that *that* is not *this*.

These misgivings about commercial recordings reflected an antitechnological unease common to early twentieth-century anthropology and ethnomusicology that viewed mass culture as a threat to folk traditions. The Herskovitses were eager to describe Toco, for example, as a place where a small phonograph is a rare "item of luxury," and one could count "only three or four radios" in total.[23] The absence of mass-media apparatuses preserves the authenticity of Toco culture and keeps the modern at a distance, allowing the Herskovitses to assure their readers that recording industries did not threaten the "vitality" of local Trinidadian calypso. In other words, this anxiety around calypso in *Trinidad Village* divulges a deeper wish to keep Toco *live* and unmediated by modern culture industries that originate from the metropole. Ironically, it would turn out, the solution to such technological corruption had a technological remedy: field recordings made possible by new phonographic technology—the very technology that threatened folk culture's liveness—could be used to preserve that liveness by documenting folk culture before its corruption by mass culture.

This paradoxical logic of ethnographic field recordings—that one could preserve the liveness and immediacy of folklore through technologies of mediation—had much more in common with Tin Pan Alley and Harlem blues than the Herskovitses would probably have been willing to admit. In his discussion of the early recordings of the ragtime craze, Bryan Wagner describes how the black singing voice entered phonographic recording as a mark of racial authenticity and liveness from its very beginnings. The pioneers of early recording technologies considered the black voice uniquely suited for demonstrating the sonic accuracy of their devices; to white ears, recorded blackness sounded "exactly like" its live precursor. When listeners heard it, they imagined themselves hearing not an imitation or a copy but "the real thing."[24] The grain of the ragtime performer's recorded voice, furthermore, distinguished him from white singers who performed so-called coon songs at the turn of the twentieth century. Common sense tells us that the faithfulness of a recording to a source can only be ascertained after the recording is made. Wagner suggests, however, that early recording innovators and folklorists inverted this common sense. Paradoxically, the black singer's voice materialized as faithful to its source *before* it was recorded, and recording technicians sought it out for its inherent suitability for recording. Wagner names this the principle of live fidelity: "if fidelity is supposed to presume a gap between sound and source," the black voice obliterates that gap as collectors came to believe "that there were voices that were true to themselves in the moment of their expression."[25] The contradiction implied in the phrase "live fidelity" lies in the fact that faithfulness should only be measurable at a temporal and spatial remove from its origin, but in the case of the black voice it comes to be measurable in the moment of its live sounding. In this way, technologies of sound reproduction substantiated a concept of the black voice as providing unmediated access to an authentic folk culture, one that was identical to itself.

This understanding of authenticity produces (a particular concept of) blackness. Because of its intrinsic recordability, folklorists and Tin Pan Alley impresarios alike heard the black singing voice faithful to itself as a pure expression of a black folk culture. Subsequently, the principle of live fidelity required the disavowal of technology for that authenticity to be secured. Such a disavowal enabled folk collectors "to translate the concept of live fidelity from a technological into a cultural idiom."[26] Mediation renders blackness immediate. The principle of live fidelity is a variation on what José Esteban Muñoz calls "the burden of liveness"—the mandate to perform that animates racial subordination and works to deny the possibility of both historicity and futurity as such performances become "a substitute for historical and political representation."[27] In Wagner's account, the irony is that the ethnographic logic of a folk purity untouched by modernization is an effect of the phonograph. The recording proleptically guarantees the authenticity of the source and the source as authentic to itself. "The aura," writes Wagner, "is made, not destroyed, by the phonograph" as technological fidelity becomes cultural fidelity.[28]

Operating under the principle of live fidelity, the Herskovitses collected hundreds of field recordings of Trinidadian musics, including religious songs, work songs, quadrilles (reels), bongos, and a few carnival songs. If the Herskovitses heard commercial calypsos as an antisoundtrack to their *Trinidad Village*, these field recordings promised a corrective. Melville Herskovits worked closely with Lincoln Thompson, the president of the Sound Specialties Corporation, in preparation for his trip, which would be the first to attempt extensive field recordings in a tropical climate. He purchased the following items to bring on his Toco expedition: 1 SoundScriber Junior recording machine, 1 special loud speaker case, 1 Western Electric "saltshaker" microphone (instead of "the usual Brush sound cell microphone which is not advised where temperatures may exceed 110 degrees"), 1 SoundScriber cutting head, 1 SoundScriber cutting head (spare, loaned), 1 Pr. Trimm Headphones, 50 feet of microphone extension, 1 pair Jones plugs on extension, 5 steel stylii, 5 Sapphire stylii, 1 set of spare tubes, 24 twelve-inch acetate discs, 1 Kato 300 watt belt drive gasoline engine for 110 volts AC, 201 twelve inch acetate discs, 3 sapphire cutters for acetate, 400 steel needles, and a specially constructed box and carrying platform for gas engine.[29] The SoundScriber was a dictation machine powered by a generator that used a steel stylus to cut a groove into a soft acetate disk. Once they arrived in Trinidad, the Herskovitses quickly realized that the device was too heavy to carry around the village, and the front room of their Toco home subsequently became an unlikely salon and recording studio where they welcomed villagers to perform songs as they recorded them.

Melville Herskovits's diary from the expedition paints an almost charming portrait of a man continually defeated by his new recording device.

Things got off to a rocky start, as the Herskovits couple received only a brief demonstration of how to use the unfamiliar recorder before their departure, and "through a packing mix-up, the Herskovitses left for the field without the instruction book for either the recorder or generator."[30] Although the manuals eventually arrived, they had to make do without them for the first portion of their trip, and Melville Herskovits's diary details his struggles with the new technology. In one early attempt to record four local village women—Lovey Gilman, Louisa Neptune, Martha Saunders, and Venice Talbott—who arrived at their residence, the SoundScriber proved uncooperative:

> Lovey Gilman and her three comrades appeared; it developed that they came to sing, but, alas, the recording machine wasn't willing. Apparently the spring that controls the depth of the cut has gone bad again, despite [Leo] Phillips' [a representative from the Sound Specialties Corporation] doctoring it at the house before we left, and before darkness set in I had got myself into a grand stew and a fine sweat trying to repair the trouble. I was finally defeated, but it was good to learn that there were plenty of African-like songs besides the hymns to which everyone seems to be addicted.[31]

In a later letter complaining to Thompson about the equipment, Herskovits described how the cutting head continued to frustrate him. He "found it impossible to get the sapphire far enough down to make a deep enough track to prevent jumping from one line to another on replaying," and subsequently the delicate machinery's needle often moved crosswise against the cut grooves. "I spent the better part of two days with it, and finally arrived at a solution of lowering the entire head. I am now recording," he allowed, "but I wish it were possible to make a finer adjustment of depth of cut."[32]

Herskovits imputes an animacy to the apparatus. It is obstinate and unwilling to cooperate with his desire to record the four women. Specifically, he describes frustration at the machinery's refusal to cut a deep enough track into the acetate disk to inscribe the singers' sound without the needle escaping from the groove upon playback and jumping from one line to another, thus scrambling the recording. We can understand the necessity for the depth of the stylus as a desire for both technological and ontological closure to the recording session. This will to closure, provided by mediation, seeks to contain the song in the groove as a fixed and unchanging sample. Equally willful (at least in Herskovits's account), the apparatus refused this closure and its stylus's arm moved freely across the surface of the disk, preventing easy playback but perhaps more accurately inscribing something of the singers' own performative force and will to openness. It took two days before Herskovits was able to devise a solution that would allow him to record the songs that, he was excited to discover, had more direct traces of African influence than the Christian hymns he had heard thus far. As we will see momentarily, this resistance to mediation's closure occurs again and again in further instances of ethnographic display, and the possibility that surface itself provides a kind of openness, even a sense of freedom, will echo later in the chapter in the discussion of Maya Angelou's cinematic performance in the calypso craze of the 1950s.

The Herskovitses' field expedition was repeatedly plagued by such technological malfunctions—the tropical moisture caused the generator's brushes to lose speed and slow the turntable revolution; the speed of the motor was at one point unknowingly set too high; the motor's carburetor mixture was too thick—but eventually the Herskovitses got the SoundScriber working well enough to record hundreds of songs from the villagers.[33] These recordings were as influential in the field of anthropology as the published text of *Trinidad Village*, if not more so. They provided substantial evidence for the Herskovitses' theories of cultural retention, adaptation, and reinterpretation of African cultural practices in New World contexts (although many scholars, most notably Zora Neale Hurston and Eric Williams, charged their study of Trinidad with overstating the African retentions in the practices they observed).[34] Melville Herskovits taught the recordings often in his courses at Northwestern University and inspired a generation of ethnomusicologists, including his student Richard Waterman, who "used these songs to develop concepts such as 'hot rhythm'—the sense of syncopation found in much African-American music—and 'off beat phrasing of melodic accents'—extremely influential ideas in the early analysis of North American jazz." Moreover, "[anthropologist and minister of culture and education for Tobago] J. D. Elder's work on the African heritage in the music of Trinidad and Tobago was influenced by Herskovits, via [anthropologists] Daniel Crowley and Andrew C. Pearse."[35] These recordings circulated through classrooms, lecture halls, and archives across North America. Lovey Gilman and her comrades reached a large audience outside of Toco, ironically following the same routes as commercial calypso from Trinidad to American cities such as Chicago, New York City, and Washington, DC.

As these recordings circulated, they bolstered the principle of live fidelity in disciplines such as anthropology, folklore, and ethnomusicology. Their afterlife continued well into the twentieth century. In 1999, the songs reached an even larger audience when prominent calypso historian and anthropologist Donald Hill oversaw the release of a selection of them onto CD. In the recording's liner notes, the scholars involved describe the laborious process of creating digital tracks from "mono analog transfers made by work study students in the 1970s" that were themselves drawn from the deteriorating originals. Despite these multiple transfers, they assure listeners that "all tracks were equalized to restore as much of the ambiance and sparkle of the original performances as possible. Again, our intent was to 'look through' the medium to the original performances. They have not been heard as clearly since they were performed."[36] In an echo of the Herskovitses' assurance that the "vitality" of calypso persists in Toco despite commercial recordings, the CD promises that it has restored the "ambiance" and "sparkle" of the original performances. So ingrained is the principle of live fidelity/the burden of liveness that the liner notes can confidently characterize the animatedness and vitality of an original performance that the CD producers themselves could not have seen or heard. The recording demonstrates the faithfulness of the source to itself. The phonograph, as Wagner says, creates rather than destroys the aura of authenticity. This is not to rebuke the deeply valuable contributions made by Hill and others in disseminating these recordings to listeners today (and which make analyses such as my own possible). In their avowed intention to "look through" the medium, the CD producers remain faithful to the original approach of Melville and Frances Herskovits, who sought to preserve an immediate contact with Trinidad folk culture in the inscription of their SoundScriber's touch of stylus to acetate. Listening to the Herskovitses field recordings today we can continue to hear ethnography's commitment to the principle of live fidelity, which depends on a disavowal of the technology that guarantees the performance's vitality, ambiance, and sparkle in the first place.

Another encounter between the Herskovitses and Lovey Gilman and her comrades, however, tells a different story about performance, the apparatus, and the principle of live fidelity. A few days after Melville's battle with the SoundScriber's cut of depth,

> the four women came again and this time everything worked, except that occasionally a particularly loud note would cause the needle to jump and on replaying go back into the same groove. I think, however, that will come with time. We did three records, both sides, for a total of nine songs—bele, sentimental songs, and reels. The women were on the porch at the side, and the songs, carried by the wind toward town, seemed to have created a minor

> sensation, for people began to drift up the hill, and when we had Margaret [another villager] shoo them away, we could see the road in the valley with many more than ordinarily. So after this singing will be indoors.[37]

On this occasion, the performers' voices frustrated the efforts to faithfully record them. The sonic calibration of the voice—let us imagine it was Lovey Gilman's, or, rather, let her name stand for the collective women's voice that sounded the particularly loud notes in this chorus—jolts the stylus's arm. The needle jumps in response to alterations in Gilman's performance, making a scratch that carries the needle backward into the groove on playback and, in this repetition, prevents closure to the song's mechanical reproduction. Even while Herskovits eventually got his recordings (three records' worth) out of this session, Gilman manipulates the scene of recording and asserts her own performative force—one that travels across the village and draws a local audience whose presence is distracting and unnerving enough that Melville decided to move his recording studio inside. The singers offer their song, but not without occasionally exceeding and disrupting the scene of recording itself. In a very real sense, Gilman can "work" the machine as well as Herskovits, who earlier got himself into a "grand stew" and "fine sweat" trying to operate it. Recording here is not something that is only done to Gilman but also something that she does. She reveals herself as a sound engineer and a not-so-distant relative to the hip-hop artist who transforms the turntable into an instrument with a scratch. As such, Lovey Gilman and other folk singers are decidedly modern (especially seen alongside Melville's own perplexed relationship with the apparatus). With this scratch and jump, Gilman violates the principle of live fidelity by marking the technology that the collector seeks to "look through" in order to hear the original performance; the recording is less a window than it is a screen. The performer in collaboration with the apparatus turns the technology against itself and slows the smooth functioning of the ethnographic program, all the while creating "a minor sensation" that calls forth a second audience at the boundaries of the property and interferes with the act of recording. Needless to say, the recently released CD of the field recordings does not reproduce any of the malfunctions or jumped needles described in Herskovits's diary. The resistance of the object—either of the SoundScriber as apparatus or Lovey Gilman as ethnographic object—is muted as the performance of the medium is minimized and subordinated to the live performance it recorded, rendered now on CD as "clearly" as at its first occasion.[38]

Muted, but not fully erased. The CD includes the recording of "Polly Say

She Love Me," a sentimental ballad sung by Venice Talbott, one of Gilman's comrades. The sample of the song recorded is a little over a minute long. At the end of the track, we hear Melville Herskovits himself ask: "You done?" This unintended capture of Herskovits's own voice—from the recording, it is impossible to tell if his question is asked out of interest, respect, confusion, impatience, greed, exhaustion, or something else entirely—reveals the one-way act of collection to be a dialogue. Or, put another way, it renders audible the dialogic nature of all ethnographic collection that early anthropology and folklore sought to disavow. The question is a response to the song; the song is a response to the question, always-already asked. The exchange between Talbott's song and Herskovits's query suggests that even when the needle does not jump, the desire for technological and ontological closure—and that closure's refusal—remains audible in the recording, then and now.

One final scene, this one of Trinidad in New York City, will further illustrate the relationship between ethnography, mediation, and black performance as it appeared in the calypso boom of the 1940s. In 1947 (the same year that *Trinidad Village* was published), renowned folklorist Alan Lomax curated a concert at New York City's Town Hall called Calypso at Midnight. This showcase resembled the ethnographic entertainments of Sam Manning's and Wilmoth Houdini's *Carnivals* staged around the same time, but with a more anthropologically explicit sensibility—think *Trinidad Village: The Musical!* This concert was part of a series presented by People's Songs (a popular front organization founded by Pete Seeger, Lomax, and others to enlist labor songs and folk music in the broader leftist struggle for social change) and points to the political investment in calypso as "the sound of the people" at the start of the folk music revival that began in the 1940s.[39] With People's Songs, Lomax curated a series of late night concerts programmed to showcase folk music for a live audience. He staged evenings such as "Blues at Midnight," "Spirituals at Midnight," "Ballads at Midnight," and, on December 21, "Calypso at Midnight."[40] As posttheater destinations, these performances took on the feel of a nightclub show more than a concert.

The Calypso at Midnight program led audiences through what Lomax dubbed a "primer in calypso" that musically introduced the fundamentals of Trinidadian folk culture.[41] The irony was that Lomax employed commercial performers and popular entertainment to stand in as representative of authentic folk culture. Lomax served as emcee and brought well-known Trinidadian performers Duke of Iron, Macbeth the Great, and Lord Invader to perform the program's songs and folklore, backed by bandleader Gerald

Clark and his orchestra. The trio of performers was familiar to US audiences, and each singer delivered a popular, Americanized calypso in order to ease the audience into the scene: "Ugly Woman," "Rum and Coca-Cola," and "Stone Cold Dead in the Market Place" (this last a popularized version of the Trinidadian bongo "Payne Dead, Payne Dead" first recorded by the Herskovitses during their time in Toco).[42] This set gradually gave way to presentations of less familiar aspects of Trinidadian culture, with a particular ethnographic tone. Macbeth explained the makeshift implement he called a Trinidadian harp (a percussive instrument made from a bottle and spoon) and sang the esoteric "Do Lai Do," a call-and-response work song that Donald Hill and John Cowley speculate Lomax first learned from the Herskovitses' field recordings.[43] Duke of Iron performed songs detailing the various religious groups of the island, including one sung in rituals of spirit possession. Following a brief intermission, a second act presented the elements of carnival: lavway (the calypso road march), tent songs, hand drumming, kalinda (ritualized Trinidadian stick fighting, demonstrated by two dancers credited only as DeLeon and Simeon), a calypso "war" in which the singers wittily insulted each other in improvised verse, and a calypso drama. This last musical form was a brief skit set to calypso that began to formalize in Trinidad in the 1930s. (Lomax's show resulted in the earliest-known recording of a calypso drama, Lord Invader's "The Lady and the G.I.")

As this program indicates, Calypso at Midnight was an embodied ethnographic text that drew freely on the mass production of calypso's postwar popularity and suggests the easy transit between ethnography and Tin Pan Alley. Like Melville and Frances Herskovits, Lomax too attempted to "look through" the ethnographic apparatus in order to hear the authentic culture it records. But unlike them, it was not the recording device but the popular performers themselves that were the mode of mediation. The show encouraged viewers (and listeners) to look through the commercial singers to see the folk culture behind them. Despite Lomax's casting of media stars, the principle of live fidelity ensured that audiences viewed the performances of Calypso at Midnight as "uncommonly true to themselves."[44] Yet as live performers in this ethnographic scenario, Duke of Iron, Macbeth, Invader, and others were able to work both with and against the principle of live fidelity. For example, shortly before intermission, Invader performed a calypso called "Tied-Tongue Baby." At the beginning of the song, Invader has difficulty hearing the band and misses his entrance. "Invader and the band are out of sync," as Hill and Cowley describe it in the recording's liner notes.[45] After a few bars of vamping, singer and band find the same groove and complete the number. But at the end of the song, Invader goes off script and offers an extemporaneous verse to address the stumble:

> Ladies and gents, just now when I started this composition,
> Don't you put no blame on the musician,
> Because I didn't get the chord, neither the tune correctly,
> That is why I stallin' the melody,
> It's my fault, Invader really have to admit,
> But in these verses, don't you see I did my bit.

Like Lovey Gilman's scratch, Lord Invader's false start, stalled melody, and improvised ending jump the groove, returning to the beginning of the sequence and refusing any easy closure. In doing so he not only displays the extemporaneous virtuosity of the Trinidadian calypso tent but also makes scratches in Lomax's staged presentation of folk authenticity. Literally of course the song ends, but not before Invader, like Gilman, thematically interrupts its will to closure by extending the song through the necessary chance of improvisation. Hill and Cowley speculate, further, that this brief misfire contains an entire history of class conflict in Trinidad between the figure of the musician, who could read music and often came from the upper classes, and the calypsonian, who usually did not read music and often came from the lower classes (an accurate description of the relationship between Invader and bandleader Gerald Clark).[46]

Such scratches—malfunctioning recorders, false starts, jumping needles, out-of-syncness, mishearings, lost chords, stalled melodies, rebeginnings, *You done?*—are haphazard but inevitable and can become the occasion for improvisatory invention. These malfunctions that Herskovits struggles against, Gilman engineers, and Invader improvises are not at all accidental in the sense that they are an inevitable and entirely expected part of any apparatus's performance, even if through the whim of chance. They are unavoidably part of the program's regular functioning. They are predictably unpredictable (it is not a question of if your computer will crash but when). One definition of a program in Flusser's terminology is "systems in which chance becomes necessary."[47] In the context of a program such as the calypso craze, "necessary chance" is one way we can define liveness. Rather than something to *look through* or *look past* in order to apprehend the performance they record, these accidents and malfunctions insist that we *look at* the apparatus as a participant in the project of race-making in the twentieth century. In this sense, Gilman reprograms the SoundScriber recorder and interrupts the principle of live fidelity that informs our understanding of black performance. Her recorded song reminds us that mediated performance, like live performance, can elude ontological closure and is not always identical to itself. Herskovits's diary compels us to hear his field recordings less as an artifact or a trace of past performance than as an emergent index of the conditions of racial reproduction. By jumping back into the same groove, the disk redirects the ethnographic desire to "look through" the technology to the putatively original performance behind it. The disruption or malfunction of the apparatus discloses its program and avows the technology that grounds the principle of live fidelity/the burden of liveness.

This desire to look through mediating technologies and reach the original source that I have described in the ethnographic scenes of Lomax and the Herskovitses had its commercial corollary in one of the mid-twentieth-century's most significant advancements in listening practices: the development and marketing of high fidelity recording technologies and home sound systems. By the mid-1950s, hi-fi referred both to an aspiration toward a purity of sound (a program) and to the home audio equipment that could deliver that purity in suburban dens (an apparatus).[48] High fidelity consoles, AM/FM tuners, turntables, and component systems with high quality speakers greatly increased sonic quality and transformed suburban rec rooms into new auditory sensoriums. Home audio culture had its own magazines, such as *High Fidelity* and *HiFi and Music Review*, and middlebrow lifestyle magazines such as *Life* and *Look* regularly covered hi-fi developments. This refinement in mass cultural technology was a key part of the calypso craze's marketing as an immersive and escapist experience. Record companies and audio systems manufacturers marketed hi-fi technology and recordings—of everything from popular and classical music to nature sounds and exotica—not as a way to bring the world into your domestic space but as a sonic transport to an exotic elsewhere beyond your staid living room. For the anthropological program, technology must be "disavowed by the ethnographic enterprise that [it is] made to serve" in order to secure unmediated access to the pure source, as Wagner puts it.[49] Similarly, hi-fi aficionados became experts in the minutiae of audio technology, which promised ever-purer sonic absorption—*as if you were there*. But the calypso craze of the 1950s avowed mediation and technology, making it a part of the spectacle. Even as record companies rushed to put out more hi-fi calypso albums, the craze itself advanced what we could think of instead as a no-fi aesthetics: one that repeatedly undermined the claim of cultural fidelity (as true to itself) that arises from the possibility of technological fidelity (as true to its source) by a continuous avowal and inevitable malfunction of the apparatus—*as if there is no there*. These are the historical, theoretical, and technological grooves cut and jumped by the calypso program. Such no-fi aesthetics characterize the craze in general and, as we will see in the next sections, its cinematic dimension in particular.

The Cinematic Calypso Craze (I): Performance without Copresence

By the calypso craze of the 1950s, the theatrical displays of 1940s ethnographic authenticity gave way to the elegant cosmopolitanism and no-fi aesthetics of the calypso revue. The calypso revue was a new genre of nightlife performance that incorporated standardized Caribbean music and dance into the black nightclub revue and made momentary stars out of women performers such as Josephine Premice, Phyllis Branch, and Enid Mosier.[50] At the height of the calypso craze, these revues were ubiquitous as upscale hotel lounges, intimate cafés, and cabarets transformed themselves into calypso rooms. The decor and costuming—fishing nets strung from

Figure 4. Calypso revue with singer Lord Flea, 1957. Photo by Yale Joel. LIFE Picture Collection/Getty Images.

Figure 5. Calypso revue with singer Pork Chop, 1957. Photo by Yale Joel. LIFE Picture Collection/Getty Images.

the ceiling; straw hats and tropical shirts—seasoned these rooms with a dash of Trinidad village, but they never encouraged their generally white and middle-class audiences to pretend they were having anything other than a stylishly urbane experience (figs. 4 and 5).[51] Like any revue, it is difficult to ascertain what new experiences, sounds, or knowledge were created in any single performance event; even when muffled, the sounds of carnival are difficult to silence. But as a genre the calypso revue dispensed with the ethnographic trappings of the 1940s and embraced artificiality.

Although the Village Vanguard in Greenwich Village invented the calypso revue in the early 1940s, the shows produced in the 1950s at Chicago's Blue Angel—the Cotton Club of the calypso craze—were the gold standard of the genre (fig. 6). Impresario Jean Fardulli, himself an accomplished opera singer, established the revue's formula: a calypso emcee (backed by a house band) hosted the evening, performed a few numbers, and introduced the acts. The entire cast would take the stage in the opening number, and the program would typically include a headlining vocalist, followed by a steel drum band, a drumming act, various dance numbers (including a male/female duet, a larger chorus number for the "heavy voodoo thing," and other novelty bits such as a fire dance or the "Dance of Possession"), and ended with "the usual Blue Angel finale, [the performers] weaving in and out among the audience with flash, noise, and speed."[52] The music was an undifferentiated mix of Afro-Caribbean and Latin American styles, foregrounding congas, bongos, and marimbas.[53] These fast-paced spectacles of "hip wiggling voodoo dancers and spicy calypso vocalists" abandoned any pretense of genuine Trinidadian culture and indulged in the calypso kitsch of the fad; one Blue Angel revue concluded by leading a donkey through the audience.[54] Eager for the opportunities to book on what was known as the "Caribe belt" that spanned major cities across the US north (and Miami), many black musicians added "island material" to their playlist to fit the fashion.

Not only were these calypso revues good work, they could also be entryways to performance in other media—specifically film and television. *Variety*, for example, endorsed one show as a "whirlwind bit of solid show-

Figure 6. Calypso Carnival postcard, Blue Angel nightclub, Chicago. Collection of the author.

manship, big for niteries, television stage work, and could be used in pictures to advantage in the right place."[55] As this endorsement suggests, the structure of the calypso revue provided the general framework for the cinematic calypso craze and represents another element of the larger calypso program.[56] Like many low-budget movie musicals of the 1950s, films produced as part of the short-lived calypso craze such as *Bop Girl Goes Calypso* and *Calypso Heat Wave* largely transported the nightclub revue to the screen. Each of these films uses the setting of a nightclub and the revue format in their plotting, and in most instances, they simply reproduced nightclub acts by performers such as the Kingston Trio, Lord Flea, Duke of Iron, and Maya Angelou. The often-baroque intricateness of the films' plots compensated for their narrative irrelevance as the story was little more than a thin pretext for a series of musical acts. A distant relative to the early cinema of attraction, which featured performance, spectacle, and sensation over narrative, these films could be thought of as feature-length soundies, the coin-operated film jukebox popular in 1940s nightclubs and amusement districts that allowed viewers to watch a short musical performance or novelty act.[57]

Although these films record some of the most accomplished and remarkable performers of the calypso craze, I do not take them here as artifacts or documents that preserve lost performances on celluloid and allow us access to (some glimpse of) the live event. Rather than separate liveness and mediation or police the boundary between them, I ask what happens when we see them as copartners in the making of performance. In doing so I also implicitly ask, following Wagner and Muñoz, what aims are achieved by keeping them separate. Because cinema shares photography's indexical relationship to its referent, it remains common sense to think of cinematic images as documenting events that have previously occurred. But to persist in thinking of it as a document is to continue to ontologically privilege the live and mark the film as derivative, obscuring the performance of the film itself. I do not, in other words, interpret these films quasi-ethnographically as something that we can "look through" to the performances they record. I take them instead as a refusal of the promise of the ethnographic gaze and the principle of live fidelity/the burden of liveness that undergirds it. Like Lovey Gilman's voice as it causes Melville Herskovits's SoundScriber to jump the groove, these films refuse this promise through their fad-governed engagement with their own technical apparatuses. In the remainder of this chapter, I look at how two of these films—*Bop Girl Goes Calypso* and *Calypso Heat Wave*—intensify the inauthenticity-effects of the calypso craze with a critical solipsism that foregrounds their own reproduction of the racial fad and the calypso program.

We know from its title that *Bop Girl Goes Calypso* is a film about the contagion and frenzy of the calypso craze. The film both presents and represents the affective compass of the fad. It follows Bob Hilton (Bobby Troupe), a graduate student of applied psychology and parody of the newly institutionalized study of mass communications who is completing an academic treatise on "Mass Hysteria and the Popular Singer." Explaining his theory that "every musical beat or style has a tendency to rise or fall in popular appeal . . . for example, a style that's on a rising trend needs only the spark of a vivid singing personality known or unknown to explode into tremendous popularity," Bob enlists a resistant club owner and his star performer, the wholesome Jo Thomas (Judy Tyler), to test his hypothesis. Armed with a scientific apparatus that he developed to measure the intensity of audience reaction to performance, Bob seeks the right performer to translate calypso into an American idiom. "As soon as I find the right singer," he tells Jo, "I'll prove my thesis and turn in my paper." He eventually persuades them that calypso will supersede rock and roll, and by the end of the film Club Downbeat transforms into Club Trinidad and the evening's performance is broadcast live over the radio.

Bob's preoccupation with scientifically measuring the intensity of fad performance is paralleled by a subplot about racial measurement pursued by Bob's fiancée Marion, a eugenicist colleague at his university. Marion looks with disdain on psychology, preferring instead the major literature in her field: "*Mating to Breed Personality. Mating to Breed Strength from the Jungle. Mating to Breed Appearance. Eugenics and the Mind of Man*. Did you get that? *Mind of Man*. Soon they'll isolate the heritable genes that affect the mentality, and then where will you and Dr. Winthrop be?" She intends to prove her thesis on biological determinism by having a child with Bob, whom she selected for his genetic profile. *Bop Girl Goes Calypso*'s explicit tension between biological and cultural determinism unfolds against the anxieties of youth culture, racial mixing, and adolescent sexuality in the 1950s and is a transmutation of racial measurement and descent that persists in various forms from the Enlightenment to the present. By the end of the film, Bob's culturalist explanations defeat Marion's eugenicist ones in a dynamic that plays out in the musical sphere. The logic of racial purity gives way to the sound of integration by the end of the film when Jo performs "Calypso Rock," a song that, as Michael Eldridge observes, is formally "a conscious hybrid [of rock and calypso], and hybrids are inevitably the product of crossbreeding." Eldridge continues to note that "the film offers no suggestion that calypso-rock's conception has taken place any way other than immaculately—which is to say, symbolically."[58] In other words, *Bop Girl*'s technologies of racial measurement are sublimated into its technologies of fad measurement, providing an imaginary resolution to the real anxieties surrounding popular music, youth culture, and racial mixture.

Solipsistically enough, then, *Bop Girl Goes Calypso* is a film about the calypso craze's concern with its own measurement and audience feedback. It not only depicts the careful calibration of performer and audience that occurs in live performance. It also participates extracinematically in the feedback loop of the calypso craze as a fad. Content follows function as Bob Hilton's measurement apparatus stands in for the reciprocal interaction between culture industry makers in Hollywood and their audiences. Performers, writers, directors, producers, and executives all receive feedback from spectators and incorporate that feedback in the further refinement of their performance. Samuel Katzman, producer of *Calypso Heat Wave* (discussed in detail in the next section) and dozens of other low-budget genre films, told reporters in advance of his calypso film that he always "keeps his well-tuned ear to the ground" and that he "tours the country twice yearly assessing public tastes and prowls the musical joints," adding that his "19-year-old son is perhaps the best barometer of juvenile tastes."[59] While this likely hyperbole gives his film the credibility of youth market authenticity (much more important than Trinidadian authenticity), it also reflects the general trend in advanced consumer culture, in which consumers are neither fed their tastes from a monolithic culture industry nor are wholly free agents but make decisions within a finely calibrated dynamic.[60]

This feedback and refinement of mass media's performance scrambles one of the distinctions between the ontology of performance and the ontology of film. The feedback loop between a performer and her audience is for many one of the defining characteristics of performance. Theater and performance studies scholars often distinguish performance from other forms of mediation by the shared time and space of the performer and the audience. This copresence allows for the reciprocal exchange of information and affect between the performer and the audience. Martin Esslin, to take one example, writes, "as regards the 'live' theatre its only true distinctive feature, and one that constitutes an immense advantage vis-à-vis the mechanically reproduced forms of drama, is its ability to establish an immediate interaction between performers and audience, a continuous feed-back of reactions." This feedback loop creates a continual calibration between audience and performer that allows performers to "immediately modify and adapt their performance."[61] To take another influential example, Erika Fischer-Lichte writes that "performances are generated and determined by a self-referential and ever-changing feedback loop. Hence, performance remains unpredictable and spontaneous to a certain degree."[62] For her, this spontaneity allows for varieties of experimentalism, for example in the play of proximity and distance and in the potential for a destabilizing role reversal between performer and spectator. In one final, concise example, Diana Taylor tells us, "the live performance can never be captured or transmitted through the archive. A video of a performance is not a performance."[63] The elision here of live performance into performance as such serves to make liveness or copresence a requirement for performance. This multidirectionality is distinct from the unidirectionality of film, sound recordings, and other media. While both live and recorded performances can affect the spectator, only in the live can the spectator affect the performer.

While satisfactory for a definition of the theater, such descriptions become parochial and partial when the rules of the stage are taken to stand in for performance as such. Esslin in particular is an unlikely yet revealing figure in this regard, for he does not commit this generalization. As we saw in this book's introduction, Esslin lamented the disciplinary division of film studies and theater studies. He sought to expand the notion of performance, as I do here, in a way that might include television and film. To do so, he proposed recuperating the word *drama* in the expansive way that scholars have come to understand *performance*. Esslin redefined drama to include not only the stage but also everything from "Renaissance *triomfi*; elaborate Corpus Christi processions in Bavaria, Austria, or Belgium involving huge puppets parading through the streets (and revived by Peter Schumann's Bread and Puppet theater)," carnival and religious processions; military parades; pageants and masked balls; circuses; and political spectacles to "contemporary avant-garde performance art; environmental theater; [and] happenings and similar experimental work."[64] In other words, Esslin proposed expanding the word *drama* to include everything that we now describe under the rubric of performance, but with one exception: Esslin also included film, radio, and television in his broad-spectrum approach.[65] For various reasons his call was largely ignored by subsequent generations of performance studies scholars, even while his general proposals accorded with the dominant direction of the field. There are numerous explanations for why this may have been the case, including Esslin's inclusion of mediating technologies. But among those explanations, I believe, was Esslin's simple retention of the word *drama*, which performance studies historically consigned to the realm of a more narrowly delineated theater studies against which it defined itself. Indeed, liveness and presence—necessary elements of theater—as they are taken for granted in performance scholarship today might be properly thought of as a return of a repressed theater studies within performance studies' institutional sedimentations.

As André Bazin suggested over half a century ago, "it is false to say that the screen is incapable of putting us 'in the presence of' the actor. It does so in the same way as a mirror—one must agree that the mirror relays the presence of the person reflected in it—but it is a mirror with a delayed reflection, the tin foil of which retains the image."[66] While the interaction between audience and spectator is a necessary requirement of performance, it is the notion of immediacy that *Bop Girl Goes Calypso* and other calypso films query. The calypso craze reminds us again and again that technological reproduction does not eliminate the feedback loop, but defers it. Indeed, we might even say that a fad, in its immediacy and mediation alike, is nothing other *than* feedback loop. The reciprocal exchange of information between performer and audience still occurs, but over the longer spatio-temporal horizon of the calypso program. Within the context of a program, Flusser explains, "the reception of technical images does not end the communication process."[67] Rather, "a feedback loop must appear between the image and the receiver. . . . The images have feedback channels that run in the opposite direction from the distribution channels and that inform the senders about receivers' reactions, channels like market research, demography, and political elections."[68] When viewed within the larger performance ecology of the fad, we can see that the programmed sounds and images of the calypso craze (recordings, film, television specials, and the like) are not passively received by consumers but are shaped in response to the earlier response of spectators, who in turn respond again, and so on. Any single film viewed, of course, does not allow for a multidirectional exchange between the performer and the audience. But when we recognize the fad as a whole scene of performance, we can see the constant calibration in its programming, staging, and production. The calypso craze as a program incorporates feedback as it reproduces and adjusts itself: from film to film, from television special to television special, from recording to recording.

Another way to describe this is performance without copresence, in which the relationship between spectator and performer is extended across space and time. To understand these deferred enactments as a kind of performance is to disarticulate liveness from embodiment. Performance continues to describe the aesthetic fashioning of the body into new roles, sounds, or forms, but here and now is only one possible spatiotemporal dimension in which that occurs. The cinematic calypso craze suggests another. To understand the stretch of black fad performance as a temporal mode is to recognize, in the words of performance theorist Rebecca Schneider, "a more intermedial history of live performance in relation to media as well as a more malleable notion of copresence informed by the complications of duration that resists determinate legislation of the boundaries of the 'now.'"[69] *Bop Girl Goes Calypso* shows us at least two temporalities at work in black fad performance: the temporality of the live performance—which happens in a circumscribed time and place, before an audience, in the plot of the movie—and the temporality of the fad's programming—which incorporates both the live and mediated performances of the calypso craze, extending the performing body both forward and backward in time, in the circulation of the film itself.

Fad temporality, as we saw in chapter 1, has an unknown but inevitable end. Commenting on *Calypso Heat Wave*, Katzman stressed to reporters that "I want to get the picture out in a hurry because this calypso craze won't last long . . . the kids like it now, but it will blow over."[70] Katzman describes a circumscribed temporality that resembles the ephemerality of live performance, but with a difference. It is not the film that disappears, as the celluloid print remains to be screened again, but the racial fad, which is itself performance. This is not a disappearance that allows performance to escape or elude mechanical reproduction; it is the performance of mechanical reproduction in fad temporality. The cinematic calypso craze thus shares at least two of the defining characteristics of performance. First, it too establishes a feedback loop between audience and performer (though over a longer duration and scale than the relatively intimate and time-bound theater performance). Second, it too is marked, as Katzman's comments demonstrate, by impermanence, fragility, and ephemerality (though within a different temporal horizon than a night at the theater). This is one way to understand the performances of mass culture, rather than performance as a romantic resistance to mass culture. Attending these calypso films was a way to participate in the larger craze and, like the early cinema of attraction, offered a sensory experience that evoked the variety theater. Any particular film was not a single event but an element of participation in black fad performance. The film does not mediate between viewer and the world but participates in the world with the viewer. The extended yet circumscribed temporal frame of black fad performance—its deferred performance—is a time that certain authorities have long claimed solely for the live and for the present. In making this time available to black fad performance, such films and recordings steal this time (back).

The Cinematic Calypso Craze (II): Projection without Representation

The self-reflexivity of Hollywood's cinematic calypso craze toggles between presentation and representation, production and reproduction. *Bop Girl Goes Calypso* is not only a story about the calypso craze but also an active participant in the calypso craze. *Calypso Heat Wave*, another critically solipsistic participant in the fad, likewise makes the apparatuses of black fad performance central to its story. Yet unlike *Bop Girl Goes Calypso*, in which the musical numbers are primarily staged in nightclubs, the musical numbers in *Calypso Heat Wave* are generally staged in a recording studio as performers record albums or broadcast live across the country. The film opens on a shot of a recording booth light blinking on, locating us from the start within the technological infrastructure of the calypso craze and alerting us that this is a recording of a performance of a recording of a performance. This first scene finds a singer and his band recording the song "Calypso Joe" in the studio, with teenagers from his fan club pressed against the glass recording room windows. Microphones and cords cut across the screen, and sound engineers monitor the record-cutting machine as it inscribes the song into a master disk. As the singer reaches the end of his song, the soundtrack stays the same but the scene dissolves to a lavishly appointed uptown apartment where a mobster, his girl, and his accountant are listening to the recording, now completed, on a jukebox.

The entire network of fad production, distribution, and consumption is neatly condensed in this dissolve from recording studio to jukebox. As this opening scene suggests, the film takes us behind the scenes of the calypso craze and makes the various technological apparatuses of the fad as much a part of the story as the musical acts. The singer is the fictional Johnny Conroy (Johnny Desmond), copartner and star artist of Disco Records. The mobster, Barney Pearl (Michael Granger), controls the jukebox distribution trade and threatens to withhold Disco Records disks from jukeboxes nationwide unless they give him a cut of their profits. Fleeing the heavy hand of the mobster, Conroy disappears to Trinidad, where he rediscovers calypso music (in the form of performer Maya Angelou) and returns to New York with a new list of singers for the label. The conclusion of the film is a live radio simulcast of a calypso revue, a musical showcase not unlike Alan Lomax's curatorial Town Hall Concert a decade earlier but without the folkloric authenticity. Throughout the film, *Calypso Heat Wave* repeatedly depicts its own program and, in doing so, demonstrates how the calypso craze projects nothing other than itself. As such, it is a project that can interrupt the principle of live fidelity/the burden of liveness that structures black performance in mass culture.

Within the calypso program, apparatuses perform whenever they assert themselves against their functionary, as the Herskovitses' SoundScriber did during their field recordings. *Calypso Heat Wave* is rich with scenes that self-reflexively avow the technological infrastructure of the calypso craze. Here I will focus on one sequence in particular. Singer and poet Maya Angelou performs the opening number for the live radio broadcast of "the first all-calypso carnival in America" at the end of the film. Several other acts follow her performance, in the style of a calypso revue. I turn to this sequence in particular because it is perhaps the only number in the film that manages to transcend the film's historical particularity as part of the calypso craze; the scene "juts out" from the film (as James Baldwin would say), even approaching Expressionism.[71] Like Josephine Premice's sound recordings discussed in the previous chapter and the Duke Ellington television special discussed in the next chapter, Angelou's screen performance fully achieves a stepping out of itself and becomes her own. It accomplishes this, as we will see, through its engagement with the conditions of the calypso program and its apparatuses. It fully realizes the possibilities of black fad performance, including its ability to mark and therefore exceed the conditions of its finitude.

The scene, in which she performs Louis Jordan's 1947 calypso hit "Run Joe," reproduces a number from her own theatrical revue, titled *Calypso Heatwave*, that ran in New York City in the first half of 1957.[72] In this context she appears in the film as herself, an index of the real, on a nightclub stage barefoot and adorned in an elegant white evening gown. Three musicians in stereotypical island garb sit in the shadows around her. Angelou herself begins singing in the shadows as a spotlight slowly opens onto her body and casts her in a brilliant circle of light. Curiously, over the course of the song the spotlight's aperture repeatedly dilates and contracts on Angelou, widening into illumination and narrowing into darkness. She is caught and fixed by this light. Planted firmly in the center of the stage, her arms reach outward in deliberate gestures of stylized struggle and restraint. The spotlight is in tension with her performance, seeming almost desperately to compel her to move while simultaneously containing that movement (fig. 7).

We could view this scene as the black fad performer's capture by the technologies of mass culture. Angelou is fixed by the spotlight, rendered

Figure 7. Spotlight opening and closing on Maya Angelou.
Calypso Heat Wave (dir. Fred Sears), 1957.

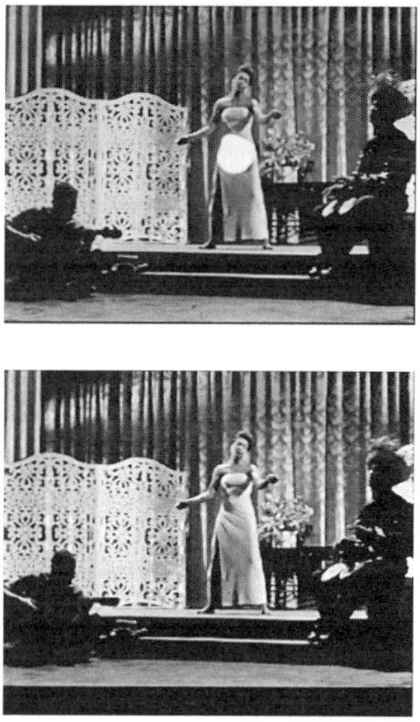

Figure 7. (*continued*)

exposed and hypervisible to the spectator, then just as quickly made invisible, only to be exposed again. The spotlight heightens the policing of the black woman's body by spectatorial regimes of racialization and allegorizes the conditions of labor for the black female entertainer in the Jim Crow era. She is continuously appearing and disappearing, repeatedly revealed and hidden. Whenever the tempo of the song slows down enough that she might escape it, the spotlight returns, compelling her to sing for the audience. The song she performs further underscores this dynamic: "Run Joe" is a song about two men arrested by the police for running a backroom fortune telling business. As one escapes, the other issues him instructions to destroy evidence and create an alibi for himself. In her third autobiography, Angelou explains how the song made its way into her nightclub repertoire and details her choreographic interpretation of it: "I knew every rest and attack of the song. I stretched my arms and waved my hands and body in a modified hula, indicating how fast Joe made his getaway. I tugged away from an imaginary policeman showing the extent of restraint imposed on Joe. I spun in place in the small area, kneeled and bowed and swayed and swung, always in rhythm."[73] She brought much of this same choreography to her cinematic performance, offering from one perspective a glimpse of what her live show might have looked like.

Alongside such an understanding of this scene's representation of blackness, however, I also want to consider how the film presents its representation of blackness in order to ask what this number from the calypso craze might tell us about the relationship between race, mediation, and performance. The image of Angelou's performance is not a mirror reflection of an objective world but a programmed projection that naturalizes racial common sense. Rather than luring us to *look through* the apparatus to the performance behind it, the film instead compels us to *look at* it and see that it obscures as much as it makes visible. In bringing our attention to the apparatuses that make the performance legible—the screen, projection, lighting, and film itself—Angelou's sequence presents race in the calypso craze not as something (mis)represented by mass media but as the very medium of representation itself: race as both the apparatus and the interval, the technology that makes representation possible and the temporal span in which certain images become animate. Understood as medium and duration rather than representation, race is that which structures sight and sound, making certain things visible and audible and others invisible and inaudible. To think of race as such an "intervening substance" for the senses is the proposal made by scholar W. J. T. Mitchell, who suggests that race is "not something to be seen, but is itself a framework for seeing through or (as Wittgenstein would put it) seeing *as*."[74]

This notion of race as a framework for seeing—as a medium—is anticipated in Frantz Fanon's well-known description of his experience going to the movies. Fanon describes film as a racializing technology and the feeling of dread that fills him as he waits for the movie to begin: "I cannot go to a film without seeing myself. I wait for me. In the interval, just before the film starts, I wait for me. The people in the theater are watching me, examining me, waiting for me. A Negro groom is going to appear. My heart makes my head swim."[75] Kaja Silverman, like many film theorists who consider this Fanonian scene, points out that the audience structures Fanon's double consciousness. "Since the film has not yet begun," Silverman writes, "the representations within which Fanon feels obliged to recognize himself seem to derive directly from the personal prejudices of the audience. The power to confer meaning seems to be immanent within the collective white look."[76] The film begins before it begins and, like a funhouse hall of mirrors, the screen transforms Fanon himself into a screen for the historical and psychological projections of the audience. This temporality of "suspended anticipation," Kara Keeling argues, traps Fanon within a "hellish cycle wherein the past constricts the present so that the present is simply the (re)appearance of the past, felt as affect."[77] The cycle "restricts by anticipating in advance the range of the black's (re)actions to his present experience."[78] The anticipation of such cinematic distortions fixes blackness within a recursive loop whose pattern is foreordained and unalterable.

In contrast to this view, however, Keeling offers a second, subtler, interpretation of this scene. Reminding us that Fanon himself never specifies the racial identity of the audience, she raises the possibility that, along with Fanon, "perhaps they simply are enduring, surviving the interval" as well.[79] Reading against the closed cycle of anticipation that must culminate with the arrival of the Negro groom, she notes that "the time just before the film starts is nonetheless a time swimming with possibilities and, less perceptible but no less immediate, impossibilities."[80] These possibilities and impossibilities refer to the range of reactions the spectator may have to the images on the screen and the excess meanings such images might convey despite themselves. Even while Fanon's scene ultimately "privileges the film's ideology over the range of possible meanings communicated by its images," Keeling detects "an insistence, however fleeting, of the (im)possibility of a different perception" that might alter the closed cycle and colonial temporality of the interval.[81] Keeling's analysis allows us to see Angelou's performance in *Calypso Heat Wave* as one that keeps open the Fanonian interval as a time swimming with (im)possibilities for a different perception.

Returning to Fanon's description with this in mind, let us consider in addition to the audience another element of this mise-en-scène that shapes Fanon's anticipatory dread and organizes the series of projections within this interval: the screen. As we have seen, Fanon's look at the blank, unilluminated screen is saturated with anticipation for the image of blackness that is going to appear. In the time before the image arrives, it is the screen that Fanon contemplates in angst. Here Fanon draws our attention not only to the inevitable representation of the black imago but also to the technological apparatuses that makes it possible—the screen and the projector. It is the expectation of projection, the arrival of the Negro groom on the screen, that Fanon dreads and anticipates in the interval. The screen is that which allows for any image of blackness or whiteness—of race—to appear at all.

Put another way, Fanon figures race itself as a screen or medium. Angelou's performance vividly extends this crucial insight into the calypso craze. Her performance of "Run Joe" reintroduces the Fanonian moment of anticipation back into the event that has already begun, though for Angelou this interval is keyed not to angst but to virtuosity. Over the course of this scene, Angelou's image undergoes a subtle but unmistakable transformation. What begins as a representation of Angelou as a calypso chanteuse modeled on her real-life persona gradually ceases to be a representation and instead becomes the very thing that makes the cinematic image possible: Angelou becomes at once the screen and the act (rather than the content) of projection. As the aperture of the spotlight opens and closes on Angelou, adorned in a white dress, throughout her song, the moment that Fanon and his audience await—the illumination of the film—is formally enacted and reenacted as Angelou is repeatedly illuminated, cast into darkness, and illuminated again. The Fanonian interval, in other words, is perpetually prolonged as the spotlight *in* the film doubles the projection *of* the film in the movie theater in which viewers sat in 1957. In this way Angelou's sequence works against its own representation by drawing attention to the temporality of suspended anticipation and keeping open the inevitable closures of this temporal structure within the stolen time of the cinematic calypso craze.

The mise-en-scène further draws our attention to this multiplication of screens, surfaces, and curtains. Angelou is positioned as a screen among a variety of other screens. She appears on stage before a curtain of heavy fabric and is flanked on either side by two ornately carved ivory screens (fig. 8). The spotlight further doubles her (or doubles her again) by cast-

Figure 8. Maya Angelou before curtain and ivory screens.
Calypso Heat Wave (dir. Fred Sears), 1957.

Figure 9. Maya Angelou and her shadow. *Calypso Heat Wave* (dir. Fred Sears), 1957.

ing a shadow figure on the curtain behind her that follows her movements (fig. 9). This other screen—this third screen; the screen behind the screen; the forms that dance on the back side of the screen—reminds us that what lies off screen is not a real blackness that might be properly represented or otherwise distorted by mass media but is the negation of that representation, an outline or silhouette that can never be properly filled in by the technologies of mass media. The screen is both something projected on and something that conceals. Ghosting her exact movements, this animated silhouette counters the indexical desire of cinematic reproduction and the principle of live fidelity that would offer the spectator the real off-screen Maya Angelou.

Even if we want to persist in viewing this scene as a representation of Maya Angelou, we must concede that it does not represent the singer in any simple way. It does not only represent Angelou but also becomes a commentary on the conditions for cinematic racial representation itself and the technologies of Angelou's own filmedness. "Run Joe" is a song of escape. The character in the song is eluding the authorities. It is possible (and in one register not incorrect) to understand Angelou's inclusion of this song in her repertoire within her own history of violence, confinement, and the elusion of police power. But in this filmic scene she also eludes the easy incorporation of her sound and body into the apparatuses of reproduction. In this sense, she is kin less to Fanon's (kinless) Negro groom than to Lovey Gilman and her comrades who altered their own entry into Melville

Herskovits's Trinidadian field recordings. Angelou marks the working of the apparatus—the projector, the screen—as it records her and in doing so eludes the principle of live fidelity the scene requires. She prolongs the Fanonian interval, turning the sequence not into the arrival of a racial distortion but deferring any such arrival by offering herself not as image but as a screen that is both empty and overfull at the same time.

A helpful example of what I mean by this last claim can be found in a brief digression on the work of Japanese photographer Hiroshi Sugimoto, specifically his series *Theaters*, begun in the late 1970s (figs. 10 and 11). According to the artist, this project was driven by a particular thought experiment: "*Suppose you shoot a whole movie in a single frame?* And the answer: *you get a shining screen.*"[82] To discover this answer, Sugimoto took a large-format camera into various movie houses and set up his tripod at the back of the theater. When the film began, he explains, "I fixed the shutter at a wide-open aperture, and two hours later, when the movie finished, I clicked the shutter closed."[83] Once developed, the single overexposed image reveals a screen that glows with an uncanny illumination. Despite its

Figure 10. Hiroshi Sugimoto, *U.A. Walker, New York*, 1978. Gelatin silver print. 47 × 58¾ in. Courtesy of the artist and Marian Goodman Gallery.

Figure 11. Hiroshi Sugimoto, *Canton Palace, Ohio*, 1980. Gelatin silver print. 47 × 58¾ in. Courtesy of the artist and Marian Goodman Gallery.

appearance, the screen is not in fact empty; rather, it is too full. It contains all the images of the film at the same moment. In its oversaturation, Sugimoto's photograph reveals the cinematic not as a series of represented images or as a narrative story unfolding sequentially but as a collection of images happening all at once, an interval of blinding vision that explodes both representation and narrative. In the artist's words: "That evening I developed the film and the vision exploded behind my eyes."[84] Sugimoto's series envisions projection without representation. It is this notion of pure projection that the cinematic temporality of linear narrative obscures.

Projection without representation is one way to understand Angelou's performance in *Calypso Heat Wave*. Just as Fanon becomes a screen for the projections of the audience, Angelou too becomes a screen. But in this case, the representation never arrives. Angelou appears as nothing other than a shining screen. This cinematic self-reflexivity interrupts the easy notion that black and white are known categories that, as Keeling explains, allow us to measure positive or authentic images against negative or inauthentic images.[85] Rather, by highlighting the materiality of the screen as medium and presenting Angelou herself as the screen, this sequence figures race not as mere representation but as the very medium that makes representation possible. Race occurs here not as something that precedes media or even as something socially constructed *by* media but rather *as* a spatial and temporal medium. Read not in terms of content but in terms of medium, race appears in this scene as a screen that is both projected on and conceals. As Mitchell puts it, the racial medium "can both obstruct and facilitate communication; [be] a cause of misunderstanding and blindness, or conversely, a mechanism of 'second sight'; [be] a prosthesis that produces invisibility and hypervisibility simultaneously, as Ralph Ellison's tale of the invisible man tells us."[86] From one vantage point, the film *Calypso Heat Wave* provides us a record of Angelou's performance. From another, Angelou's cinematic presentation provides a record of technology's performance, avowing that which relies on its own disavowal. Rather than "look through" the technology to the performance it records, Angelou's sequence refuses such accessibility and remains open, swimming in (im)possibilities.

Writing decades after the calypso craze in her 1976 autobiography, Angelou revisits her first performance of "Run Joe" at a San Francisco nightclub. It was this number that launched her brief but significant career as Miss Calypso. In her reminiscence, however, it is the live audience that becomes remarkably like a screen:

> I realized that I could not see the people. No one had warned me that a combination of spotlights and nerves would cause blindness. The aisle down which I had walked still lay open and unobstructed. I looked at it once, longingly, then turned to the pianist and nodded. And although I did not know it, another career for me had begun.[87]

Angelou's troping of screens and surfaces, visibility and blindness, and the play of looks may well be a feature of black female performance under Jim Crow more generally, an aesthetic stance and a survival strategy that we also saw, for example, in Josephine Premice's performance in the previous chapter and will see again in Lena Horne's in chapter 4. I include Angelou's autobiographical retelling of this song here as a variation on this trope, one that shows its rewriting by Angelou decades later under different aesthetic and historical conditions. The point of view of the autobiography, written long after the fact, replaces the position of the spectator of the film with the inner experience of the performer being looked at (Horne will similarly rewrite the calypso craze in her autobiography after the fact), and provides a depth and interiority that the film does not. Yet tellingly the effect is the same. The immediate feedback loop that characterizes live performance is momentarily cut off by the technology—here, the spotlights—that make her visible on the small stage, isolating her as if she were on screen and removed from her audience. At the same time, these spotlights paradoxically cause a loss of vision, a saturated blankness that recalls Sugimoto's screens as Angelou looks out into the glare. We might also pause on the longing look Angelou makes toward the open aisle/isle from which she arrived. She may, in this moment, have been thinking about her maternal grandfather, who came to the United States from Trinidad. Or she may have been thinking about the life that, in retrospect, was about to change with her new turn to calypso performance.

Although she did not know what her future held at the time this scene took place, Angelou looks back on it following her epochal career as a poet and life writer. In this vast body of work, including seven autobiographies, Angelou demonstrated again and again her commitment to the project of authentic selfhood and the perpetual rediscovery of her voice. We can see her navigating these imperatives in nascent form as Miss Calypso, the short-lived persona that opened a new future to her through the inauthenticity of the calypso craze.

In these three motions—the longing look, the turn toward the pianist, the nod—Angelou marks in her autobiography the gesture of diaspora itself. In the literary account of this calypso number, the position of the spectator, obscured by the spotlights, thus also becomes a screen on which Angelou can imagine her past and future. The films of the calypso craze, by contrast, withhold such exposure of interiority. This is another way of saying that the performances of the calypso craze do not offer access to an authentic folk culture or black interiority but constitute an aural and visual screen that continually prolongs the Fanonian interval and Angelouian nod. In refusing to gesture to anything outside the fad, the film interrupts the system of representation that would seek to arrest Angelou (singing, not by accident, "Run Joe") and provides the space and time for Angelou and others—including Lovey Gilman, Venice Talbott, and Lord Invader—to determine how they might fashion themselves, rather than be fashioned by, the calypso program: projection without representation. In *Calypso Heat Wave* we can never look through the film to the live performance behind it. We remain, for better or worse, with the performance of mediation itself. By posing and sounding as the apparatus of cinematic reproduction, Angelou's performance provides a key way to understand the calypso craze as a projection without representation.

It is not necessary that anybody working on the film meant to do this "intentionally," as the accusation goes (though, in fact, somebody intended to have Angelou's performance filmed through the frame of a recording both, and somebody intended to surround her with screens, and somebody intended to open and close the spotlight on her throughout the number, and Angelou's own autobiographical reminiscence suggests that *she* had thought carefully about her staging and choreography in performance). Similarly, it is not necessary to claim that Melville Herskovits's phonograph had agency to willfully work or not work, or that it chose to jump its needle. The critical solipsism of black fad performance and the performance of the apparatus do not require conscious intention by actor or director; it is programmed into the calypso craze. "Programs," Flusser writes, "despite being projected by programmers, become autonomous. *Apparatus always function increasingly independently from their programmer's intentions.*"[88] The calypso craze of the 1950s, like other race crazes, was autogenerating and tautological. It referred to nothing other than itself. There was never even a failed promise of an authentic blackness that was corrupted by the craze; blackness was already rendered inauthentic in the fad's films and recordings. The racial fad was a screen that projected itself onto itself, continuously revealing that it was nothing other than screen. Within such a spotlight, Maya Angelou draws attention to the function of race as medium and helps us to imagine the cinema not only as a project(ion) of racial representation, to be celebrated or contested, but also to imagine race as the very condition for such a project(ion) and the potential explosion of vision and sound.

As we have seen in this chapter, technological and epistemological links between race, entertainment, and ethnography recur throughout black fad performance in the Jim Crow era. The black voice is figured by entertainment and anthropology as always-already recorded, its sound evincing its fidelity to itself. But while the ethnographic displays of the earlier calypso craze of the 1940s rely on this principle of live fidelity, the critical solipsism and self-reflexivity of the calypso craze of the 1950s displaces this principle and makes visible the role of technology in racial (re)production. My argument in this chapter has not been that live performance and film are identical. I have sought instead to show that the cinematic calypso craze disrupts the conflation of liveness and performance in order to better grasp the range of practices and effects that make up black fad performance. Liveness is a possible but not necessary element of performance. Cinema is one element in a broad spectrum of performances that make up the calypso craze. Like the calypso revue and other spectacular displays, *Bop Girl*

Goes Calypso and *Calypso Heat Wave* share aspects that scholars have long identified with performance, such as ephemerality and a feedback loop between performer and audience. But unlike live performance, these cinematic performances occur over a deferred temporal scale. As such, these deferred performances interrupt the principle of live fidelity/the burden of liveness. Like all programs, the calypso program disrupts the easy location of agency, domination, and resistance. But its quasi-automation creates vital "challenges to improvise" and offers performers multiple if fleeting ways to disrupt racial common sense and imagine blackness differently.[89] Its critical solipsism frustrates the ethnographic desires of black fad performance's consumers and holds out possibility for diasporic self-making as suggested, for example, by the gesture of Angelou's turn and nod. Such gestures, often overlooked, are part and parcel of the calypso craze and its disclosure of authenticity through inauthenticity.

THREE

Carnivalizing Jazz: Duke Ellington's Calypso Theater and the Diasporic Instant

In 1950, NBC executive David Sarnoff wrote an editorial for the middle-brow magazine *Look* that celebrated television's potential for spreading democracy overseas, battling communist ideology across the globe, and building an international community; he called his vision "Transoceanic TV."[1] Seven years later at the height of the calypso craze, Duke Ellington and Billy Strayhorn presented their own vision of transoceanic TV, one that took advantage of liberal ideological investments in television such as Sarnoff's. On May 8, 1957, over five million US households tuned in to the *United States Steel Hour*'s primetime CBS broadcast of Ellington and Strayhorn's *A Drum Is a Woman*. This live presentation was an hour-long theater-dance-music suite filmed deliriously across four soundstages that combined elements of Afro-Caribbean rhythm with swing and bebop to tell a fable about the history of jazz and visualize the African diaspora. Narrating from his piano bench on one stage with his orchestra, Ellington told the story of Madam Zajj, the drum-turned-woman of the title, who is discovered in a tropical island jungle by an archetypal figure called Caribee Joe (fig. 12). Zajj—"a funny way," Ellington said, "of spelling jazz backwards"—invites Joe to travel the world with her.[2] When he chooses instead to stay in the jungle, she sets forth in search of other musical partners and chronicles the history of jazz as a series of substitutions in a journey of perpetually deferred reunion. On the other three soundstages, she flies from the Caribbean to New Orleans to Chicago to the jazz clubs of Fifty-Second Street and finally the moon and back in a story that marks her transformative presence at key moments in and as the history of jazz. As Madam Zajj materializes in these different times and places, from drum to woman and back again, her dizzying travels trace the development of various musical styles including calypso, rumba, Dixieland, bebop, and swing. Following Madam Zajj up to Ellington's present day and beyond, *A Drum Is a Woman* visualizes diaspora as a distinctly temporal formation that comes into being through musical enactment, appearing always just ahead of itself and lingering in/as its dispersal.

Like sound recording and film, television was a significant medium for the performances of the calypso craze. Harry Belafonte's *Calypso* album of 1956 originated a year earlier during an appearance on NBC's *Colgate Variety Hour* (newly renamed from *Colgate Comedy Hour* in order to emphasize its expansion into drama and more serious fare). These 1950s variety shows exemplify what historians call the "golden age" of television. With radio as a model, they simply transferred nightclub and vaudeville acts to broadcast studios and presented them to a mass audience. Emphasizing the liminal status of these mediated-yet-live performances, industry commentators dubbed them "vaudeo": a combination of vaudeville and video that, historian Susan Murray explains, promised variety theater's "immediacy,

Figure 12. Duke Ellington and His Orchestra on the set of *A Drum Is a Woman*, 1957. CBS Photo Archive/Getty Images.

intimacy, and spontaneity" through the medium of television.[3] Having just starred in Twentieth Century Fox's film *Carmen Jones* (1954) and having just released his first album of folk songs from RCA Victor (*Mark Twain and Other Folk Favorites*, 1954), Belafonte signed to perform on at least five episodes of the *Colgate Variety Hour*.[4] His first appearance on October 2, 1955, was a twenty-minute segment called "Holiday in Trinidad" that the show promoted as an "integrated musical trip thru the West Indies"—as much a theater piece as a variety sketch.[5] Dressed in kitschy calypso clothes, Belafonte debuted variations of four Caribbean folk songs, including "Day O (The Banana Boat Song)," which became the kernel of his record-breaking album released seven months later.

While Ellington had been thinking about the musical project that would become *A Drum Is a Woman* since the early 1940s, the creative possibilities offered by television and vaudeo in the mid-1950s recast his vision for the musical suite.[6] He worked closely with Strayhorn, composing the work in 1956 with the avowed intention of making creative use of the new possibilities afforded by television. The mostly live theater piece (some vocal tracks were prerecorded and lip-synched) they created found a home on the middlebrow anthology drama series *US Steel Hour*, and *A Drum Is a Woman* remains an important early experiment in the interplay between jazz sound, image, and narrative. Cutting back and forth between Ellington's orchestra and Expressionistic scenes of theater and choreography, the performance showcased an array of black artists to a national audience. Cuban percussionist Candido Camero joined the Ellington Orchestra, sitting in on congas and bongos. Madam Zajj was given multiple forms: she was alternately sung by soprano Margaret Tynes and jazz vocalist Joya Sherrill, and was danced by Carmen de Lavallade, a classically trained dancer with the Metropolitan Opera. Other featured performers included nightclub singer Ozzie Bailey and acclaimed dancer/choreographer Talley Beatty.

At the same time as the broadcast showcased experiments in black performance, the entire event was also an impressive achievement of corporate cross promotion. The *Drum Is a Woman* LP recording was released a few months earlier, and the CBS broadcast was a tie-in for its recording subsidiary, Columbia Records, to which Ellington was signed in the 1950s and 1960s. Columbia Records and US Steel heavily promoted the broadcast in television, radio, and print markets throughout the nation (including urban and rural markets across the South). US Steel pressed a special promotional 45-rpm recording with excerpts from the suite and sent copies to television and radio stations around the United States as well as to thousands of US Steel customers.[7] Staged publicity stills from the show appeared in national and local print media (figs. 13 and 14). While not identical to how the live broadcast appeared to viewers, these images give a sense of the tone and mood of the performance as it was promoted around the country: an upscale gentility and supper club feel with a dash of exoticism (though Candido appeared in these promotional photos with Ellington's orchestra in "primitive" garb, he donned a tuxedo for the live broadcast).

Focusing on the Columbia Records LP of the suite, most Ellington scholars describe *A Drum Is a Woman* as a minor Ellington undertaking or neglect it altogether.[8] It had an uncharacteristically truncated afterlife, with only a couple of full concert performances in the late 1950s and a staged revival in 1988 conducted by Mercer Ellington. Yet *A Drum Is a Woman* was more than a whimsical Ellington project or a canny advertising scheme.

Figure 13. Duke Ellington and His Orchestra on the set of *A Drum Is a Woman* with Candido Camero, 1957. CBS Photo Archive/Getty Images.

Figure 14. Joya Sherrill, Duke Ellington, and Margaret Tynes on the set of *A Drum Is a Woman*, 1957. CBS Photo Archive/Getty Images.

And it was more than a national platform for a number of brilliant performers during the Cold War. When we view the Columbia recording of *A Drum Is a Woman* within the context of the calypso craze and consider its full range of dance and dramaturgy on the *US Steel Hour*, Ellington and Strayhorn's project takes on new dimensions. Inasmuch as the television show was a cross-promotional project designed to capitalize on the various venues of the Columbia Broadcasting System, we can see the broadcast and the recording as versions of each other. What listeners bought was different in significant ways from what they saw on TV. The album, for example, contains more detailed and discursive explorations of black musical history than were able to fit on the television show. And, conversely, purchasers of the album were unable (except perhaps in their memory) to see the choreography and scenography that distinguished the broadcast. Ellington himself recalled that "what could not be experienced on the Columbia album was the radiant presence of Carmen de Lavallade, who danced so superbly in the television version."[9] When we think of *A Drum Is a Woman*, it is important to take both presentations of it side by side as two elements of the larger project of *A Drum Is a Woman*. By restoring movement, choreography, videography, and scenography to the history of the piece and returning it to the faddish conditions for its broadcast, it can be seen as a more significant and substantial contribution to Ellington's oeuvre and to black musical history.

By the time of the calypso craze and *A Drum Is a Woman*'s television broadcast, the Jim Crow logic of racial disenfranchisement was in undeniable conflict with US Cold War policies of democracy promotion. The persistence of Jim Crow and the violent reactions to the civil rights movement contradicted a postwar image of the United States (against the repressions of the Soviet Union) as a bastion of freedom, liberty, and individualism.[10] This paradox of midcentury US liberal internationalism was both managed and heightened by the US State Department's program of "cultural ambassadorship" that sent African American musicians abroad and deployed jazz performance as a kind of freedom publicity (including, in the 1960s, Ellington). Historian Penny Von Eschen describes the origins of this government program in the mid-1950s as the unlikely time that "Ike got Dizzy": the time when President Eisenhower endorsed the bebop music of Dizzy Gillespie and other jazz musicians as a sign of American democracy in State Department-sponsored foreign tours.[11] The musicopolitical dizziness of this moment—its Diz-orientation—requires us to approach Ellington and Strayhorn's figure of Madam Zajj in relationship to the paradoxes of the calypso craze and US liberalism in the early Cold War/late Jim Crow era. The composers' bebop reshuffling of space and time disturbed a national narrative of jazz as a homegrown American invention. In its place, they extended histories of migration beyond national boundaries and sketched a diasporic philosophy of the history of jazz, one that advanced not by a logic of developmental teleology but by the swell and dissolution of a transitory collectivity in contact with West African rhythm.

Here I consider *A Drum Is a Woman* in relation to the larger context of the calypso craze, showing how the production worked within the constraints of mass media to compel the de-historicized and undifferentiated calypso fad to reckon with its own history and difference. Rather than amplifying the fad's critical solipsism, Ellington and Strayhorn used the recording opportunities the fad afforded to extend the craze beyond the craze. Locating jazz in the scene of encounter and transformation between people, the composers posed important questions about the relationship between nation and diaspora; African American and Afro-Caribbean cultural exchange; white commercial culture and black performance; and the sounds and gestures that reshaped cultural geographies in the twentieth century, in particular the role of calypso and its routes as a significant artery for jazz. They also (inadvertently?) posed a crucial question about the role of female sexuality, homoeroticism, and misogyny within these new cultural imaginaries.

I will return to this last question at the end of this chapter. First, I contextualize *A Drum Is a Woman* within 1950s television culture and elaborate a particular strategy of black fad performance that I describe as *radical counterprogramming*: an alternative to the middlebrow's exploitation of blackness in the project of Cold War internationalism and a fundamental rewriting of the calypso program. Working against the ideological conventions of the middlebrow anthology drama—what media theorist Anna McCarthy describes as a liberal postwar tactic of "governing by television"—I argue that the CBS broadcast sounded and visualized a black expressive line of flight as it moved across the Atlantic to Barbados, New Orleans, and the urban north.[12] Through their musical-theatrical-televisual experimentation, Ellington and Strayhorn created a hybrid performance in the mode of calypso fantasia: a formal and thematic engagement with diasporic aesthetics and the calypso craze—particularly with the history and form of New World carnival—to visualize diaspora as a temporal formation that coalesces and disperses within the sounds and movements of black music. Their fantasia sounded and staged a philosophy of the history of jazz predicated on the production of a people that emerge as a refusal of the national population addressed by US Steel and CBS. In doing so, Ellington and Strayhorn displaced the specter of the fad consumer with a vision of a diasporic people. Borrowing extensively from Afro-Caribbean and Latin American sounds and making use of new televisual broadcast technologies, they performed a theory of diaspora as constituted in time—the diasporic instant—as much as in space. As Madam Zajj appears and disappears in various eras and geographies, diaspora itself is visualized on television as an appearance and dispersal that is occasioned in the instant of performance. By focusing on the television broadcast's dance and dramaturgy, this chapter shows how *A Drum Is a Woman* imagined a decorporealization of the body and a queer transubstantiation of sound that contested the corporate body of national citizenship and the regularized body of Jim Crow.

Notwithstanding the fact that there is only one song in *A Drum Is a Woman* that could properly be called a calypso, the calypso craze and the more general conditions of black fad performance I described in earlier chapters are crucial contexts for this broadcast. It appeared within and against the larger calypso program. There is, first, its calendrical occurrence, broadcast in mid-1957 while the craze was still robust, and its proximity to Belafonte's performances of calypso on variety shows such as the *Colgate Comedy Hour*, the *Ed Sullivan Show*, and the *Nat King Cole Show*. Television critics at the time saw the broadcast as an overt bid for the calypso craze's youth market.[13] Second, its plot (which traces Madam Zajj's origins in the Caribbean and includes a calypso number) and the performers it features (Talley Beatty and Carmen de Lavallade, both associated with the craze) locate it within the calypso craze's gravitational pull and the opportunities opened up for performers by the fad cascade. More significantly, as we will see, the broadcast takes the occasion of the calypso craze to measure the relationship between the US jazz tradition and the musics of the Caribbean, including Latin jazz, cubop, and calypso. It places jazz in a diasporic rather than a national history, especially through dance as a mark of a Caribbean carnival aesthetic that animates the jazz tradition. This is not the Old World carnival of inversion but a New World carnival of emancipation.

Digging a little deeper, we find that *A Drum Is a Woman* exults in a particular stance toward itself and a self-reflexive mood that I argue throughout this book is characteristic of black fad performance. While researching *A Drum Is a Woman* in the Duke Ellington Collection at the National Museum of American History, I came across a piece of archival ephemera that suggests the specific ontological conditions of black fad performance were on the mind of Ellington and Strayhorn as they adapted it for television. Tucked between pages of a draft script for *A Drum Is a Woman* is an unidentified verse composition titled "La Conga Samba Rhumba Chica Chica Bomba." This poem is a parody of race crazes and Latin music manias that were popular in the 1940s and 1950s. A sample:

> La Conga Samba Rhumba Chica Chica Bomba
> Was inspired by Carmen Miranda,

Every Brooklyn seniorita
Loves its spic and Spanish meter,
And it's played on every juke box in the landa,
But in Uruguay and Chile
It's considered rather silly,
Though it's done on every campus,
Not a gaucho on the pampas
Is a victim of its Yankee propaganda . . .

It is positively peachy
When it's sung by Don Ameche,
But in Ecuador and Quito
They have marked it with a veto,
You won't see it in Havana,
Panama or Tia Juana,
Down in Montivedo
It's a song they never playo,
It el floppoed in Bogota,
But they love it in Dakota.[14]

A song about a song, "La Conga Samba Rhumba Chica Chica Bomba" is a mashing together of at least four different Latin American musical crazes. It traces itself to the manufactured persona of Brazilian singer Carmen Miranda (a prominent figure in a samba craze of the 1940s) and the screen performances of Italian American actor Don Ameche, who performed with Miranda in the schlocky 1941 movie musical *That Night in Rio*. These figures mark "La Conga Samba Rhumba Chica Chica Bomba" as a product of the culture industry, with a tenuous nonrelation to the various musics by which it names itself. Although a huge hit in cities and college campuses across the United States, according to itself, the people of South America neither recognize it nor fall prey to its "Yankee propaganda." The author(s) of the verse playfully develop a rhyme scheme that works by alternating geographies of consumption with geographies of exploitation, such that every affirmation of the song is undone within its next lines by negation.

Its reference to Carmen Miranda further embeds this verse within a tradition of race crazes, recognizing her as a forerunner and fellow traveler in the complexities of fad culture. The song signifies on one of Miranda's numbers from *That Night in Rio*, "Chica Chica Boom Chic," which itself comments on race crazes in South America: "It don't make sense, the Chica Chica Boom Chic, / but it's immense, the Chica Chica Boom Chic." Like the presence of Candido in *A Drum Is a Woman* and other performances of the calypso craze described in this book, Miranda stretches the avowedly inauthentic and through it imagines opportunities for "serious" musical work in commodification (its "immensity"). The non-sense of the race craze, as Miranda demonstrated throughout her career, is an immense and overdetermined occasion for pressurizing epistemologies of race and imagining new aesthetic possibilities-within-constraint. These songs are further examples of fad performers, like Josephine Premice (chapter 1) and Maya Angelou (chapter 2), theorizing the performance of their performance in their performance. "La Conga Samba Rhumba Chica Chica Bomba" is a kind of wink from one fad performer to another, a not-so-secret handshake in song that recognizes affinities in each other's practices.

Whether anyone intended "La Conga Samba Rhumba Chica Chica Bomba" to be set to music or not is unclear. Unclear, too, is its provenance and authorship, though its references to *That Night in Rio* likely date it to the early 1940s. These lines are unattributed, but they closely resemble Ellington's style in other literary experiments with verse and poetry.[15] If it was, as I believe, written by Ellington (and/or Strayhorn), its inclusion with the *Drum Is a Woman* papers at the National Museum of American History may not be a case of misfiling a wayward document. It would indicate that Caribbean and Latin music crazes of the 1940s and 1950s and their complex relationship to (in)authenticity were at the forefront of Ellington's mind while he was composing *A Drum Is a Woman*. Using the form of a fad song to playfully mock fad songs, it delights in clever rhymes and word play and captures the sensibility of black fad performance with precision as a song about itself. As a shadow song to *A Drum Is a Woman*, "La Conga Samba Rhumba Chica Chica Bomba" should be understood as an important document of black fad performance—a mocking and self-reflexive avowal of the inauthenticity that characterizes mass cultural race crazes.

Liberal Governance and Radical Counterprogramming

In the shadow of the calypso craze, *A Drum Is a Woman*'s televisual fantasia counterprogrammed this tradition of black fad performance in the Jim Crow era. When the broadcast aired, there were approximately forty million televisions in homes across the United States. This wide reach of television provided a new form and opportunity for black fad performance's stolen time. Specifically, television offered new ways of monetizing (and thus conceptualizing) time. In an important analysis published in 1951, radical economist Dallas Smythe delineated mass media's new economic model. He proposed that the product television stations sell to advertisers such as US Steel is best understood in temporal terms. It is a combination of what he called "station time" (the actual timespan of an advertisement) and "audience loyalty," or the projected time (measured by ratings) that audiences commit to regularly watching a broadcast. As this audience loyalty to a program includes within it "the possibility of developing audience loyalty to the advertiser," the logic of television advertising assures that the program "is paid for twice": first by the sponsor and then by the viewer-turned-consumer who buys the sponsor's products.[16] Given this double loyalty, Smythe anticipates the instrumentalization of television in the Cold War era by asking "is it any wonder that our traditional view of our cultural values, including freedom of speech and freedom of the press, may be reshaped increasingly into the likeness of the cultural values of the advertisers?"[17]

In the 1950s, the cultural values of corporate America were closely aligned with Cold War public policy in both foreign and domestic spheres. Even while New York intellectuals such as Dwight Macdonald and Clement Greenberg lamented what they saw as the stultifying culture (or anticulture, as they described it) of middlebrow television programming, the media industry eagerly promoted television as a technology for cultivating postwar values of civic responsibility, free market principles, and the liberal democratic state. Taking stock of the undeniable ascendance of television over radio and other media by the mid-1950s, *Variety* magazine claimed that TV had "imposed a new dimension on Americans everywhere" and that "the ability and the capacity of TV to influence the minds of its viewers can no longer be questioned."[18] NBC president Pat Weaver seconded this thinking when he declared in his 1955 address to NBC affiliates that "every NBC show should serve a purpose beyond diversion, and every time we can increase information, contacts, facts, knowledge, and we deliver a fact somewhere to a mind somewhere in the country, we have added one more tool, one more weapon in the fight against bigotry, stupidity, intolerance and prejudice. . . . We are moving up as individuals, as a society, and we are doing it by improving ourselves"[19] As these comments indicate, media corporations recognized the possibilities of television to influence the conduct and values of its viewers and shape the idea of American citizenship in the early Cold War.

In other words, as media theorist Anna McCarthy puts it, television in the postwar era presented new methods for governing the population. Through culturally uplifting programming and broadcasts that combined entertainment with instruction in economic, domestic, and foreign affairs, middlebrow television shows and advertisements influenced the self-conduct of the postwar citizen-consumer. In doing so, such shows addressed themselves to the individual viewer as part of a national population. The concept of population emerged as a conceptual category and political technology new to modernity as a way of ordering and regularizing the heterogeneities of large groups of people based on the distribution of their life processes. For philosopher Michel Foucault, the regularization of the population is a tactic of power that takes life itself and its cultivation as a site of application (across his writings, Foucault described this concept as "biopolitics"). Population in this sense is distinct from either "a collection of a subject of rights," as political philosophy would have it, or a labor force, as political economy would have it.[20] Through new administrative and health knowledges such as demography, sociology, hygiene, epidemiology, birth and death rates, and the like, biopolitics developed as a form of liberal governmentality: a political-economic rationality of self-governance that since the late eighteenth century promoted freedom, autonomy, and enterprise while advocating minimal interference from the state.[21] Thus the population as a site of the application of power "provides a hold for concerted interventions," Foucault writes, not only through laws but "also through changes in attitudes, ways of doing things, and ways of living that may be brought about by 'campaigns.'"[22] It was to this entity whose "attitudes, ways of doing things, and ways of living" could be guided and modified that much postwar television addressed itself. Middlebrow television, long understood to have a pedagogical dimension and designed to reach a mass audience, was particularly suitable for guiding viewers through the concerns of the Cold War era.

This background begins to help explain the incongruous coupling of US Steel and Madam Zajj. One particular form by which television programming helped to naturalize free-market values and to establish a relationship between corporate interests and national well-being was through the practice of corporate sponsorship. With its mass audience, consumer frenzy, and geopolitical veneer, the calypso craze and its offshoots were prime material for this project. In sponsoring the *US Steel Hour*, US Steel followed other corporations such as Kraft and General Electric in using television to promote not any specific product but a corporate ethos and a positive image. To do so, such corporations took up the form of the anthology drama series. Anthology drama programs presented canonical drama and original teleplays crafted for primetime television that associated its sponsor with high-quality, aesthetically ambitious theatrical programming. These programs are important and understudied moments of drama and theater in the 1950s, when live television came to merge with and expand the conventions of live theater. The *US Steel Hour*, for example, distinguished itself from its competitors by its association with the esteemed Theatre Guild (formerly the Washington Square Players), which selected and produced most of its programming.

By sponsoring Ellington and Strayhorn's *A Drum Is a Woman*, US Steel not only advanced a liberal governmentality but also allowed African American viewers to participate in the project of corporate citizenship as a type of symbolic activism. Gaining access to mass public spheres, promoting the cultural accomplishments of African American artists, and challenging the representational regimes of Jim Crow were a common and often effective civil rights strategy during this period. The broadcast was successful at promoting goodwill toward the company from black political and cultural spokespeople. The black weekly *Pittsburgh Courier* wrote that "U.S. Steel and the Theatre Guild must be commended for their efforts in throwing light on Negro music."[23] The head of the National Urban League, Lester Grange, declared, "the public is indebted to U.S. Steel, CBS and Duke Ellington for a three-way collaboration which established a healthy precedent in the television industry and brought pleasure to millions." Channing Tobias, chairman of the NAACP, praised the "commendable" steps of US Steel and CBS. And Jackie Robinson, Langston Hughes, Marion Anderson, and Mahalia Jackson all echoed approval not only for Ellington but also for US Steel (Anderson: "Hail to the pioneering spirit of the sponsors"; Jackson: "Thank you US Steel and CBS, too").[24]

This praise vividly illustrates the larger political economy of corporate sponsored television programming within which Ellington and Strayhorn developed their project. Enmeshed in the temporal economies of television that Smythe diagnosed, *A Drum Is a Woman* can be understood as a theft of television's double time and its tie to Cold War liberalism. Within and against the liberal governmentality of the corporate-sponsored anthology drama, Ellington and Strayhorn presented their own radical counterprogram that not only took the time and form of the anthology drama toward different ends but also contested its biopolitical address to the population. Radical counterprogramming is a crucial dimension of black fad performance that used the conditions of mass media to advance a response to fad culture different from the solipsism, tautology, and recursivity that we have seen thus far. Stolen time in this example does not so much expose the representational cul-de-sac of the calypso craze as it steals the time of the craze to do something different.

In the case of *A Drum Is a Woman*, Ellington and Strayhorn used the opportunity of the *US Steel Hour* to present a temporal theorization of diaspora itself as time stolen (back) and simultaneously always just ahead of itself. In doing so, their counterprogram visualized a different conceptualization of collectivity than the population subject to the demographic management and regularization of biopolitics. In the same lectures in which Foucault details the emergence of "population" as one new technique for regulating the heterogeneities of a nation, he also briefly sketches the emergence of an alternative collectivity that he calls, repurposing an old term, "the people." He outlines but does not further develop this concept of a collectivity that appears in clear opposition to the management of the population and the conduct of the consumer-citizen:

> the people comprise those who conduct themselves in relation to the management of the population, at the level of the population, as if they were not part of the population as a collective subject-object, as if they put themselves outside of it, and consequently the people are those who, refusing to be the population, disrupt the system . . . We see a division being made in which the people are generally speaking those who resist the regulation of the population, who try to elude the apparatus by which the population exists, is preserved, subsists, and subsists at an optimal level.[25]

Foucault characterizes "the people" in the opposite sense of liberal political philosophy, for example, for whom the people is the unified body politic whose consent legitimizes the sovereign. Here, the people appear instead as a refusal to be the population. Foucault stresses that the relationship of the people to a population is not analogous to the relationship of a delinquent subject to an obedient one. The people's act of refusal is not a violation of law or contract. Rather, it imagines new ways of inhabiting the relationship between individual and collective that seeks to elude "the regulation of the population" and "the apparatus by which the population exists." This positive and productive project of the people is signaled by the subjunctive mood in which it appears in Foucault's lecture: the people operate "as if" they were outside the population and in doing so disrupt the processes of regularization. This "as if" signals that the work of imagination is central to the work that brings the people into being.

Foucault did not elaborate on this hazy notion of the people as that which eludes the apparatuses of the population and imagines alternative configurations of collective subjectivity—but Ellington did, especially in a trilogy of musical compositions that reimagined black history. His suites *Black, Brown, and Beige* (1943), *A Drum Is a Woman*, and *My People* (1963) constitute an ongoing project over three decades to visualize black collectivity within and as history. *Black, Brown, and Beige* traces the black presence in the New World from slavery and emancipation, to the battles and wars fought by the United States, to West Indian migrations to northern cities, and finally through the interwar period to its current moment.[26] *My People,* performed for the centennial of the Emancipation Proclamation, revisits these same themes by staging the interplay between the sacred and the secular in black history. In *My People,* Ellington even revised some of the compositions from *Black, Brown, and Beige* and extended its historical pageant through the civil rights movement (this centennial production also featured Joya Sherrill and Talley Beatty among its large cast, each of whom had earlier appeared in *A Drum Is a Woman*). According to Ellington biographer Barry Ulanov, Ellington chose the cyclical and looser form of the suite rather than the more unified totality of the symphony because it was "the form which best expressed his ideas and emotions about his people."[27] His adaptation of the "apparent formlessness" of the suite, as Ulanov described it, and his combination of dance, theater, poetry, narrative, and different musical genres gave provisional shape to the philosophy of history and vision of the people that Ellington advanced.[28] As we will see, like these other suites *A Drum Is a Woman* presents the people as an insurgent collectivity through the musical migrations of black music.[29]

The Futuriginal Circle: Staging a Philosophy of the History of Jazz

In doing so, *A Drum Is a Woman* advanced a contrapuntal performance that offered a radical counterprogram to the privatized conduct of liberal consumer citizenship promoted by US Steel and the *US Steel Hour.* While some viewers were invited to see *A Drum Is a Woman* as an enjoyable moment of black entertainment, Ellington and Strayhorn approached it as a possibility to invent new aesthetic forms within the conventions of what such entertainment allowed for (Strayhorn was deeply involved in the composition and arrangement of the suite, but much less engaged with the *US Steel Hour* broadcast). *A Drum Is a Woman* not only staged their take on the history of jazz but also sketched a philosophy of the history of jazz, one that imagined the production of a collective black subjectivity-in-difference—a people—through the transformations of West African rhythm across the New World. This production reached beyond early Cold War attempts to enlist jazz in US State Department propaganda and restored a transnational, Caribbean dimension—a Spanish tinge and carnival impulse—to the development of jazz. More specifically, what emerges over the course of *A Drum Is a Woman*—both the Columbia LP and the CBS broadcast—is a *speculative* philosophy of the history of jazz that resists the developmental telos of liberal historiography.[30] As a particular vision of the past and the future—Madam Zajj and her journey from the Caribbean to New Orleans to New York to the moon—*A Drum Is a Woman* approaches history as a simultaneously cyclical and inventive process in which a people becomes visible to itself through the performance of black musical production. The shape of history here, in its recurrent swell and crash, takes the form of what Caribbean theorist Gordon Rohlehr (glossing a line by Saint Lucian poet Kendel Hyppolite) describes as a "futuriginal circle": "a Whitmanesque world, a sensibility, a people, an aesthetic, a form of the future; a totally original and wholesome growth which yet partakes of the cyclical firstness of man's heritage. So runs the dream."[31] Although Ellington did not schematically articulate such a philosophy of the history of jazz in his writings or performance, we can nonetheless discern such a project in his personification of Madam Zajj and his vision of a people produced through the occasion of her arrival. In the next section, we will see how *A Drum Is a Woman* visualizes this futuriginal circle through narrative and choreography that take their cue from a carnival aesthetic and calypso feeling. First, I pause to elaborate the philosophy of the history of jazz advanced by the suite and the aesthetic innovations of the broadcast developed to present it.

Alongside Zajj's journey through English-speaking Caribbean islands to the United States, early scripts for the *Drum Is a Woman* broadcast suggested a second, parallel itinerary for Madam Zajj's travels through Spanish-speaking islands that was ultimately not developed on either the LP or the television broadcast. In this early version, a narrator describes how African music in the New World arrives from across the Atlantic and branches off in two different directions: one westward across the Gulf of Mexico through the port city of New Orleans and northward to Memphis, Saint Louis, and Chicago; and a second that branched eastward across the Caribbean to Cuba. This is a musicolinguistic fork in the road, and the route Zajj ends up forging on the *US Steel Hour* broadcast carries the sound and movements of Caribbean carnival into North America. These two branches, the narrator explains, eventually reunite in the migratory vortex of New York City, where African American and West Indian musicians compared, competed, and collaborated:

> Each branch went a different way
> To meet again on another day,
> To converge—New York—splurge—New York—get the urge—New York.
> To meet—New York—greet—New York—entreat—New York.
> The West hobnobbin' with the Eastern mob and
> They blew some and grew some.
> They made a handsome twosome.[32]

In the end, Ellington and Strayhorn set aside this particular approach to their story and emphasized instead a cyclical rather than evolutionary development that foregrounded the people who emerge through musical movements. Elements of this previous plotline, however, remained audible as a musical presence in the suite. For example, in one of *A Drum Is a Woman*'s final songs, "Rhumbop," Ellington and Strayhorn's composition marries the Caribbean/Cuban (rumba) and continental (bebop) influences of Zajj's travels as they make a handsome twosome in the song ("bebop and rhumba bumpin' rolled into one"). "Rhumbop" stands in here for the branch of Latin jazz known as Cubop pioneered by Afro-Cuban performers such as Mario Bauzá, Machito, and Candido working with African American musicians such as Dizzy Gillespie in the early 1940s. This number, which I describe further in the next section, occurs when Zajj appears in New York City in the current moment of the broadcast.

The 1950s was the decade when the history of jazz first began to be written in a systematic way. Ellington and Strayhorn's approach to jazz historiography in *A Drum Is a Woman* can be usefully juxtaposed to other contemporaneous histories, including Nat Shapiro and Nat Hentoff's oral history *Hear Me Talkin' to Ya': The Story of Jazz as Told by the Men Who Made It* (1955), Marshall Stearns's *The Story of Jazz* (1956), Studs Terkel's *Giants of Jazz* (1957), and Shapiro and Hentoff's *The Jazz Makers: Essays on the Greats of Jazz* (1957).[33] Each of these books describes the movement of West African rhythm to the New World and documents the migrations of black music across the same geographies through which Madam Zajj moves. But, as their titles suggest, these histories are biographically organized around the "giants" and "greats" of jazz history who advanced the tradition through New Orleans, Kansas City, Chicago, and New York. In contrast, Ellington does not tell the history of individual musicians who stand out in the history of jazz (with the key exception of Buddy Bolden, described below). Rather, he charts the emergence of a people through the migrations, repetitions, and transformations of black music. *A Drum Is a Woman*, that is to say, does less to recount a history than to imagine what might be thought within and through that history.

Ellington sought not only to tell this philosophy of the history of jazz but also to enact it via the mediated spectacle of televisual music and performance. In an interview, Ellington described this creative challenge of bringing *A Drum Is a Woman* to the small screen:

> You mention jazz on Madison Avenue and they quake. Then when they come down to earth, they'll say, "Of course, I dig it the most but how can you make jazz visual?" Visual is the key word with television people. But their idea of visual is pathetic; it's elementary and unimaginative. They put a camera on the brass section—so you see the horns waving. Then down to the saxes and then the camera lights on the fingers coming down on the piano keys—and that is "visual." We tried to do a good deal more in "Drum Is a Woman," meanwhile telling the story of jazz, in simple fashion, as we went along.[34]

Jazz, Ellington suggests, poses a problem for television, even as television poses an opportunity for jazz. As he puts it, Madison Avenue executives' idea of the visual is "pathetic." This "elementary and unimaginative" notion of the visual is simply a depiction of musicians and their instruments. Ellington aspired to visualize a "good deal more" than the band at play, and it is something separate from the "story of jazz, in simple fashion," that he tells along the way. *A Drum Is a Woman* undertakes the more ambitious project of visualizing what is communicated sonically: black history in the New World as the production of an oppositional people through music, image, voice, and movement. More: Ellington sought to visualize the process of visualization itself and expand its possibilities. Rather than translating a floorshow to television, Ellington worked with a theater director, choreographer, and television writer to adapt *A Drum Is a Woman* for the *US Steel Hour*. Although the final shooting script was a streamlined version of Ellington's more intricate drafts, he retained musical control over the program, and his conception of the story was largely realized in the broadcast despite financial, formal, and technological constraints. The result was an aesthetic experiment that mixed drama, music (swing, calypso, Dixieland, bebop, rumba), dance, and scenography to create a hard-to-categorize production violating the generic conventions of music and theater.

Even as civil rights organizations and black entertainers praised the broadcast, music and television critics had a more mixed response to this theater/musical hybrid. One critic pondered: "Is Duke a Musician—A Playwright—or Both?"[35] Another, recalling Ellington's performances during an earlier racial fad, proposed that it should be shown "in a major night club on Broadway. It's the first really big and worthwhile thing to come along in Negro show business since the old Cotton Club."[36] And another, expressing surprise that Ellington "could have conceived such a travesty as this musical amalgam," complained that "to call this hybrid a folk opera would be an injustice. Indeed, I find it difficult to categorize a work which at one end of the scale degenerates into a conception of jazz such as one might hear at the local music hall, and which at the other makes a self-conscious attempt to emulate writing more fitted for the concert platform."[37] While such confusion was a common response to the mixed-brow modes in which jazz was performed in the 1950s—sometimes middlebrow, sometimes avant-garde, sometimes popular, sometimes all at once—each of these attempts to bring generic coherence to *A Drum Is a Woman* underscores Ellington and Strayhorn's formal experimentation and the attempts (and failures) of existing categories to easily contain it.

Calypso Theater and Carnival Aesthetics

Keeping their diasporic vision and their proximity to the calypso craze in mind, we might seek affinities between *A Drum Is a Woman*'s formal experimentation and the aesthetic traditions of carnival and calypso theater. In his important study, *The Trinidad Carnival: Mandate for a National Theatre* (1972), Errol Hill describes the development of short skits that occurred in Trinidadian calypso tents beginning in the 1930s. These skits evolved from a variety of calypso lyric forms, including the kalinda, the belé, the calypso ballad, and the calypso duet. Although "abbreviated," such skits "contain the elements of a full-scale theatrical presentation and may be considered miniature operettas," and share features with Ellington's jazz suites, including generic hybridity and narrative economy.[38] We might even imagine Ellington and Strayhorn as mock calypsonians—as Hill reminds us, the calypsonian "is not merely a singer, but he must also be a poet, musical composer, and actor. He not only writes lyrics and creates melodies, but he also stamps each performance of his song with his own powerful histrionic talent."[39]

These minidramas, like calypso itself, developed from the practices and milieus of nineteenth-century Trinidadian carnival, including its street masquerades and calypso tents. Historically, this carnival made a subjugated people visible to itself, disorganized the logics of city planning, rehearsed scenarios of social inversion, and created corporeal resistance to everyday conditions of colonization. From the nineteenth century forward, colonial administrations in Trinidad sought to manage this potential insurgency through official ordinances, edicts, and modifications. With this history of regulation in mind, musicologist Jocelyne Guilbault argues that the history of Trinidadian calypso "has been inextricably linked to socioeconomic projects and political technologies to govern, manage, and improve the conduct of racialized subjects."[40] Drawing on the theories of power and governmentality discussed earlier in this chapter, Guilbault's study of calypso reminds us that the cultivation of life as a vector of power occurred as much through cultural and aesthetic practices as it did through the procedures of social science and the administration of biological processes. Trinidadian carnival, for example, was never banned outright, though aspects such as stick fighting and masking were from time to time. As Guilbault explains, "the white colonial administration, which would have preferred to ban Carnival altogether, could not do so for at least two reasons: it feared a genuine revolt by the former slaves, and it wanted to avoid the open hostility of members of the colored middle class who would see such a state intervention in Carnival as blatantly excessive."[41] Instead, carnival was instrumentalized as a practice that could improve public behavior and cultivate civic values and middle-class sexual mores through the introduction of "respectable" masquerade balls (known as "fancy mas"); the promotion of (European-based) string instruments in place of (African-based) percussive instruments; the marketing of carnival to middle-class Creoles and tourists; the sponsorship of calypso tents and calypsonians by local businesses; and the awarding of prizes for calypso performances that were judged according to more respectable standards.

The objects of these "improvements"—the people and cultures of the lower classes of Port of Spain—resisted these modifications in various ways. The calypso, for example, developed into a more pointed but coded expression of complaint, dissent, and parody. Another significant instance of creative resistance was the invention of new percussive instruments in response to colonial ordinances that regularly banned the drumming associated with former slaves. Deprived of drums in the early twentieth century, the lower classes modified bamboo stems into percussive instruments that were stamped on the ground. By the 1930s, Donald Hill explains, these "bamboo instruments were gradually augmented with instruments made from assorted metal containers, especially biscuit tins."[42] Following the US occupation during World War II, musicians repurposed left-behind fifty-five-gallon oil drums into the steel pan drums that are closely associated with midcentury calypso music. As this history suggests, the calypso ethos—including experiments with its styles and forms—developed both within and against colonial attempts to cultivate a self-governing, compliant population.

A Drum Is a Woman can be seen as a similar improvisation in mass media that performatively conjures a people within and against the population's management, as if they put themselves outside of it. By calling this performative, I mean to emphasize that the broadcast's representation of a people enacts that very people in its visualization. Each sequence of *A Drum Is a Woman* begins with Madam Zajj materializing in a New World locale and draws on carnival aesthetics to visualize a diasporic counterpopulation.[43] In each number her appearance calls forth from seemingly empty streets, marketplaces, clearings, squares, nightclubs, and moonscapes a crowd of musicians, dancers, revelers, and spectators—a people. At the beginning of the program, Zajj encounters Caribee Joe in an island jungle. Gradually, a large chorus joins them in a clearing. When Zajj leaves Caribee Joe in search of other musical partners, she arrives in a Barbados marketplace. The quiet space is again quickly filled with black dancers as performer Ozzie Bailey sings a calypso number. This pattern—the arrival of Zajj and the subsequent emergence of a chorus of dancers that fills the visual field and then disperses following her flight—repeats itself in each of the musical sequences.

The broadcast provides something that the sound recording or concert presentation of *A Drum Is a Woman* does not: choreography. While the soprano Margaret Tynes and the jazz vocalist Joya Sherrill both gave voice to Madam Zajj and can be heard on the recording, it is the dancer Carmen de Lavallade who most fully realized her—as a character and a philosophy—on the *US Steel Hour* broadcast. Prior to *A Drum Is a Woman*, de Lavallade danced in films such as *Carmen Jones* (1954) and the Broadway calypso musical *House of Flowers* (1954), where she met her lifetime partner in art and marriage, Trinidadian dancer-choreographer Geoffrey Holder (the subject of chapter 5). She studied at the Lester Horton Dance Theater in Los Angeles—where she became Horton's protégé and close friends with dancer Alvin Ailey—which provided training not only in modern dance and ballet but also a panoply of dramaturgical arts: acting, painting, music, lighting, set design, and others.[44] Although Broadway choreographer Paul Godkin designed the large chorus numbers for *A Drum Is a Woman*, there was significant room for play and improvisation during the live broadcast. The dancers often had the occasion to fill sequences with their own steps, and de Lavallade in particular brought her own imagination to Zajj's movement.[45] Thus despite this chapter's title—a concession to editorial economy—*A Drum Is a Woman* as it was broadcast on the *US Steel Hour* was as much the product of de Lavallade and Strayhorn as it was Ellington, and her choreographic conception of Madam Zajj is a crucial part of this suite's creative labor.

The sequence that brings Zajj to New Orleans Mardi Gras and then Congo Square exemplifies the carnival aesthetic I am describing. The New Orleans sequence begins on an Expressionistic set that suggests a quiet French Quarter street at dawn. A solo clarinetist opens the scene, sitting against a steel pole below a wrought iron balcony. A woman in silhouette with a basket passes by and greets him; they pantomime a friendly exchange. A second man passes by on his way to the market carrying caged chickens. Slowly the street begins to come to life as carnival revelers fill the stage in turn-of-the-twentieth-century costume. In his narration, Ellington gives this scene specific coordinates: "Basin Street, Rampart, Perdido, Bourbon . . . all through that side of New Orleans, they're waiting to hear just *one* piece of news. Who's going to be king this year!" Like Trinidadian carnival, Madam Zajj's Mardi Gras exceeds the ordinances and edicts that would keep it segregated from official city parades and confined to the historically black districts of the city.

The exuberant crowd makes way for a Mardi Gras float bearing Madam Zajj, a jazz band, and this year's King of Mardi Gras, Buddy Bolden (performed by trumpet player Clark Terry). The historical Buddy Bolden is a key figure in the story of jazz. The turn-of-the-century New Orleans cornetist is credited in many histories as the "father of jazz" for incorporating greater improvisation and blues sounds to ragtime music. Bolden occupies a quasi-mythological location in jazz lore; he left no recordings and was committed to an asylum for schizophrenia at the age of thirty. He does not provide a verifiable origin for US jazz history but marks the perpetually incomplete and unreliable lineage in any attempt to establish a definitive jazz tradition. His inclusion as a character in the story thus keeps it in the realm of speculation and fable rather than fact (a draft of the script includes the lines: "Like Paul Bunyan and his legendary ax / Buddy Bolden blew his horn and blew the facts"), and is consistent with the description of this performance as enacting a philosophy of history of jazz rather than a historical account.[46]

By locating this parade in New Orleans' historically black neighborhoods, Ellington invokes the city's Zulu parade, the African American Mardi Gras celebration that ridicules the pretensions of white New Orleans society and mocks the official King of Carnival (on the Columbia LP, Ellington names the Krewe of Zulu explicitly and narrates a brief history of its traditions; this is simplified for the CBS broadcast). Significantly, Ellington and Strayhorn's Zulu parade does not feature scenes of parody or symbolic inversion but instead foregrounds the sonic and visual production of the carnival crowd. The arrival of Madam Zajj and her contact with Buddy Bolden brings into being a people who become legible (to themselves and others) not through the science of demography or the partitions of Jim Crow, but through musical performance and black dance. The shooting script for the sequence (adapted from Ellington's script by screenwriter Will Lorin) describes it for the director:

> Perhaps this music should be played live too, so that the lonesome clarinet solo can drift naturally and easily into the march tune in this section. Another street musician joins the clarinet player, and adds on his instrument, then another, then another. . . . By the time the sixth—and last—musician is in the group, they're swinging away on the marching tune, and a crowd begins to gather. . . . The music begins to infect the crowd; little by little, perhaps one by one, they begin dancing.[47]

This gradual accumulation of music and its conjuring of a people is, ultimately, what Madam Zajj stands for: the moment that comes just before the downbeat; the intake of breath; the animation of jazz in performance. In each number, Madam Zajj's arrival conjures out of stillness a chorus of bodies in motion that signals a pleasure and a potential insurgency—a pleasure-in-insurgency and an insurgency-in-pleasure. While the narrative focuses on the romance between Zajj and the various musical partners she encounters on her migration, the main character and visual focus of the broadcast is more accurately the people that she brings forth as she moves through various black Atlantic lifeworlds. These sequences do not stage a preexisting population that can be known in advance or, like the commercial messages that interrupted the show, one figured in relation to a corporate norm. They instead stage a people who come into existence through the productions of black performance.

On the LP recording of *A Drum Is a Woman*, the New Orleans sequence is followed by Zajj's appearance in Congo Square, the public space in New Orleans that was historically set aside for the enslaved to gather and socialize. Congo Square was an important location for the visualization of a black public and the development of African music in the New World. Ellington relates much of this history on the album, but it is not included in the television broadcast. Instead, it is suggested but not named in a sequence that finds Zajj and a Caribee Joe figure in an unmarked public space that quickly fills with dancing revelers. This is perhaps the most extensive and complex choreographic scene in the broadcast. A feast is held as Mardi Gras masqueraders deliver baskets of fruit and cakes. Dancers couple up and pull tightly to each other, moving their hips. Others glide across the camera shot. The jazz band flows among and through the crowd of dancers as the clearing becomes a dance floor. One man lifts his partner, who reclines gracefully over his shoulder. Couples dance together as the camera swirls among the crowd. Camera dissolves create an echo of bodies moving, fading, and superimposed over others. At times, only limbs are seen as the dancers seem to overtake the camera: arms, legs, elbows, hands, necks, shoulders. The camera itself is completely immersed in the crowd and dizzyingly swirls among the chorus. It then rises above the crowd and gazes down on it as couples come together and drift away, laughing, chasing, and tugging at each other. The chorus parts for Zajj, who enters with a parasol. One dancer kisses her hem. She moves languidly in the circle as the crowd again begins to dance. When the camera returns to Zajj, we find she has left again, leaving a drum in her place.

This carnival aesthetic is not confined to the warmer climates but continues through Zajj's journeys. Now she is in New York City: de Lavallade appears on a set designed to look like Fifty-Second Street, famous for its jazz clubs, dressed in a gown and feather boa. The chorus gathers around her, and she leads them dancing through two large art deco doors that open onto the soundstage where Ellington and his orchestra have been performing the broadcast. At this moment, the telling and the tale become one as Zajj and her chorus perform accompanied by Ellington's orchestra. In this number, Zajj is represented on screen by two performers at once: jazz vocalist Joya Sherrill stands at Ellington's piano singing "Rhumbop" with the orchestra while de Lavallade dances with the chorus. Sherrill provides Zajj's voice and de Lavallade provides her movement on the dance floor (this doubling occurs again with a difference at the end of the show, when opera singer Margaret Tynes appears with Ellington and his orchestra to sing the recitative "A Drum Is a Woman" prior to the credits).

Now she is on the moon: near the end of "Rhumbop," a pair of waiters lifts de Lavallade-as-Zajj and carries her to a booth in the corner, where she appears both bored and longing for Joe. Following a song written for the broadcast but not included in the original recording ("Pomegranate Suite") that temporarily reunites the lovers, Zajj finally gives Joe the moon. With dancer Talley Beatty, she commences Strayhorn's instrumental composition "The Ballet of the Flying Saucers" on a surrealist fog-covered moonscape filled with bejeweled trees and alien flora ("a diamond-encrusted hothouse," Ellington narrates). These sequences take Zajj's migrations from the past to the present and into a future marked by fantasy and unlimited imagination. As de Lavallade and Beatty dance, the chorus again appears around them dressed in gowns and top hats and tails. The ballet slowly accelerates into a swing dance as the scene fades back to Ellington's orchestra and the program concludes.

A Drum Is a Woman's counterprogram thus advances a fundamentally choreographic view of carnival, an aesthetic element that Trinidadian writer and calypso dramatist Rawle Gibbons characterizes as the "impulse to 'fill up the space': instinctively inclusive, [carnival] achieves this in several ways, from the enlarging of self in costume to the prancing and swaying, jumping up and rolling on the ground that claim the horizontal and the vertical dimensions of space. Through performance, mas and mass (the movement of crowds) claim the streets, asserting the freedom intrinsic to carnival."[48] As de Lavallade remembered it, filming the broadcast was an exhilarating commotion. It was filmed in one studio across four different soundstages, and the cast hurried from scene to scene, stepping over sets and making costume changes where they could.[49] This tumult is legible in front of the cameras as well; the chorus, notes scholar Lynn Spigel, adopted a stance toward the cameras that was indifferent to the home viewer.[50] They slipped in and out of the static shots, and many performed with their backs to the camera. One bewildered television critic described the chorus numbers as so many "mob-dancing scenes where no viewers within this corner's reign were willing to admit understanding what was going on."[51] Other reviews, however, recognized the centrality of the choreography to Ellington and Strayhorn's project. "One of the brightest elements in the show was the chorus," according to one review. "Loaded with ability, this fresh-spirited group breathed fire into the production numbers. Though relegated to background accompaniment, they can be credited with a good portion of the success of the undertaking."[52] Another approvingly noted that "some of the dances looked as if they were made up as the dancers went along."[53] Rather than view this tumult as mislaid choreography, a limitation of televisual technology, or the exigencies of live broadcast, we should see it as marking the boundaries of US Steel's visual field and suggesting a more expansive vision beyond its reach.

Through this carnival aesthetic, *A Drum Is a Woman* performed the contradiction between the corporate-sponsored anthology drama and the unruly, unregularized production of a diasporic people-in-music. Such an ephemeral and improvisatory counterpopulation, produced through the transformations of black performance in the Americas, is finally what Ellington, Strayhorn, de Lavallade, and the rest of the cast visualized on television during the calypso craze. In the diasporic instant, Madam Zajj occasions a collectivity that cannot be regularized by a concept such as population. It is instead a people governed by the aesthetics of carnival and black music. Despite the descriptions of the chorus by television critics, this aesthetic should not be mistaken as spontaneous or natural. Carnival, as folklorist Roger Abrahams importantly reminds us,

> is not an event that serves as a point of discharge for the players, but more a culmination of a year's work of planning, sewing, rehearsing, tuning the instruments, and, for the calypsonians, finding that right note that will cause the muse to descend upon them for the song-combat to come. This anticipation is far from any catharsis for the participants; *emancipation* rather, even more than *carnivalization*, is the more appropriate analytic term for the sense of wild energy arising during the Carnival moment. The history of Carnival playing makes this clear: this is an event that celebrates not only the historical act of slave liberation, but uses the emancipation as a way of establishing and reinforcing a community of feelings and meanings.[54]

In its vision of a people brought into being in the instant of dance and its music, yet whose dispersal eludes the regulating technology of population, *A Drum Is a Woman* imagines diaspora as a temporal form that exists in its doing. As Abrahams proposes of Trinidadian carnival, "perhaps, as in many other places, the Trinidadian community exists only as Carnival is played."[55] The choreodramatic tour of Madam Zajj through the expressive geographies of jazz put this production of a people at the center of the history of jazz. This speculative philosophy of the history of jazz was more thoroughly developed on the Columbia LP (where Ellington's narration provides greater detail and complexity to Zajj's travels and relationships) but more deeply realized on the CBS broadcast, where de Lavallade's performance and the overall choreography presents the production of a people that is not a population or a community or a unified body politic. Rather, Ellington, Strayhorn, and de Lavallade visualized black musical history as the production of a people that appears in and through the interstices of population, exceeding its optimal conduct and performing as if they were not a part of it.

Madam Zajj's Queer Transubstantiation

Yet what does it mean that such dizzying imaginaries occur by way of a figure that is both a woman and a drum? Despite its commercial success, the title of the show and several of its numbers left (and continue to leave) audiences uneasy. "The thought kept plaguing me," wrote one music critic at the time, "that maybe television now is spreading the unsophisticated philosophy that a woman should be beaten regularly—like a drum."[56] The single calypso number in the show made the point in explicit terms: "It isn't civilized to beat women, / no matter what they do or they say. / But will somebody tell me / what else can you do with a drum?" Fortunately, the song never caught on, but the metaphor lingered in the jazz imagination. In the early 1980s, the jazz poet Jayne Cortez recorded a black feminist spoken-word piece titled "If the Drum Is a Woman" that used Ellington and Strayhorn's title to unflinchingly confront a casual approach to violence against women and foreground the homosocial production of the metaphor. In counterpoint with a trio of male drummers (including her son, Denardo Coleman), Cortez asks "If the drum is a woman / why are you pounding your drum into an insane babble." After invoking historical conditions of violence and impoverishment, she shifts registers and transvalues the image that structures Ellington's philosophy of the history of jazz:

> If the drum is a woman
> then understand your drum
> your drum is not docile
> your drum is not invisible
> your drum is not inferior to you
> your drum is a woman
> so don't reject your drum
> don't try to dominate your drum[57]

The poem-performance is governed by the conditional clause—"if the drum is woman"—and therefore engages without necessarily conceding the basic premise of Ellington's own poetic vision. Thus, as scholar Aldon Lynn Nielsen understands it, Cortez's contrapuntal address "is a raid upon the aestheticization of the figure of woman and a return to the same metaphor, reclaimed, that served as the vehicle for that aestheticization. What she demands, and what she accomplishes on this recording, is a sweeping redefinition of the place of woman's voice in the communal creation and circulation of tropes."[58] It is not a negation or refusal of the trope but a transvaluation of gendered troping as such. De Lavallade's choreographic agency in the television broadcast anticipates Cortez's protest and discloses her critique as immanent to the philosophy of history of jazz that *A Drum Is a Woman* visualizes. In this way, Cortez can be seen as a further incarnation of Madam Zajj who—like de Lavallade—materializes her presence in jazz history not just within but also against its often masculinist and misogynist conditions of production.

Ellington's own understanding of the metaphor draws further attention to the complex formations of gender and sexuality that shape *A Drum Is a Woman*. In the weeks surrounding the broadcast, critics often called on Ellington to clarify the title of the show. In response, he repeatedly offered the following explanation of its sexual and gender politics:

> [Madam Zajj] is the spirit of jazz, which comes about as a result of this tremendous romance that goes on between a musician and his instrument and his music—and this is a big thing, and this is how we arrive at our statement that a drum is a woman. We've seen a lot of guys who would leave a real pretty chick so that he can go off in a corner and blow his horn. And you see guys like [Ellington Orchestra member] Sam Woodyard, who is a drummer, and when he takes a solo, he'll be grunting and closing his eyes and caressing that drum and feeling the skin of its head—and it couldn't be hotter. That's what they call their drums, skins. A drummer is a skin whipper. And a woman is the most important accessory a man has.[59]

In another explanation, Ellington further mused on this scene:

> Any real jazz cat . . . is in love with what he plays. A cat says to his wife, "Here's $2, chick, go out and have a ball." He says it to her so he can be with what he loves, his horn or whatever it is. Why, you can hear those hot romances up in the air shafts at night . . . a sax cat standing there all alone in a lonely room, blowing against a wall just to hear the sound bouncing back. Maybe he doesn't drink or gamble or play around with the chicks. But he can be real dirty and mean when he gets alone with what he's in love with. He's a schizo. That's why a drum is a woman.[60]

Far from clarifying the issue, these comments only leave things more problematic and, potentially, more interesting. In trying to describe the relationship between a musician and his instrument, Ellington unsurprisingly heterosexualizes the erotics of musical production. His comments are grounded in the same casual misogyny that would view women interchangeably with objects or accessories and foreclose the possibility of a woman as a music maker herself. Yet tellingly, the erotics here are not all that straight. The woman in the schizo scenes Ellington describes is quickly ushered out. No longer an object of desire or domination, she becomes extraneous. This is no less misogynistic, perhaps, than the woman as a drum, but it complicates the erotic scene it conjures. The familiar structure of male homosocial desire routed through the possession of a woman underwrites Ellington's anecdote ("between instruments," as it were), and the logic of such homosociality entails that it can easily and unpredictably slide into a disavowed homoerotic desire.[61] A number of displacements shape these scenes—from woman to man, from drum to horn, from allo- to auto-, from hetero to homo, from touch to breath—and suggest a homoerotics that is pivotal to the transformations of Madam Zajj and thus the history of jazz. This queer reading of Madam Zajj is furthered by Strayhorn's own outness and his thoughts about gender and sexuality. Recalling their many long conversations, Strayhorn's closest friend, Lena Horne, described how they "talked about everything. We talked about what it was like to be a woman and what it was like to be a man, and we talked about how mixed up each of the sexes were and how better off we'd all be if we were even more mixed up together."[62] Moreover, Strayhorn was not the only out gay figure associated with *A Drum Is a Woman*. In a queer twist of casting, out cabaret performer Ozzie Bailey sang the part of Caribee Joe, Madam Zajj's love interest, disrupting the story's romantic narrative with some behind-the-scenes irony and further scrambling the routes of *A Drum Is a Woman*'s desire.

Given all of this, we might then think of Madam Zajj as a transnational, transgendered, transhuman body that stands in for the (philosophy of the) history of jazz, which is itself a history of the production of subjectivities-in-resistance. This queer critique is crucial to a full understanding of Madam Zajj's biopolitical performance. In the *US Steel Hour* broadcast, Madam Zajj is already a multiple body: as we have seen, she is sung at different moments in the piece by soprano Margaret Tynes and jazz vocalist Joya Sherrill, each providing a different musical inflection, and danced by Carmen de Lavallade. She appears again in Cortez's later troping of the drum/woman trope. This proliferation of Madam Zajjs allows us to consider her elusive embodiment as she refuses the corporeal reduction to an individual body that could be disciplined by the title of the piece or the violence that the title implies. The feminist agency of de Lavallade's choreography and the queer energy of Strayhorn's sensibility counter-counterprogram Ellington's *A Drum Is a Woman*. In her choreographic, musical, vocal, and poetic transformations, Madam Zajj (and/as de Lavallade) eludes the dominant logic of the metaphor that would fix her.

Irving Townsend, Ellington's close confidant and producer at Columbia Records during the recording of *A Drum Is a Woman*, might have contextualized this image of Madam Zajj's plural body within what he called "the total Ellington personality." Shortly after Ellington's death, Townsend wrote: "The longer I knew Duke, the more convinced I became that he needed many bodies, many separated minds and fingers, to reveal himself. This multibodied personality," he concluded, "was most apparent in the Ellington-Strayhorn unity."[63] This Ellingtonian multitude invites us to see Madam Zajj as a de-corporealization of the body and a queer transubstantiation of sound that emerges against the corporate body of US Steel's consumer citizenship and the regularized body of Jim Crow. A queer carnival reading of Madam Zajj suggests that the production of a people will necessarily elude or contest the sexuality *dispositif* of regulatory biopower and state racism by inventing different configurations of sexuality and embodiment. As a live telecast, *A Drum Is a Woman* enacted yet another de-corporealization of Madam Zajj as it broadcast her across the nation via radio transmissions to be decoded and reassembled in postwar middle-class living rooms. With the *Drum Is a Woman* broadcast on the *US Steel Hour*, Ellington and Strayhorn appropriated the time of the calypso craze and counterprogrammed the fad to visualize and enact an understanding of the time of diaspora and diaspora as time. Their calypso fantasia reimagined the historiographic modes of jazz, diaspora, and migration and displaced a population with a people who become manifest through musical movement and transformation. As a sound, a gesture, a Diz-orientation of time and space, a futuriginary circle, an immense nonsense, a history and a philosophy of history, a queer fever dream, mas and mass, Madam Zajj both represents and enacts the de/materialization of a people through an aesthetics of emancipation that extended New World carnival through technologies and ontologies of black fad performance.

FOUR

Surfacing the Caribbean: Black Broadway and Mock Transnational Performance

Lena Horne almost didn't star in the Broadway production of *Jamaica*. Intended to capitalize on the calypso craze, the 1957 folk musical was originally crafted as a vehicle for performer Harry Belafonte following the release of his best-selling album *Calypso* the previous year. With lyrics by blacklisted Jewish lyricist E. Y. "Yip" Harburg, libretto by Harburg and Fred Saidy, and music by Harold Arlen, *Jamaica* was conceived as a sharp political satire that parodied postwar consumerism and the commercialization of the calypso craze (of which *Jamaica* was a part) using the form of the calypso musical. A socialist fable told through a musical-comedy love plot, it depicts what happens when an unscrupulous Harlem businessman, Joe Nashua, introduces capitalism to a small, self-sustaining fishing village on Pigeon Island, a fictional British colony off the coast of Jamaica. After depleting the island's natural resources and devastating its social relations, Joe attempts to return north, but is prevented by what at first appears to be a nuclear explosion (though later we learn it was a hurricane) that cuts the island off from the rest of the world. Charged with reinventing the world in act 2, the residents of Pigeon Island, led by the local fisherman Koli, come to reject Joe's model of social organization and choose an alternative mode of economic production. In numbers like "Yankee Dollar" and "Leave de Atom Alone," *Jamaica* parodied the colonial system, Caribbean tourist economies, and the ideological struggles that subtended a cold war that was never very cold. It may be the only Broadway musical to stage, just before intermission, a mushroom cloud.

But this script was hastily retooled when Belafonte dropped out of the production months before opening night, citing prior engagements that would conflict with an extended Broadway run.[1] Scrambling to find a marquee name to replace him, the producers turned to Horne, who had recently captivated New York in an extended engagement at the Waldorf Astoria's Empire Room. Her role in *Jamaica* as the island girl Savannah was the singer's only stage performance in a book musical. To showcase its new star, the show underwent a series of revisions, often against the strenuous objections of its writers. As the company rehearsed in out-of-town previews, the production team shifted the focus from a male lead to a female lead, reassigned songs to Horne (by opening night she was singing more than half of them), and streamlined the book. These changes muted Harburg's political content, though it remained audible as a whisper in the story and somewhat more loudly in the song lyrics, which for the most part remained intact. With Horne in Belafonte's place, *Jamaica* opened to huge popular—though not critical—success and was the longest-running black-cast Broadway musical up to that time. Despite (and also because of) the writers' intentions, the show appeared as a typical instance of midcentury Broadway Caribbeana: a tourist production that traded on recycled notions of an undifferentiated Caribbean landscape and a tropical aesthetic of pseudo-calypso rhythms, moonlight romance, and folk simplicity (fig. 15).[2]

Figure 15. Lena Horne, Ricardo Montalbán, and the company of *Jamaica*, 1957. Photo by Friedman-Abeles. © Billy Rose Theatre Division, New York Public Library for the Performing Arts.

Like other calypso craze productions, it would seem that *Jamaica* had nothing to do with Jamaica or the larger Caribbean scene. As theater historians such as Errol Hill and Allen Woll have argued about midcentury commercial stagings of Broadway Caribbeana, "such productions have provided work for black actors, including those from the Caribbean. As is indicative of Caribbean life, however, these works are seldom significant as they tend to avoid dealing with issues that daily confront people of the region."[3] Clearly, as we have seen, this claim extends to most of the calypso craze. Yet if calypso craze performances have little directly to say about the daily issues of those who live in the Caribbean, they never pretended otherwise, and this very avowal of inauthenticity was one way that they engaged with diasporic history and aesthetics. While *Jamaica* was not about Jamaica, it was also not-not about Jamaica. As part of the calypso craze, it participated in an ongoing representational project in which popular US conceptions of the Caribbean were shaped, perpetuated, and disavowed. If the calypso craze films discussed in chapter 2 spent more time on the nightclub stages or recording booths of New York City than island locales, and if Ellington's televised spectacular discussed in chapter 3 offered an impressionistic tour through a New World soundscape, musical theater (and *Jamaica* in particular) staged Caribbean geographies more directly in the calypso craze and its critical engagement with the inauthentic.

Through Broadway productions, mass-produced soundtrack recordings, and paratheatrical publicity, musical theater was another performance medium like film and television in which the calypso craze developed. Returning to this musical in light of the larger context of the black fad performance that we have seen thus far, I describe *Jamaica* as an exemplary instance of black fad culture's deep tradition of mock transnational performance. I use the term *mock transnational* to describe a theatrical mode and performative stance that takes up the misuse of diasporic cultural indices to critique and refigure the politics of the nation-state and racialized national formations. Mock transnationalism developed in response to the ontological, epistemological, and representational conditions of black fad performance that we have seen in earlier chapters. It is another iteration of black fad performance's stolen time: a bait and switch in which the inauthentic is foregrounded to further force the question of existential and cultural authenticity in the time of the fad. Where we might expect national and racial identities to be buttressed and secured by *Jamaica*'s touristic presentation of alterity for profit and amusement, we find instead that, much like Duke Ellington and Billy Strayhorn's *A Drum Is a Woman*, the musical's songs, sound, and staging provided a surface for constantly shifting and destabilizing configurations of nation and race. To demonstrate this, I track *Jamaica*'s articulation of the mock transnational in three different loci of its production: first, in the critique of multinational capital and colonial tourist industries that persisted in incongruous lyrical moments of its otherwise conventional musical-comedy libretto; second, in Horne's auditory maneuvers and performative vocal strategies, which sounded the paradoxes and tensions in the musical's score; and last, in the networks of professional support and social activism cultivated in the musical's backstage relations.

Jamaica's mock transnational performance allowed for these political alternatives to be staged, sounded, and embodied, even in the face of the tourist economies and minstrel traditions in which black fad performance trafficked (fig. 16). While the aesthetic strategy of the mock transnational appears across a range of media during the calypso craze, it develops most fully within the tradition of black Broadway, by which I refer not only to the emergence of black theatrical productions and performers in New York City's midtown commercial theater district, but also to the more general structure of feeling that foregrounds the complex relationship between commercial theater and black musical performance in the

Figure 16. *Jamaica* dancers in an island scene, 1957. Photo by Friedman-Abeles. © Billy Rose Theatre Division, New York Public Library for the Performing Arts.

Jim Crow era.[4] Locating *Jamaica* within a tradition of mock transnational performance provides the occasion to consider what happens when black Broadway becomes—or fails to become—a part of the Caribbean archipelago.[5] Hill, Woll, and other theater historians argue correctly that midcentury Broadway Caribbeana, and the calypso craze more specifically, worked to displace contemporary political concerns in both the United States and the Caribbean. But like all displacements—psychic, social, representational, political, geographic—*Jamaica*'s displacements had a number of unexpected and unpredicted effects that provided opportunities for performers to steal (back) the time of the musical. Despite *Jamaica*'s romanticization of the Caribbean folk and the exploitation of a "calypso mood," we will see that an anticolonial politics, diasporic consciousness, and socialist possibility nonetheless surfaced in the increasingly outmoded form of the black musical revue, which returned to Broadway under the auspices of the calypso craze. Stuart Hall proposes that this intrinsic contradiction is what characterizes black fad performance as a site of "strategic contestation": "However deformed, incorporated, and unauthentic are the forms in which black people and black communities and traditions appear and are represented in popular culture, we continue to see, in the figures and the repertoires on which popular culture draws, the experiences that stand behind them."[6] Through various elements of performance, Hall contends, "black popular culture has enabled the surfacing, inside the mixed and contradictory modes even of some mainstream popular culture, of elements of a discourse that is different—other forms of life, other traditions of representation."[7]

At first glance, we might understand Hall to be saying that we can often discern, beneath the distorting waters of mass media, the outline of the true culture that it covers over, traces of its authentic origin that speak to us from below. But throughout his work, Hall was wary of the ruses of popular culture that could lead to essential notions of cultural authenticity. Close parsing of this passage suggests that the "experiences that stand behind" deformed representations of blackness need not necessarily refer to a pure or authentic cultural form but might describe instead the signifying chain of representations and the "game of cultural 'wars of positions'" that define black popular culture as a site of struggle.[8] In the context of the calypso craze, this would include the play of inauthenticity and authenticity that defines black fad performance. Thus we might understand his use of *surface* as a transitive verb: to give a surface *to* something, or to cover a surface *with* something. *Jamaica* (and the calypso craze more widely) enabled the surfacing of other forms of life and different discourses not by recourse to what lies below it but by reassembling and rearranging the elements above—*surfacing* as making-a-surface rather than emerging-from-beneath. Instead of seeking the true performance behind black popular culture, Hall directs us to the new performances made possible on its surface. And, as we will see at the end of this chapter, paradoxically but appropriately it was in this musical's backstage region that performers invented new forms of life and different discourses.

On stage, too, paradox structured the musical's formal project. It used a story of a folk culture outside of commodification to issue a political critique of capitalism through a form—black Broadway's midcentury calypso musical—that undermined the fictions of authenticity on which it relied. But if Yip Harburg misrecognized the ontology of black fad performance (to his deep frustration with this production), the actors did not. The performers' stance toward the musical brought a black fad sensibility to Harburg's Old Left cultural politics. To put this another way, this production staged an errant *Jamaica*: one wayward and in error, but also one that wandered, in the sense that Édouard Glissant proposes, unmoored from its point of origin. It was an excess *Jamaica* that lay beyond the national boundaries of its referent, avowing its inauthenticity and constituting new relations in the black fad performance of the calypso craze. For Glissant, such errancy is enacted as a series of detours, substitutions, and decenterings. The Caribbean archipelago provides an exemplary model of such errancy for him, "a place of encounter and connivance" that refuses autochthonous origins and the founding legitimacy of filiation.[9] We will see by the end of this chapter how the performance of *Jamaica*, by way of and in excess of the calypso craze, remains faithful to what Glissant describes as a poetics of relation: the rhizomatic networks of a diasporic consciousness that bring into being new forms of connection and subjectivity through unexpected and rerouted associations. In what follows, I invoke Caribbean theorists such as Hall and Glissant in order to mark (and mock) the erasures of Caribbean history, knowledge, and philosophical thought within the production of *Jamaica* and, at the same time, to recognize a certain decolonial pulse, New World consciousness, and socialist unconscious—a calypso ethos—that surfaces on and as the representational cul-de-sac of black fad performance.

Black Broadway's Mock Transnationalism

In early drafts of Harburg's book for *Jamaica*, the expectation of voodoo exoticism that typically organized Broadway and nightclub stagings of the Caribbean is at once raised and disappointed. The island matriarch, Grandma Obeah, seems to satisfy a number of stock requirements for mid-century Caribbean kitsch. With a name evoking island sorcery, she stands as the moral center of the musical and dispenses oracular folk wisdom on matters of love and island life. Her particular method of deciphering portents takes the form of reading cloud formations over the sea, which provides her with knowledge of future happenings. Grandma Obeah is a more respected figure than the colonial Governor, who relies on Grandma Obeah to keep order and ensure the smooth functioning of the island. In this relationship, the musical foregrounds questions of geopolitics and governmentality that emerge in the conflict between indigenous cosmology, on the one hand, and colonial administration, on the other. At *Jamaica*'s start, Grandma Obeah has called off fishing for the day because the clouds portend dangerous seas. Concerned by the loss of a day's tax revenue, the Governor arrives at her village to investigate, exasperatedly explaining that "we can't run a social order based on clouds." Deferring to the supernatural, Grandma Obeah adamantly maintains her position.[10]

Shortly after this scene, however, Grandma Obeah confides to her grandson that in fact there is no such thing as magic: "I'se not foolin' de folks, I'se only tryin' to help dem see wid their eyes what they feel in their hearts. Some times dey don't listen to an old woman—so I calls on de clouds to make it official." While in one sense this scene simply exchanges one stereotype for another (replacing voodoo magic with the gravitas of folk authenticity), it is important to note that Grandma Obeah's performance as a seer works not only for dispensing love advice but also for manipulating matters of state and capital. By appealing to a higher authority than that of the British Crown, she uses the clouds and the colonial uncertainty about her powers to authorize a day off from fishing, deceiving the colonial administration and gaining time for rest for the island laborers.[11]

This ambivalent satire of colonial relations and its demystification of the representational codes of black theatrical characters are prime examples of the tradition of mock transnational performance developed within the exigencies and constraints of musical theater in black fad performance. This mock transnationalism is not a simple inauthentic presentation or caricature of diasporic cultural practice. Rather, mock transnationalism describes a certain stance toward transnational movements, sounds, and scenes as they were commodified, exchanged, and faddishly circulated through various channels of capital. In other words, mock transnational performance's referent is not something we might identify or imagine as "the transnational," but the inherent limitations of transnational imagination as such. Even as transnational movements of performances, politics, and practices generated productive alliances and exchanges, they also created what Brent Hayes Edwards describes as the "unavoidable misapprehensions and misreadings, persistent blindnesses and solipsisms, self-defeating and abortive collaborations, [and] a failure to translate even a basic grammar of blackness" that are part of any diasporic culture.[12] Mock transnationalism developed within black fad performance as one theatrical response to these necessary breakdowns and incommensurabilities. As *Jamaica* demonstrates so well, the mock transnational occurs through these accidents, miscastings, mistakes, and unforeseen confluences. It is a theatrical "encounter and connivance" that makes use of the mistranslations of transnational diasporic imaginaries as they circulate through systems of fad production and consumption.[13]

As such, this stance relies on the double sense of "mock" as imitation or parody—with the senses of falseness, mimicry, inauthenticity, and ridicule—and "mock" as assemblage—with the senses of a mock-up, a model, an aggregation of disparate sounds, signifiers, images, gestures, and representational bits. Even while it suggests something artificial, it invokes a kind of creative making-do, the bricolage of something like mock turtle soup, the eighteenth-century British culinary improvisation that sought to imitate the texture and taste of expensive turtle meat with discarded portions of cows or pigs. This double sense of mock transnational performance opens up a space of contradiction and disjunction in which the false starts and dead ends of transnational commodification could themselves be productive of new political and cultural possibilities. We see this double sense of mock in earlier black fad moments, for example, in Josephine Baker's "Danse sauvage" (1925) or her later film *Princess Tam Tam* (1935). In both cases, Baker's performance refers not to African cultural practices, but rather parodies the Parisian vogue for Africanist primitivism. Yet this referential displacement is also a performance of relation that expands racial formations beyond simple satire. In the national indeterminacy of their diasporic identity, Baker's performances hold open space for other configurations of race and nation.[14]

Mock transnationalism can be heard as a leitmotif that recurs throughout the extended score of black fad performance across the Jim Crow era, especially in musical theater that staged blackness under diasporic banners such as "Africa" (most commonly in the early genre of the back-to-Africa musical) and "the Caribbean." This tradition began with the inauguration of black Broadway itself during the first cycle of Jim Crow fad performance: Bert Williams and George Walker's *In Dahomey* (1903), one of the most successful musical theater productions associated with the turn-of-the-century ragtime craze. *In Dahomey* follows a crooked investor (Walker) and his guileful sidekick (Williams) who attempt to defraud their shareholders with a back-to-Africa scheme and the promise of repatriation. Over the course of the plot, the musical plays with African American diasporic geographies—beginning in Boston, then shifting to Florida, and finally arriving in Dahomey—to question competing constructions of African American racial and cultural identity.

Like other black musicals in this tradition, *In Dahomey* pressed the relationship between signifiers such as "Africa" (or "the Caribbean") and the gestures and sounds that made up its staging, the light and colors that illuminated its scenic design, the fabrics that covered (or didn't cover) the dancers and actors, and the conditions of its scripting. The fraudulence that drives William and Walker's characters' financial scams in the libretto, for example, points us to some of the musical's larger baits and switches. As the cast transforms the stage into an African pantomime to signify their arrival in Dahomey in act 3, the scene, according to performance historian Daphne Brooks, is "not so much about literally being present 'in Dahomey.' Instead, it is what happens in the brief yet startling transmutative sequences when one is 'there' that serves as a catalyst and a recurring, figurative trope that repeatedly critiques and rewrites racial categories and conventional notions of identity formation."[15] This use of Africa "not only competed with conventional representations of an 'uncivilized' frontier but it also threatened to revise how Africa might be narrated and ultimately who would narrate that mysterious land in Western cultural consciousness."[16] This reading is confirmed by Louis Chude-Sokei, who argues that the Africa staged at the end of *In Dahomey* "certainly was not real but a discursive space constructed to enable a simultaneously local and global critique by way of a black imagination that was diasporic in its reach."[17]

What Brooks describes as *In Dahomey*'s "disquieting double-vocality" and what Chude-Sokei calls its "deliberate falseness and unreality" are characteristic of mock transnational performance from the early twentieth century to a production like *Jamaica* and beyond.[18] We can further trace the strategic misuses of diasporic geographies in *Abyssinia* (1907), Williams and Walker's follow-up to *In Dahomey*, as well as in later back-to-Africa productions such as Flournoy Miller and Aubrey Lyle's *Rang Tang* (1927) and Trinidadian-born writer and composer Donald Heywood's *Africana* (1934).[19] Each of these productions used diasporic imaginaries in order to explore and complicate the relationship between African American racial consciousness and theatrical form, on the one hand, and African diasporic histories and fantasies, on the other. As Brooks and Chude-Sokei have argued about *In Dahomey*, these musicals were not about Africa, but about the very construction of diasporic thought and the terms of racial representation. Such mock transnational strategies developed a way to advance a diasporic imagination that shaped relations between the multiplicity of black ethnicities within the United States and beyond its shores.

To further illustrate the possibilities and limitations of black fad performance for such transnational relationality, we can view *Jamaica* alongside two contemporaneous Broadway performances of the popular Caribbean that predate the calypso craze of the 1950s: Anglo-Trinidadian William Archibald's *Carib Song* (1945) and Truman Capote's *House of Flowers* (1954), both of which prefigured and made possible the production of *Jamaica*. Although conceived and written by librettist and lyricist Archibald, *Carib Song* was in actuality the creation of dancer-anthropologist Katherine Dunham, who codirected the show, choreographed the dance numbers, and starred in the lead role. Set during carnival season on an unnamed island, *Carib Song* is about an unfaithful wife who is cast out of her community by a campaign of vicious gossip and at the end murdered by her husband. Mingling Trinidadian folklore, ritual, and ethnographic dance, Dunham's choreography drove the production more than plot or song, so much so that one critic complained that the show "should have been billed as a dance recital."[20] As we saw in chapter 2, this turn to the ethnographic was common during calypso's 1940s miniboom in New York City, of which *Carib Song* was a part. Dunham's attempt to bring Afro-Caribbean movement to the popular stage was most spectacularly realized in the first-act climax, which featured a stylized recreation of a Shango ritual (a number adopted into Dunham's repertoire and performed in subsequent dance programs, including her more successful 1946 revue, *Bal Nègre*). These syncretic compositions and voodoo pantomimes, based on her anthropological fieldwork, tried to transform a stock bit of Broadway exotica by bringing to it some anthropological detail and Caribbean movement. This choreographic project confounded most critics, who found it a misguided presence in the context of the black Broadway musical revue.[21]

House of Flowers, by contrast, made no attempt to incorporate Caribbean culture or history into its story. Capote wrote the lyrics and book, based on his short story of the same name, and *Jamaica*'s Harold Arlen composed the music. Although to this day more critically celebrated than *Jamaica*, *House of Flowers* had none of its successor's social consciousness or self-awareness. The musical portrayed the comic conflict between the madams of competing brothels on an unnamed island in the French West

Indies inspired by Capote's own recent trip to Haiti. The show was padded with local-color exotica and easy jokes that traded on unearned laughter at illicit sexuality, and the overall effect was one of an unhistorical and undifferentiated Caribbean fantasy. Although a crucial professional opportunity for performers such as Pearl Bailey, Diahann Carroll, Enid Mosier, Carmen de Lavallade, Josephine Premice, and Alvin Ailey (the last two of whom would later appear in *Jamaica*), the book shamelessly indulged Capote's cosmopolitanism and cast a knowing wink to Caribbean sex tourism. The *Boston Globe* found it "too naughty for this city," and critic Miles Jefferson lamented unnecessary details such as scenes of "young boys working up a sexual lather in a house of ill-fame" and "a representative of the law emerg[ing] from [a brothel] buckling his suspenders and putting on his coat."[22]

There was, however, one moment of rupture in *House of Flowers'* otherwise exoticized story, in which the surface cracked to reveal not the true culture concealed in the depths behind it but another form of life and representation beside it. The young Trinidadian dancer Geoffrey Holder, newly arrived to New York City with his own dance company, performed a solo dance number of his own creation for the musical's spectacular second act "voodoo ballet" sequence. In this number, Holder appeared as the Haitian spirit Baron Samedi (listed in the program as Baron of the Cemetery). Baron Samedi is a vodou deity of fertility and death, recognizable by his top hat and the tailcoat he wears over his shirtless torso. Holder appeared with his face painted half white and half black to further suggest Baron Samedi's skull-like visage (fig. 17). Holder based his dance number on his recent encounter with vodou dance in Haiti, where he witnessed the great Haitian choreographer Jean-Léon Destiné perform the *banda* dance. Although one review found Holder's dance solo "thin in places, casual with respect to form," it nonetheless praised his "impressive ranginess, his great movement facility and the remarkable head-spins (the rotating head looked as if it would fly off the neck)."[23] As dance historian Celia Weiss Bambara observes, in the context of *House of Flowers'* stereotypical depictions of the Caribbean, Holder "drew upon American and Haitian culture to create a dance-based representation that expressed a new Caribbean identity."[24] In this musical, too, he introduced for the first time on the US stage the Trinidadian steel drum band.[25] Holder was one of the central performers of the calypso craze and would go on to develop this *House of Flowers* choreography into a full-length modernist dance composition over the subsequent decades. With these brief bits of sound and dance, Holder stole (back) the terms of Caribbean representation from *House of Flowers* to

Figure 17. Geoffrey Holder as Baron Samedi in *House of Flowers*, 1954. Jerome Robbins Dance Division, New York Public Library for the Performing Arts, Astor, Lenox and Tilden Foundations.

stage forms of life and different discourses that anticipated, as we will see in the next chapter, his later stance toward the calypso craze.

Following in the mock transnational tradition inaugurated on the Broadway stage by *In Dahomey*, *Jamaica* staged a different relationship to the transnational than either *Carib Song* or *House of Flowers*, which stand as emergent instances of popular Caribbeana before its rapid consolidation into the calypso craze. As I will demonstrate in the next section, *Jamaica* was different than a musical like *Carib Song*, which staged its relationship to the Caribbean as an intercultural dialogue between the aesthetics and practices of Caribbean music and dance and the tradition of the black musical revue, calling on Dunham's ethnographic experience for its authenticity claims. It was likewise distinct from a musical such as *House of Flowers*, which provided a touristic fantasy of colonial erotics and a depoliticized calypso vision of tropical life (Holder's invocation of Baron Samedi notwithstanding). Unlike *Carib Song*, *Jamaica* made no attempt to work within the traditions and histories of Caribbean diasporic cultures. Unlike *House of Flowers*, it undermined its own commitment to exoticism and critiqued the touristic and colonial conditions of its own existence as a popular fad. The theoretical category and aesthetic posture of the mock transnational, we will now see, provides one way to think about the ontological context and unfixed middle ground of black fad performance that *Jamaica* often inhabits, connecting it to a deeper tradition of black fad performance's strategic misrecognition of diasporic locales, peoples, and sounds.

Jamaica's Calypso Mood

In the mock transnational tradition of black fad performance, *Jamaica* appeared as a parody of a travesty, a representation of a misrepresentation that threw into stark relief the failures of transnational representation as such: *this* is not *that*. Moreover, the musical's lyrics and its performances depended on the audience's recognition and knowingness of these failures in order to launch its critique. *Jamaica*'s use of knowingness and its displacement of a grounding authenticity—achieved in the erased socialist politics of its book and in the vocal disarticulations and self-reflexivity of Horne's performance—put pressure on the ties that bind national identities to racial formations, disrupting and expanding those formations under the sign of the mock transnational and surfacing new relations of performance in the calypso craze.[26]

The title of Harburg and Arlen's musical points to the acts of deferral, substitution, and displacement that shape histories of mock transnational performance. While *Jamaica*'s name marks the absent presence of Belafonte as a trace in the show's origins (whose Jamaican heritage was a significant aspect of his star image), it also foregrounds the production's musical distance from the history of Trinidadian calypso—a history that it both invokes and obscures. Arlen's score borrowed musical techniques and tone patterns from forms such as the beguine, the rumba, and the blues, as well as from the calypso, to create what one theater critic characterized as *Jamaica*'s "calypso mood."[27] As we would expect by now, this is a calypso explicitly unmoored from any particular political or geographic context, buoyed by the Caribbean faddishness occupying supper clubs, airwaves, and movie screens across the United States. Arlen confirmed as much in a profile published shortly before *Jamaica*'s opening, which confided that

> because he finds calypso boring and repetitious, Arlen has merely flavored the *Jamaica* score with it, feeling that a full evening of calypso would be mighty dull. Before he began writing songs for the show, Arlen characteristically made a study of calypso and decided that using the authentic form would prove ineffective in the theatre.[28]

Just as earlier generations of white corporate songwriters (including Arlen himself) appropriated "the blues"—as mood, as marketing device, as sign, as song—the Caribbean-tinged popular compositions of the calypso craze standardized a musical tradition, rescoring it in a different form and sound that nonetheless failed to fully write over the form and sound it claimed. This would prove to be both enabling and encumbering for Caribbean musicians throughout the twentieth century as the calypso craze transformed and reformed Caribbean music, and its performers modified their stance to the cultural conditions of musical production.

In contrast, the political poetry of Harburg's lyrics bears a closer resemblance to the Trinidadian calypso tradition of coded protest, topical commentary, and cutting mockery. While Harburg was never the doctrinaire radical his redbaiting critics accused him of being, he was a committed leftist who was blacklisted during the 1950s for his support of social justice and global economic equality. Early in his career, he disrupted the easy entertainment of the musical revue with his 1933 ballad "Brother, Can You Spare a Dime?," politicizing Broadway with a subtle satire of the failures of the American Dream. Such socialist yearning emerges again and again in Harburg's oeuvre and structures the political consciousness of *Jamaica.* In its lyrics and earliest versions of the book, Harburg and Saidy made use of a calypso mood to demystify the construction of the Caribbean as a tourist paradise, to voice a critique of Cold War ideologies, and even to undermine its own complicity in the calypso craze.

Two examples will demonstrate how this calypso mood functioned as a critique of the calypso craze itself, drawing on Trinidadian calypso traditions even as it erased them. In the first, a scene from an earlier draft of *Jamaica* whose content was muted but survived in the Broadway production, the colonial Governor's native assistant Cicero (performed by Ossie Davis) arrives at the wharf where tourists dock for day trips from Kingston. The stage directions describe a "customs shed" and "a series of souvenir stands nearby," locating the scene between the mutually reinforcing institutions of the state and the market. In his role as native assistant to the colonial Governor, Cicero is a character derived from the tradition of the blackface dandy: he functions as a figure of ridicule for his pretensions to leadership, his malapropisms, and his faux cosmopolitanism. Yet like many black performances of this stock figure, he also becomes the voice of critique and mockery of white attitudes toward blackness. Announcing himself as the self-appointed chief of the "In-Tourist Department," Cicero reports that Pigeon Island is in financial crisis because it has failed to draw a tourist trade and is losing money to other islands in the region.[29] To redress the situation, he instructs the dockworkers and souvenir sellers in how to attract American tourists. Reading from a decree, he announces the blueprint for what he calls "Operation Greenback" (a play on Puerto Rico's postwar economic modernization project, Operation Bootstrap):

> WHEREAS, we is all broke, be it resolved we set up this In-Tourist department to create for the tourists the kind o' quaint native atmosphere that they expect from the Hollywood movies.
>
> ITEM NUMBER ONE—clothes. Be on guard night and day for the approach of a tourist. That mean—wear your festival costumes at all times.
>
> ITEM NUMBER TWO—No more homemade souvenirs. From now on we is importing genuine authentic mementoes from Hackensack, New Jersey—stamped Jamaica.
>
> ITEM NUMBER THREE—Sing whenever possible. If a tourist ask you a question—answer in Calypso.[30]

Taking his cue from Hollywood, Cicero directs the workers how to dress and sound and finds in the culture industry's calypso craze an opportunity for the island's own economic growth. The importation of souvenirs from New Jersey, yet bearing the stamp of Jamaica, calls into question the very grounds of the "genuine authentic" (a telling redundancy). Here we see the reciprocal dynamics of black fad performance's founding disavowal: the distinction between the calypso craze and "true calypso" makes both *this* and *that* less self-evident than they at first seem.

Having issued this decree, Cicero rehearses Operation Greenback with the vendors by play-acting the part of a tourist. In response to his stock tourist question—"Chappie, could you direct me to the nearest banana boat?"—the vendors perform their new and improved Caribbean personas by "answering in calypso." Singing to the tune of Belafonte's "Day O (The Banana Boat Song)," they reply: "Dey no more banana boats in de sea / Dey all belong to Harry Belafonte."[31] With these familiar notes from Belafonte's recent hit, the musical marks his conspicuous absence and playfully but pointedly questions the ownership, origins, and authenticity of the current calypso fad (as we will see, this was one of many ways that Belafonte's calypso image haunted this production). Such a scene queries not only the staging of *Jamaica* and the calypso craze, but also the more general production of the Caribbean by an emergent mass-tourist industry that, writes David Timothy Duval, was "characterized by undifferentiated products, origin-packaged holidays, spatially-concentrated planning of facilities, resorts and activities, and the reliance upon developed markets such as the United States, Canada, and Britain."[32] Cicero's subsequent order to the vendors to "turn on de naturalness" denaturalizes the calypso mood that sustained this industry, mocking the global circulation of the calypso vogue and the iconicity of Belafonte as the voice of a popular Caribbean in the United States.

The following musical number, "Yankee Dollar," realizes the mock transnational critique of Operation Greenback. Performed by the vendors and Cicero's love interest, Ginger (played by Josephine Premice, whose contributions to the calypso craze I detailed in chapter 1), this mock calypso names the relations structured in dominance that shape US-Caribbean relations—relations that extend to the audiences at *Jamaica*'s theater. In other words, among the things being satirized in this scene is *Jamaica* itself:

> Big boat in de bay,
> Small boat give salute.
> The tourist arrive
> in grey flannel suit . . .
>
> Hooray for de Yankee dollar
> Beautiful Yankee dollar.
> And I like de one
> Wid George Washington . . .
> And also de one
> Wid Mr. Lincoln.
>
> Banana won't fall
> Papaya won't stir
> Till Yankees arrive
> With legal tender.

This commentary on midcentury US-Caribbean cultural relations foregrounds the economic dependence of the local economy on the global market. Even as Caribbean colonies achieved political independence, the tourist trade substituted one mode of colonial administration for another. "Yankee Dollar" ventriloquizes a political critique that was often voiced in postwar Trinidadian calypso. We might, for example, hear this song alongside calypsonian charges against the global market such as Lord Invader and Lionel Belasco's "Rum and Coca-Cola" (1943, famously stolen and recorded by the Andrews Sisters in 1945) and Mighty Sparrow's "Yankees Back Again" (1958). Each of these calypsos named the Yankee dollar as the sign of US military occupation, sexual exploitation, and economic colonialism.[33] Yet while these Trinidadian calypsos voiced an explicit protest against the Caribbean's structured dependence on the United States and the impact of US troops on Trinidadian life, the self-referential black fad performance of "Yankee Dollar" directs its critique toward the tourist occupation of the Caribbean that the military occupation underwrote. Sardonically celebrating the flood of US currency, the scene implicates the US tourist—including the vicarious ones at Broadway's appropriately named Imperial Theater, where *Jamaica* played—in the systems of economic exploitation by revealing the popular Caribbean itself to be a carefully rehearsed commodity, an export that circulates in the same way as natural resources such as fruit and coffee. Furthermore, this US tourist in his "grey flannel suit" alludes to the protagonist of Sloan Wilson's bestselling novel *The Man in the Grey Flannel Suit* (1955), a penetrating existential chronicle of postwar suburban existence and the purposelessness of material culture that would have resonated with the show's ticketholders. The song, in other words, ironizes *Jamaica*'s own conditions of possibility within the context of Broadway's tourist production of the popular Caribbean, which is itself the rehearsed commodity it depicts.

Cicero's transformation of Pigeon Island's tourist industry is a side plot to the larger economic transformation that occurs on the island in the course of the musical. In *Jamaica*'s primary narrative we see a second example of Harburg's anticapitalist critique and socialist yearning voiced in a calypso mood. The arrival of Joe Nashua, a Harlem businessman, disrupts not only Savannah and Koli's love story but the island's mode of production as well, as the fishing village abandons their trade to become pearl divers for Joe's corporate schemes. Joe's attempt to slip away from the island, with both its pearls and Savannah in hand, is interrupted by an unnatural cloud formation—what Grandma Obeah calls an unreadable "man-made weather"—that blackens the stage, brings winds and thunder, and cuts off contact with the rest of the world. Thinking that the world has been destroyed, the inhabitants of Pigeon Island believe themselves the sole survivors of nuclear war. With the island's fishing fleet destroyed by the storm and the food supply depleted, Koli allows himself to be momentarily transformed into a monopoly capitalist. The unexpected scarcity of fish makes his own catch, maintained while the rest of the village was pearl diving, of sudden value. Temporarily corrupted by his newfound power and the misguided impression that Savannah will marry him if he can provide her with a comfortable and luxurious lifestyle, Koli accepts Joe's offer to purchase the fish with his wealth of pearls. But the islanders interrupt this transaction by forcefully taking the pearls back in order to make Koli's fish available to all. With the communally redistributed fish, the villagers throw a collective fish fry. An exchange, cut from the Broadway production but later restored for subsequent revivals, makes explicit this scene's implied political message: as an outraged Joe names the reappropriation of his pearls "gangsterism," Grandma Obeah calmly corrects him: "No . . . that's nationalization."[34]

Harburg and Saidy couch this economic burlesque within the existential threat the Cold War posed as this errant Caribbean island briefly becomes a Pacific atoll. Under the mistaken belief, in the shadow of act 1's mushroom cloud, that the survivors on Pigeon Island represent a new genesis for world history, Ginger (Premice) leads the chorus in a complex lyric that plays on familiar Edenic constructions of the Caribbean as an uncorrupted paradise. Retelling the biblical story, Harburg depicts atomic research as another kind of forbidden knowledge that, once achieved, can only bring about destruction:

> Ever since de apple in de garden with Eve
> Man always foolin' with things that cause him to grieve.
> He fool with the woman, the rum and hot blood,
> And he almost wash out with de forty day flood.
> But not since the doom-day in old Babylon
> Did he fool with anything so diabolical
> As the cyclotron . . .
>
> Don't mess around, you dopes
> Lay off the isotopes
> Don't you fuss with the nucleus
> Don't go too far with the nuclear
> Don't get gay with the cosmic ray
> You'll burn your fingers, lose your hair
> Leave big smog in the atmosphere . . .
>
> Go back to Eve but leave the atom alone.

Harburg draws on popular calypsos such as Sir Lancelot's "Atomic Energy Calypso" (1947) and "Atomic Nightmare" (1957) by the Talbot Brothers of Bermuda to speak directly to the antinuclear protest movements of the early Cold War as the musical stages what the characters think is a post-nuclear apocalyptic world. In songs like "Leave de Atom Alone," "Yankee Dollar," and more generally in the figures of Harburg and Horne, *Jamaica* stands as an important hinge between a residual cultural front politics of the Old Left and the emergent new social movements of the 1960s.

In a discussion of an earlier Harburg-Saidy collaboration, drama critic George Jean Nathan fussily dismissed the persistence of this political emphasis and its intrusion into musical comedies. Disdaining those "who profess to see in a patch of a comedians' pants-seat an analogy to the revolt of the downtrodden against dictatorship," he warned that "if the time comes when chorus girls kick up their indignation instead of their legs, when the hero instead of going back to Maxim's will go back to Union Square, and when the heroine will start singing about Clement Attlee instead of about moonlight on the Caribbean—if that time comes, I'll buy myself a tambourine and stay home."[35] In this admonition, Nathan's postwar critique expresses tedium with the residual framework of a cultural front politics shaped during and after the Depression. What we find in *Jamaica,* however, are adaptations and modifications to this tradition made within a mock transnational calypso mood that updates the leftist musical revue for a global context and gives the lie to Nathan's fantasy of Caribbean nights as harmless musical fare. With lyrics and sentiments that, as Harburg's biographers put it, were "addressed directly to a new audience whose existence Yip might not yet have discerned," Harburg brought his investment in the social and economic critique of the cultural front to bear on emerging geopolitical exigencies and new social movements in the songs for *Jamaica*.[36]

Lena Horne's *Jamaica*

While some of Harburg's political critique surfaced in the retooled script, the show nevertheless failed to stage the dissension its authors imagined. To Harburg, the book had been so thoroughly reimagined to benefit from Horne's marquee name and star power as to be unrecognizable from his original intention. In protest, he refused to attend the opening-night performance. Declaring that he was "brokenhearted," Harburg described *Jamaica* as a show at odds with itself, a theatrical spectacle that he felt "fights the book at every instance."[37] Under the intrusive management of producer

David Merrick and director Robert Lewis, musical numbers were reassigned to Horne and the book was streamlined. Almost universally, reviews commented on the weak book while lauding the fact that the show essentially functioned as a musical revue for Horne. But even while Horne's casting indirectly diluted one political vision for *Jamaica*, I propose that it created others. Horne's substitution for Belafonte—who himself functioned as a surrogate for an "authentic," if illusory, Jamaican object of the calypso craze—proliferated new and unexpected meanings in *Jamaica*.[38] Among other effects, Horne's substitution for Belafonte displaced what Michelle Stephens calls "the fetish of black masculinity represented by the calypso crooner" and marked the blacklisted erasure of socialist and antiracist longings in the popular culture of the 1950s.[39]

The trace of Belafonte is everywhere present in and around the production of *Jamaica*. His previous association with the musical, his groundbreaking 1956 album *Calypso*, and his role in the 1957 social significance film *Island in the Sun* cast a shadow—and shadowed the cast—on *Jamaica*. By the 1950s, as we have seen, the calypso craze's presentation of Belafonte—through the promotion of his Jamaican ancestry, his television specials and recordings of popularized West Indian music, and the fashioning of his body in the public sphere—produced him as an icon of racial, ethnic, cultural, and sexual indeterminacy. His calypso image presented a vaguely exotic sexuality and feminized masculinity that was central to his public success at a time of increasing civil rights activism. Analyzing mass-cultural representations of Belafonte from this period, Lisa McGill illustrates how his simultaneous evocation of African American and Caribbean cultural codes "exploited a Caribbean heritage to both engage and challenge the anxieties of integration between African Americans and whites."[40] Stephens similarly argues that Belafonte's calypso image functioned as an overdetermined figure of cultural doublings, substitutions, displacements, and affinities. She shows, for example, how Belafonte's folk persona intentionally evoked Paul Robeson, and how his performance in the film *Carmen Jones* (1954) thematically evoked Richard Wright's Bigger Thomas (though in both cases, Stephens sees Belafonte's performance as lacking the radical promise of either Robeson or Wright).[41] His well-publicized absence from *Jamaica* and his replacement by Horne stands as another instance of Belafonte's displaced and displacing calypso persona.

Horne's performance of Savannah made use of her own public persona in the space made by the absent Belafonte to build on Harburg's politics and enact her own, rerouting the story through her bodily repertoire and vocal acts. Particularly through practices of speech and elocution, she rendered Savannah as a deferred character, an island girl who never fully materializes. From the moment she emerged onstage, Horne was never Savannah but always Lena Horne, the sophisticated and elegant nightclub chanteuse (fig. 18). Theater critics noted this incongruity in her performance, none more succinctly than Brooks Atkinson, who dryly noted that "nobody is going to mistake Miss Horne for a Jamaican native living in a

Figure 18. Lena Horne, Josephine Premice, and Ossie Davis in *Jamaica*, 1957. Photo by Friedman-Abeles. © Billy Rose Theatre Division, New York Public Library for the Performing Arts.

beach shack."[42] This failure to become Savannah was not due to the thinness of the book after its revisions, but rather through certain vocal and stylistic subversions that surfaced new diasporic configurations in Horne's performance and supported Harburg's satirical lyric. Horne achieved Savannah's perpetual deferral by the use of a black performance strategy that Daphne Brooks has theorized as "Afro-diasporic alienation effects."[43] Such acts are "a critical form of dissonantly enlightened performance" that "draw from the tactics of heterogeneous performance strategies . . . in order to defamiliarize the spectacle of 'blackness' in transatlantic culture."[44] This Afro-diasporic alienation has been central to the tradition of mock transnational performance. Brooks, for example, elaborates this notion in her reading of the early mock transnational musical *In Dahomey*, in which she finds Williams and Walker's ethnographic aesthetics reflecting back on the spectatorial practices of racial exhibition.

In another instance, critics observed Afro-diasporic alienation effects in Katherine Dunham's performance of Caribbean dance in *Carib Song* (discussed in the previous section). Lewis Nichols of the *New York Times* found Dunham's performance especially self-conscious, opaque, and disappointing. After a tepid assessment of the show as a whole, he turned to Dunham:

> A lively dancer when she tries, [Dunham] prefers to wander casually through the story rather than take active part in it. There is no insistence that she be an actress like Miss [Ethel] Barrymore, of course, but she could settle for less posturing, less repetition, in a cooler manner, of the things she has been doing for years.[45]

Rather than take Dunham's "wandering" as the casual and uninterested saunter Nichols describes, we might instead understand it as a kind of errancy as she moves through the gestures of Caribbean ritual. In doing "the things she has been doing for years," Dunham ignores the immediate demands and fleeting temporality of popular tastes. Instead she deploys strategies of alienation like quotation, repetition, and stylized indifference as she wanders through the story, distancing herself from its narrative. With condescension, Nichols bristles at her "posturing" and "repetition," but in doing so inadvertently describes Dunham's success at widening the gap between Caribbean movement and its dislocated staging in *Carib Song*. Much to the critic's disappointment, Dunham disrupted the spectatorial pleasure in Caribbean alterity. She rendered its conditions of presentation inseparable from its easy consumption on Broadway.

Similar acts of Afro-diasporic alienation shape Horne's performance in *Jamaica*. We can hear this most clearly in "Push de Button," a migration narrative she performs early in the musical. In examining her auditory maneuvers in the number, I draw not only from contemporaneous descriptions of the show and textual cues, but also from the cast recording, released during the run of *Jamaica* and a supplement to the stage performance. Just as did "Yankee Dollar," "Push de Button" mocks the calypso craze even as *Jamaica* participates and profits from it. The quintessence of the sophisticated black supper-club performer, Horne sings as an island character longing for sophistication. Manhattan itself becomes defamiliarized, cast as the kind of exotic and leisurely destination that the Caribbean represented in the calypso craze:

> There's a little island on the Hudson,
> Mythical, magic and fair;
> Shining like a diamon' on de Hudson,
> Far away from worriment and care.
>
> What an isle, what an isle,
> All the natives relax there in style.
> What a life, what a life,
> All de money controlled by de wife.
>
> On this little island in de Hudson,
> Ev'ryone big millionaire.
> With his own cooperative castle
> Rising in de air-conditioned air . . .
>
> All you do is
> Push de button!
> Up de elevator.
> Push de button!
> Out de orange juice.
> Push de button!
> From refrigerator come banana shortcake and frozen goose.

In the song's calypso mood, Horne ventriloquized a Jamaican patois, but the precision of speech that was the trademark of Horne's song stylizations—her expert control of her voice as instrument—heightened the artificiality of the lyric's dialect. Horne's elocution and diction, her relationship to Savannah's syllables and consonants, became a way in this performance of sounding the gap between the fictional character and the actress. In doing so, Horne also underscored the significance of the musical's setting: Pigeon—a play on "pidgin"—Island maps the Caribbean as a space where languages are mixed and cobbled together to invent new forms of communication across difference. Pidgin languages exist only in contact, and though they have their own usage rules and norms, they are measured by their effectiveness in practical use rather than by abstract principles. In her vocal performance of this creolized language, Horne sounds the irreconcilability of herself and her character, multiplying the meanings of blackness on the Broadway stage. In so doing, she repurposes *Jamaica* to tell a different story from the one sounded in its score or written in its script.

Achieving this deferral further depended on Horne's formal disruption of the frame of the Broadway musical by transforming *Jamaica* into a nightclub revue. Critics noted that Horne sang most of her songs standing center stage in the style she had perfected in hotels and cabarets, and *Life* magazine announced that the audience had "the satisfaction of seeing a glorified nightclub show without the bother of dealing with headwaiters."[46] We might even say that Horne used the Broadway stage to evoke a mode of black-Jewish leftist musical collaboration that emerged from the scene of Café Society, the integrated Greenwich Village nightclub where performers such as Billie Holiday, Hazel Scott, Josh White, and Horne herself performed in a cabaret style that inscribed the intimacy of nightlife with a radical political character. The irony was that, though Harburg was disappointed by the production's emphasis on Horne, her transformation of the theater into quasi-political cabaret in fact reintroduced the politics he felt were eliminated from the show.

Bracketing the island character and holding her at a distance, Horne became the chanteuse. In these acts of deferral and Afro-diasporic alienation, she shifted her character from one of typology to one of singularity. Her practices of speech and elocution deferred the arrival of the character she was playing. Horne offered a quotation not only of Savannah, but also of Belafonte, who in his calypso performances was quoting Jamaican laborers he reported hearing as a child in Jamaica.[47] Her stance toward Savannah created a gap between the performer and the performance, the actress and the character, Manhattan and Jamaica, African America and the African Caribbean. In opening this gap, *Jamaica*'s mock transnational performance resignified a minstrel dialect to become the mark of black multiplicity and dissonance, with blackness functioning in this instance less as identity than as relation. This multiplicity and dissonance, wandering errantly through Harburg's cultural-front protest, rescores *Jamaica* as something more than a bit of kitschy Broadway Caribbeana, a footnote in the career of Horne, or a misdirected Harburg musical. In occupying the space of mistranslation and disavowal, *Jamaica* marks and mocks the fissures within national and diasporic cultural imaginaries through the tones, tempos, images, stories, syllables, and gestures of the calypso craze on the Broadway stage.

This disruptive reconfiguration of race, nation, and gender also displaced the love plot of the musical, rendering Horne/Savannah a decidedly queer figure. Horne's staging divulges a camp sensibility within the staging of *Jamaica* and the queer undercurrents that often course through black fad performance. With the sting of his disaffection still fresh, Harburg reflected candidly near the end of *Jamaica*'s run on what he felt had gone wrong with the production. Not surprisingly, Horne and director Robert Lewis come in for the brunt of his criticism. For Harburg, Horne's status as a sex symbol and what he understood as Lewis's queer relationship to it corrupted the love plot. While at times he grudgingly acknowledged Horne's talent, Harburg dismissed her as "just a singer and can't act . . . and is really a bad singer except for night clubs, where she sells mainly flesh-pot, her sex, her grimaces. This has nothing to do with the songs, nothing to do with the lyric quality. It's all a sexual sale."[48]

This sale, however, was voided in *Jamaica* by the queer directorial vision that organized Horne's staging, which Harburg thought transformed his "sweet, intimate, meaningful little thing" into a 1920s-style musical extravaganza that pivoted on Horne's celebrity.[49] He accused Lewis of coarsely "amputa[ting]" and "butchering" his story.[50] Lewis, a founding member of the Group Theatre in 1931 and the Actors Studio in 1947, later served as head of the Yale School of Drama Acting and Directing Departments and had an important role in popularizing and disseminating Stanislavski's System in the United States.[51] He was also, as Harburg put it, "a little—how shall I say?—a queer."[52] In this reminiscence, Harburg continued with an assessment of the unfortunate homosexual influence on the theater:

> Look, I know a lot of homosexuals, and there are all degrees of homosexuals, and they have as much right to live as they do as the big masculine guy has. I have no intolerant attitude toward them, *but*—a lot of them have attributes that just hit certain values of life completely wrong. For example, sex relationships between men and women, love relationships or romantic relationships, such as we write, which have twinkle and fun, even though there is conflict, which always makes for drama. It's earthy. They interpret it as violent, and mayhem, and embarrassment. Their approach to sexuality is a mechanical one, because they don't know what sex is, therefore they theorize

> about it. . . . Within that medium, the whole thing becomes a real obscenity. But these people don't know it. Not that they mean evil, but they can't think otherwise. I mean, their enzymes are built that way. [William] Inge does the same thing with his themes, right. And unfortunately, the stage is now in the hands of these people, so that anybody who wants anything interpreted that's written from a masculine point of view, or from a natural point of view, let us say, has to see it now interpreted through the eyes of these people who don't intend to destroy your thing, but do. They can't help themselves.[53]

In one register, this complaint reflects a common conflict between a writer and a director and reveals Harburg's frustration at his inability to realize his vision of *Jamaica*. In another, it sums up phobic midcentury attitudes toward sexual minorities in leftist artistic enclaves. Harburg describes Lewis's genetic inability to recognize "twinkle," "fun," and "earthiness" in male/female romantic relationships. Because of their sexual inversion and distance from masculinity (which gives them a distorted relationship to romance), gay men in his view can only understand the masculine as violence, mayhem, and destruction, as William Inge's drama exemplifies. His allusion to a gay conspiracy in the fine arts is symptomatic of midcentury antihomosexual attitudes toward queer artists, especially at the height of the Red and Lavender Scares (he later describes Lewis as a "Svengali" who manipulates Horne to turn against him and adopt Lewis's queer understanding of sexuality).[54] We can also hear in Harburg's tirade echoes of some of the masculinist tendencies of the Old Left, which subordinated women's voices, queer voices, and racialized voices to a dominant narrative of class struggle.

While it is easy to dismiss the paranoia, resentment, castration anxiety, and homophobia that fuel this rant, I suggest that Harburg perceives something fundamental to the production despite himself. Harburg misrecognizes a certain queer aesthetic and politics that functions in *Jamaica* and throughout much of the calypso craze, a queer way of seeing things that cannot help but to pervert or destroy naturalized notions of masculinity and heterosexuality. Although he misrecognizes this queer dismemberment of the heterosexual and racially essentializing love plot, he does discern an alternative vision of race and sex at work. One way to describe what Harburg fails to recognize is Lewis's camp relationship to Savannah/Horne, one that draws from the Caribbean kitsch of the calypso craze more generally. This calypso camp—in *Jamaica* and elsewhere during the craze—annihilates not only the heterosexual love plot but also the colonial erotics on which middlebrow itineraries of the Caribbean folk relied. Both Lewis's directorial stance toward Horne and Horne's alienated stance toward her character drain sincerity and innocence from the love plot, rendering it, as Susan Sontag would say, "in quotation marks."[55] In the end, the spectacular staging of Horne and her deferral of Savannah turns what Harburg called "our wonderful love thing, the relationship . . . between this boy Koli and this girl Savannah" into "a horrendous and violent thing of such anger and such bitchiness: that was not included in the thing! That's only one aspect of the thing. But the whole show takes on a frenetic frenzied thing that this guy sees in it, because it's a musical, that we don't. We see in it charming folk people, not doing dances, but living up to an anthropological fact of earthiness and saltiness . . . you don't get that here."[56] Harburg could not offer a better account of black fad performance. It is exactly the failure of the "anthropological fact" that Horne's performance of Savannah—and Lewis's staging of *Jamaica*—offers.

Backstage Relations

Jamaica exists in and as a Caribbean–African American cultural matrix that stages blackness as a possibility for diasporic political consciousness. In the negotiation of this matrix—here, specifically, in the palimpsestic politics of Harburg's leftist lyrics, the substitution of Horne for Belafonte, and her dialectal inscription of island patois and acts of Afro-diasporic alienation—a politics of "encounter and connivance" emerged in performance that pressed national racial formations and staged blackness as multiplicity and relation.[57] Although there was a cast recording that partially disseminated this mock transnational content across the country, Broadway performance had an inherently more limited audience than the mass-culture performances on film, radio, television, and sound recordings during the calypso craze. Yet at the same time, the conditions of live theater had distinct opportunities for the performers caught up in the calypso craze's fad cascade. The kinds of relations this musical sounded and staged occurred not only before an audience but also in the backstage region of the theater itself. As Stuart Hall insists, despite the distorted sounds, stories, and movements of blackness in popular culture, we often "continue to see . . . the experiences that stand behind them."[58] In the exemplary case of *Jamaica*, what stands behind the repertoires on stage is not a more authentic Trinidadian culture but rather the relations enacted backstage during the production's run. Turning from *Jamaica*'s spotlight to its wings points us toward a different location of black politics, one that might worry the line between black fad performance and political protest.

Jamaica's cultural politics functioned not only on the terrain of representation and imagination (which are themselves no minor site of struggle), nor only on the ontological terrain of stolen time, but also on a political terrain of access, organization, and activism. Reflecting on his midcentury Broadway career, political activist Ossie Davis (*Jamaica*'s Cicero), recalled that

> Broadway had a kind of social as well as a cultural function, which we [black actors] took quite seriously. At the end of a performance every night, somebody would say "let's go over to so-and-so's, they're raising funds to defend William McGee," or somebody had been lynched in the south, or some atrocity had happened. . . . And we were determined to force the issue of justice for everybody onto the public consciousness.[59]

The many stories of *Jamaica*'s backstage life substantiate the claim that this show reached a wider political horizon beyond its own performance. Dance historian Thomas DeFrantz reports that Horne "lobbied producers to allow [chorus member Alvin Ailey] to use the stage between performances to develop movement ideas. It was during the extended run of this show that Ailey was able to rehearse the dancers who worked with him in the 1958 YM-YWHA concerts that began the Alvin Ailey American Dance Theatre."[60] Horne and producer David Merrick, meanwhile, used the production to compel integration of backstage labor, threatening not to open the show unless the defiant stagehands' union hired black workers.[61] Their success included the employment for *Jamaica* of Broadway's first black stage manager, Charles Blackwell.[62] The show's extratheatrical politics also extended to a number of benefit performances that raised money for the Legal Aid Society, the Play Schools Association, the New York City Mission Society, the Morningside Community Center, and the Henry Street Settlement. Each of these acts points toward the "succulencies of Relation" that Glissant suggests are often "already at work in an underground manner," shoots concealed but ready to flower with unanticipated possibilities.[63] At the end of the day, these transitory networks of professional opportunity, personal support, and political connection (often, in the case of many of the dancers, elements of a queer worldmaking) may be any black fad performance's most significant and lasting legacy.

Hence, even as the commercial changes made to *Jamaica* gradually eroded the political protest of the script and subordinated the book to celebrity, political energy flourished backstage and in the wings. These backstage relations find their poetics in Horne's personal reminiscence of the show and the rhetorical use to which she puts it in her 1965 autobiography, *Lena* (coauthored with Richard Schickel).[64] Horne felt that *Jamaica* was significant less for its musical, theatrical, or even ideological presence on Broadway than it was for enacting and staging a poetics of relation among performers, a space of collaboration and pedagogy in the wings that could potentially be transformed into a collective political consciousness. In her account, she turns her attention backstage, where she describes her relationship with the integrated company. Rehearsal time with the dancers provided Horne not only with theatrical inspiration but also with a political, even utopic feeling: "When we worked together I had the sensation of being a part of their bodies, that we were almost physically touching one another. I was so impressed with their dedication, their ability to go without something in order to pay for a dancing lesson—the Negro kids and the white kids in an association of creativity."[65] In this association of creativity, Horne describes a sensation of contact and touch—of feeling herself "a part of their bodies"—that momentarily disorganizes the boundaries between self and other in the experience of making a collective formation (fig. 19).

Figure 19. Lena Horne and *Jamaica* dancers, 1957. Photo by Friedman-Abeles. © Billy Rose Theatre Division, New York Public Library for the Performing Arts.

Like Maya Angelou's similar autobiographical reinscription of her calypso craze turn (described in chapter 2), Horne's personal reminiscence works to both revive and revise *Jamaica* in a shifted historical context. Against the death-bound trajectory of black fad performance, Horne uses her autobiography to continue *Jamaica* into the 1960s and restage a performance of relation that allows the production to inform both cultural and movement politics. In this autobiographical restaging of *Jamaica*, the show emerges as a rehearsal for the greater collaboration and felt experience of 1960s political protest. Training her eye closely on the dancers backstage, rather than on the spectacle of the show or the scenes in the spotlights, Horne sketches an important historical lesson for her readers through the narrative of her own deepening racial consciousness:

> Those young, modern kids from the show, both black and white, had a kind of dedication to their art that simply amazed me. I couldn't help but compare their way of life to the life I had led at their age. There had been so few openings in the theatre then that it would never had occurred to us at the Cotton Club to scrimp and save and do without in order to take singing or dancing or acting lessons. Consequently, we missed a whole experience of ambition or involvement in our work that these youngsters had. Now they struggled and trained, undaunted by the usual lack of jobs. The opportunities in the arts, for Negroes in particular, have not expanded very much. Still, those among them who were Negro were trying, and ready to offer psychological support to one another. They brought a thing to my life that had been missing, that I had never seen as a child and that I certainly never experienced in cabarets. . . . Now I saw *Jamaica* people devoting themselves to this kind of preparation for their career and, far from finding it embarrassing, finding new strength in it. I knew how tough their lives were, and I'm certain many of them faced personal problems as difficult as any I'd faced. Yet they had found new techniques for dealing with these problems, a spirit, a dedication that sustained them.[66]

If *Jamaica* pretended to expand Broadway to the Caribbean only to find itself washed up on its own shores, Horne's personal reminiscence suggests that the backstage country it founded anticipated the felt experience and organizing of the burgeoning civil rights movement. *Jamaica*'s choreography made visible to Horne a new historical subjectivity in this younger generation. These backstage relations within and across generations opened up new ethical, social, and cultural possibilities. *Jamaica* becomes in Horne's account a rehearsal for a different singing of the nation-state, sounding what Judith Butler and Gayatri Chakravorty Spivak term a "sensate democracy" that can conjure different modes of belonging, feeling, and politics. For Butler and Spivak, this sensate democracy poses questions about the "relationship between song and what is called the 'public.'"[67] Horne's song, as we have seen, explores this relationship, as does her intimate and felt relationship to *Jamaica*'s dancers, which aspires to a nonhierarchical relationship and pedagogy.

In subsequent decades, Horne would speak very critically of her professional collaborations across the color line. She mostly remembered *Jamaica* as an exhilarating and exhausting event that had little artistic merit or lasting impact on her career. In light of this, we should read Horne's autobiographical account of these backstage relations not as a truth claim about what "really occurred" in the production, but as a performative act of political rescripting that uses her autobiography to extend *Jamaica* and continue its poetics of relation into the civil rights movement. This revival and revision suggests that *Jamaica* was available as imaginative material for new ways of being together in the world, ways that Horne describes as literally unimaginable to her a few decades earlier. In her retelling, these backstage relations conjured a future horizon through the dedication and labor, the commitment and collaboration of the dancers.

The practice and poetics of this dance ensemble quickly give way to the practice and poetics of mass movement, as Horne's autobiography rhetorically links the backstage relations of the dancers to her increasing commitment to the protests and marches of the civil rights movement. The "new techniques" and "spirit" of black collaboration and movement that Horne describes, cultivated backstage in mock transnational productions such as *Jamaica*, served as a rehearsal for the kinds of relations and contact that would mobilize collective protest. This is one key way that *Jamaica*'s mock transnationalism allowed for the surfacing of other forms of life and different discourses.[68] Horne's account further amplifies the double function of black Broadway that Ossie Davis described: that of the representational and ontological politics of black performance, on the one hand, and of collective organization and social remaking, on the other. This double function can still be heard in the cast recording of *Jamaica*—a middlebrow trace of the performance of relation that brought Horne and Belafonte together, by way of the lyrics of Yip Harburg, as overlapping figures of black fad performance's mock transnational song and dance.

FIVE

Working against the Music: Geoffrey Holder's Elsewhen

Walking through the streets of New York City, Geoffrey Holder cut a figure. The Trinidadian dancer was six feet six inches tall, with large, heavy-lidded eyes that looked out keenly below his bald-domed head. In winter months, one could instantly recognize him gliding across town, his lanky frame flamboyantly draped in a black cape (a practical as well a stylistic choice, as it was difficult to find warm coats to fit his build). His soft basso profundo voice carried a Caribbean lilt of studied precision, a result of the childhood stutter that he worked hard to overcome. He brought his striking presence and shy extroversion to vaudeville and concert stages during the years surrounding the calypso craze, inflecting both vernacular and modern dance with elements of Caribbean movement and mythology. In the mid-1950s, after he emigrated from Trinidad at the age of twenty-three, he seemed to be everywhere. There he was on Broadway, dancing in Harold Arlen's *House of Flowers* or starring in an all-black production of *Waiting for Godot*. Here he was exhibiting his Caribbean-themed oil paintings at the prestigious midtown Barone Gallery. Now he was a solo dancer in Verdi's *Aida* at the Metropolitan Opera, now featured on the *US Steel Hour*'s TV adaptation of Robert Louis Stevenson's "The Bottle Imp," now recording an album of Caribbean folk songs, now at the 92nd Street YMHA showcasing his choreography, now at the informal Friday night salon he hosted at his West Eighty-Eighth Street apartment where he "welcomed all comers, usually dressed in a flowered caftan, serving them fish and good conversation as he painted and drank pink rosé from a huge goblet."[1] When he was not in New York City, he might be found at storied laboratories of modern dance such as Jacob's Pillow in Massachusetts or the White Barn Theatre in Connecticut. By the end of his life, he was a celebrated painter, dancer, choreographer, actor, director, and costume designer. This boundless imagination—extending across stage, dance floor, canvas, and screen—made him a fixture of the black theatrical and modernist dance scenes of midcentury New York City (fig. 20).

Like Josephine Premice (and even more so than Harry Belafonte), Geoffrey Holder was a central figure of the calypso craze. Like most calypso craze performers, he distinguished the calypso craze from Trinidadian calypso with the defining disavowal of black fad performance: *this* is not *that*. In a widely read *New York Times* article published at the height of the fad,

Figure 20. Geoffrey Holder: dancer, choreographer, painter, director, costume designer, actor, 1958. Photo by John D. Kisch. Separate Cinema Archive/Getty Images.

Holder pronounced that "a lot of what you hear now is amusing oh, yes, but not true Calypso."[2] Locating the calypso craze in a long tradition of imperial race crazes in the United States, Holder described the fad instead as "an American version of West Indian melodies and lyrics, similar to American versions of Hawaiian music, for example. It is slicked up, prettied up and sophisticated up. It is not spontaneous; it is calculated." The sophistication and calculation involved here, as we have seen throughout this book, refer less to the tastes of the postwar white middle-class consumers of calypso than to the knowingness and creativity of black fad performers themselves. He called it "Manhattan Calypso" and noted that these performances "must more nearly conform to the popular music Americans know than to the West Indian music they don't know."[3]

Yet Holder's disavowal of the calypso craze, here and elsewhere, did not inhibit his participation in it. While Belafonte created distance between himself and the calypso fad, Holder kept one foot firmly planted in its center. He participated in calypso revues, promoted a makeshift calypso dance to accompany the music of the fad, performed in an early calypso musical (*House of Flowers*, discussed in the previous chapter), and recorded an album of calypso songs accompanied by members of his dance troupe (*Songs of the Caribbean*, by Geoffrey Holder and his Trinidadian Hummingbirds, on jazz label Riverside Records). If Holder echoed Belafonte in disavowing the calypso craze, he also disavowed his own disavowal. In his calypso craze performances, Holder toggled back and forth between "Manhattan calypso" and "true calypso," reminding us of the performativity of the disavowal as a speech act and the production of inauthenticity/authenticity—*this* and *that*—in the total context of its utterance. Through the shifting referents and epistemological uncertainties of black fad culture, Holder developed choreographic opportunities to steal (back) Caribbean cultural forms and advance a calypso ethos shaped by Trinidadian national culture within and beside the calypso craze. Inhabiting the movement between disavowal and avowal, Holder's dance made explicit the premises on which (in)authenticity rests.

In other words, to say that *this* is not *that* is not to say that *that* is not also *here*. This chapter shows how Holder repeated this double disavowal through dance—first in his invention of the popular "Limbo-Calypso" dance and then on the modernist dance stage—to engage what Édouard Glissant called the "nonhistory" of the Caribbean past. By nonhistory, Glissant describes the disruption of Western historical narrative by the "context of shock, contraction, painful negation, and explosive forces" of the Middle Passage, slavery, and colonialism. This "dislocation of the continuum" of history in the New World demanded new methods to conceptualize "a painful notion of time and its full projection forward into the future, without the help of those plateaus in time from which the West has benefited."[4] The calypso craze was simultaneously a colonialist contribution to this Caribbean nonhistory and a creative corrective to it. Even while it continued an imperial relationship to the cultures of Trinidad that evacuated the Caribbean of history and self-determination, black performers such as Holder inhabited and departed from that "apparent 'historylessness'" (in the words of writer Wilson Harris) through performances that drew on these diasporic conditions.[5] Holder's dance and choreography responded to this situation by repeatedly enacting a disavowal of disavowal. Neither *this* nor *that*, neither true calypso nor synthetic calypso, Holder's choreographic work demarcated a temporal domain that emerged to the side of both an unchanging ethnographic then and the fleeting present of the fad's now: an elsewhen carved out of movement and music.

To turn to Holder is thus to locate the calypso craze in relation to modern black concert dance in the 1940s and 1950s, when black dancers developed new techniques by which to engage the ongoing encounter between Africa, Europe, and the New World. Dancer-choreographers such as Katherine Dunham and Pearl Primus made use of ethnographic research and broad cultural study to fuse movement elements from African and Caribbean dance with Western movement vocabularies. Then described as "Negro dance" or "ethnic dance," these new experiments in black modernist dance treated diasporic movements as aesthetic forms to be stylized and presented not in vaudeville shows but on concert stages (fig. 21). While the commercialized calypso craze seems far removed from the high art context of black concert dance, they were in fact coextensive with each other, and dancers moved between these spheres. Albeit in very different modes, both the calypso craze and black concert dance staged the African diaspora in performances that rerouted the assumptions of racial authenticity toward new aesthetic expressions.

Holder spanned both of these worlds, and it is helpful to detail some of his biography here in order to better understand his work both within and apart from the calypso craze. Born in Port of Spain in 1930, he grew up under the influence of his older brother, Boscoe, one of Trinidad's most significant contemporary painters and a pioneering dancer and musician. From an early age Holder's artistic aims exceeded any one form, though he fundamentally understood himself as a dancer. "All the other things," he wrote, "the painting, the designing, the singing, the acting, oh, everything else, just

Figure 21. Geoffrey Holder in *Aida*, 1957. Jerome Robbins Dance Division, New York Public Library for the Performing Arts.

grew out of the dancing."[6] Brother Boscoe founded one of Trinidad's first professional dance companies in 1947, of which Geoffrey was a member. Their company performed to local audiences, sometimes at a small movie house and other times at a local museum. Their performances mixed folkloric dance, observed at funerals and weddings, with movements picked up from Hollywood films and from other Trinidadian dancers who had traveled along performance circuits to New York City and back.[7]

When Boscoe moved to London in 1950 to seek greater opportunities in the metropole, Geoffrey took over direction of the dance company. Like his brother, he explored Trinidadian folk culture and Caribbean history in his work. Three interrelated pieces composed in 1951–52 stand out in this early period of his choreography: "Ballet Congo," "Bal Creole," and "Bal Nègre."[8] As their titles imply, these revues collectively traced the historical and social geographies of the black diaspora. Their success generated significant notice across the Caribbean and in 1952 brought Holder and his troupe to the First Caribbean Festival of the Arts in San Juan, Puerto Rico, where they represented Trinidad (alongside his compatriot Beryl McBurnie's Little Carib Company).[9] At the festival, Holder had a decisive encounter with the choreographer Jean-Léon Destiné, the acclaimed performer known as the "father of Haitian professional dance," and the dancer-percussionist Louis Celestin, who performed Destiné's *banda* dance.[10] Transformed by his exposure to the work of Destiné, Holder began a lifelong study of Haitian vodou that would shape his choreography throughout the 1950s and beyond, in particular his own version of the *banda*.

This expressive route—from Trinidad to Haiti by way of Puerto Rico—shaped Holder's pan-Caribbean consciousness, and these early experiences aligned him with similar projects in black modern dance undertaken by similar pioneers such as Asadata Dafora, Primus, and Dunham. "Too many islanders are aping Picasso and Gene Kelly and the rest of the world," he declared. "The Carib world has a culture uniquely its own—basically African, spiced with French, Spanish, English, Portuguese, Indian, and Chinese. And it's from this we must create a Carib renaissance, not from New York or London."[11] His subsequent study of the Caribbean's folkloric and syncretic cultures shaped both his vernacular and theatrical dance. His success at the Caribbean Festival of the Arts brought him extended exposure on the so-called coconut circuit, booking engagements at tourist hotels in Puerto Rico and the British Virgin Islands. These performances gained the fortuitous notice of choreographer Agnes de Mille (then vacationing in Saint Thomas), who arranged for Holder to audition in New York City. Although nothing came of the audition, it provided the occasion for Holder to permanently settle in the north.

He arrived in New York City at the age of twenty-three, bringing seven members of his company with him (among them, notable dancers Leonard Reyes and Scoogie Brown, who would also go on to participate in the calypso craze). Shortly after their arrival, The Holder Company had their US premiere at the White Barn Theatre, then a fledgling institution for experimental theater and performance (fig. 22). On the program were a comic piece about a dice game, a composition about a village love affair destroyed by vicious gossip, a pantomime about an artist who discovers that the model he loves is already married, and a retelling of the myth of Pandora's box in a Caribbean setting. The show also included two musical interludes that featured a steel drum band (then largely unfamiliar to US audiences) and a vocal performance of folk songs by Holder and his company.[12] The next year, Holder and his troupe recorded these folk songs on an album that one critic described as "noticeable for the absence of the overly commercial calypso style."[13]

Figure 22. Trinidadian members of the Geoffrey Holder Company, 1954. Photo by Geoffrey Holder. © 2017 Estate of Geoffrey Holder/Artists Rights Society (ARS), New York. Jerome Robbins Dance Division, New York Public Library for the Performing Arts.

During this time Holder moved effortlessly between popular culture and high culture. After teaching for six months at the Katherine Dunham School, Holder was cast in the 1954 Broadway musical *House of Flowers*, where he introduced the vodou figure Baron Samedi and the Trinidadian steel drum band to New York audiences. There he also met his lifetime partner in marriage and dance, Carmen de Lavallade, who was a member of the *House of Flowers* chorus (fig. 23). This appearance led to subsequent roles as the Ethiopian Prince in the Metropolitan Opera's production of *Aida* and as Lucky in an all-black Broadway production of *Waiting for Godot*. During his run with *House of Flowers*, his paintings were displayed at the Barone Gallery, and he would go on to have three more exhibitions there in the next few years. He received a John Simon Guggenheim Fellowship for his painting in 1956, the first Trinidadian so honored. "It was a very exciting time," he recalled. "I'd be done with the Met—*Aida* was on early—by 7:30. I'd jump in a cab and go to *Waiting for Godot*. Then *The Tonight Show* on television. Nobody knew who I was, but everybody knew my name."[14] With one foot in the calypso craze and one foot in the world of modern dance and theater, Holder undertook an exhilarating if precarious balancing act that invented new forms of Caribbean movement within and against the stereotyping constraints of black fad performance.

Throughout this period, Holder's dancing body was routinely presented as an erotic object and primitive fetish—often with the knowing collaboration of Holder himself, who appeared on more than one occasion in the 1950s dressed only in a loincloth. Reviewing dance programs for predominantly white audiences in venues such as the Metropolitan Opera House, Broadway theaters, and the 92nd Street YMHA, critics routinely praised his performance in deeply fetishistic and eroticizing terms. "To anyone who has ever watched this restless young man dance," noted one writer for *Dance Magazine*, "there is no need to describe the impact his long dark body, suggestive of Egyptian tribal kings, makes as it twists around a rhythm seemingly unrestricted by the usual bonds of bone and muscle, or struts in sexual insolence against the rhythms of a drum. Then there is something elemental on the stage. Something unfettered and free."[15] Another review declared that an "animal energy, intense passion, muscular virtuosity and the chilling presence of magic were almost continuously present" in his performance.[16] Describing his "stunning" appearance in *Aida*, foremost dance critic John Martin labored to reconcile Holder's supposed savagery with his grace. Praising both the Met's choreographer and Holder's interpretation of the dance, he found that the choreographer had "given

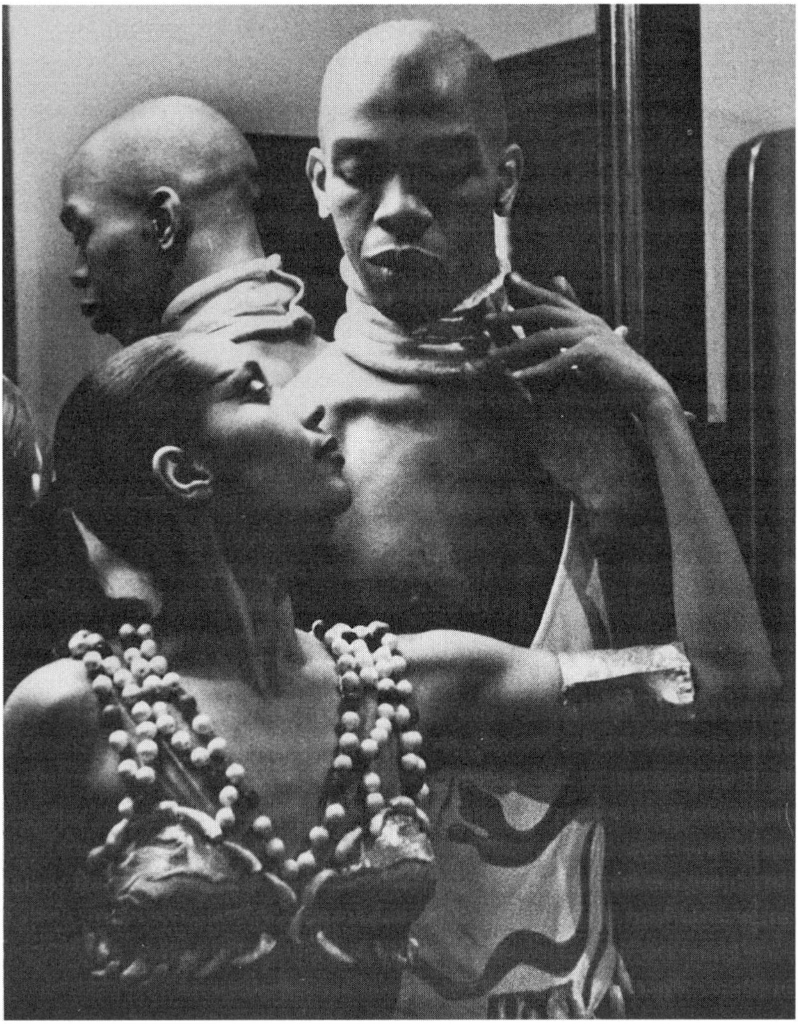

Figure 23. Geoffrey Holder and Carmen de Lavallade, around 1957. Jerome Robbins Dance Division, New York Public Library for the Performing Arts.

[Holder] enormous dignity; but he has also made fine use of his curious, primitive, Negroid movement, partly erotic, partly ceremonial, altogether personal. Mr. Holder has responded eloquently. For all the grotesqueness of the vocabulary in which he moves, he achieves a genuine elegance and proves himself an artist of unsuspected quality."[17] Such descriptions were depressingly common for even the staidest midcentury performances of "ethnic dance," but the fetishization of Holder's dancing body was even more hyperbolic than that of most other black male dancers.

Holder was well aware of the field of desire into which his staged body entered, and he used his physicality to great and often playful effect. Knowing the spectatorial conventions of the black male dancing body, he stage-managed concert dance's exoticist outlook and the middlebrow's sexual sublimation of interracial desire by defiantly confronting and laying bare the white theatrical gaze.[18] In one piece, for example, Holder staged a "reverse strip tease" where he began the performance barely clothed and, fusing the gestures of an erotic dancer with modern dance, slowly got dressed and walked off the stage.[19] Holder transformed the reverse strip tease, a novelty dance familiar in burlesque shows, into a commentary on the prurient erotics of the modern dance stage by suggesting that his fully clothed body would itself be the real taboo and revelation for his audience. In the choreography for his concert piece *Banda*, to cite a later example, Holder has the vodou figure of Baron Samedi (the deity of debauchery and death) make his entrance shuffling backward onto the stage in pants that have the seat cut out, exposing the body beneath.[20]

While these instances illustrate how he played with and against his audience's expectations, Holder also unabashedly celebrated the form and beauty of the male body throughout his career. He did this not only in his dance but also in his painting and photography, including his 1986 large-format art book *Adam*, which collected a series of his portraits of abstract black male nudes; a photo of his own torso graces the volume's cover.[21] As with Belafonte's celebrity image, Holder's midcentury performances became a way for white US consumers to approach and displace racial desires and anxieties onto a highly stylized, mass-mediated Caribbean body. As I argue in this chapter, Holder manipulated such middlebrow sexual sublimations through performances that either disappeared his body from the scene of dance altogether, leaving a phantom in its place (as we will see in his choreography of the Limbo-Calypso) or by relocating the scene of dance from exotic displays of an ethnographic past to a mythic elsewhen that reached beyond the finitude of black fad performance (as we will see in his concert dance choreography).

Holder explained his relationship to these conditions of performance in an appearance he made with de Lavallade on the arts radio program *Musically Speaking with Mildred Kayden* in 1957, shortly after his appearance in *Aida*. Kayden was a composer, lyricist, and professor of music at Vassar College who hosted a weekly arts program on WEVD New York from the mid-1950s through the early 1960s. On this broadcast, Holder described the overall aesthetic philosophy and practice that informed his midcentury creative work and that characterizes one of the tactics of black fad performers more generally: a practice of "working against the music." Kayden began her interview with a discussion of his debut in *Aida*, aggressively contributing to the sexual and racial fetishism that shaped the reception of this performance. Holder gracefully ignored the comments (and de Lavallade, sitting beside him, held her tongue) as Kayden sensationally described his performance of Verdi's Ethiopian Prince for her audience. Then, after playing a portion of *Aida*'s second act "Triumphal March," they discussed Holder's approach:

> KAYDEN: Well I'm sure that everyone who just heard this music of Verdi would wonder how, against this sweet kind of music, you would portray this savage, ceremonial, dignified triumphant Egyptian . . . not Egyptian, but—prince, Ethiopian prince?
>
> HOLDER: I worked against it.
>
> KAYDEN: *Against* the music?
>
> HOLDER: Against the music. You see, the music is all flowery and all in the air, but I had to be the earth beneath it.
>
> KAYDEN: Well this is the fascinating—this is the *new*, you see, interpretation of adding this. The music is the old and you, by working against the music, create the new.

Holder speaks both technically about his dance and metaphorically about his stance toward the performance. He describes a choreographic tension between relatively more formal and rigid forms of European dance and relatively more earthbound, bent-knee African movements that were performed across the Caribbean (in Trinidad, *chipping*—a dance movement that draws from "the union of man to earth, where the feet embrace the bountiful ground to give praise and draw from its additional power and strength," as anthropologist Patricia Alleyne-Dettmers puts it).[22] A low center of gravity and a largely earthbound orientation are marks of Africanist retentions in creolized Caribbean dance, and Holder's response to Kayden that in *Aida* he worked against the European score by being "the earth beneath it" reflects a more general practice of embodied memory. Holder's announcement that he was working against the music describes his engagement with the Africanist aesthetic of "embracing the conflict" that dance scholar Brenda Dixon Gottschild identifies in dance practices around the Caribbean, an aesthetic that "can be construed as a precept of contrariety, or an encounter of opposites" in and as a performance that is simultaneously "ludic and tragic"—like the calypso craze itself.[23] Holder's particular phrasing, moreover, reminds us that this working-against is not only an aesthetic principle but also an act of labor that finds productive force in an oppositional stance. Holder's approach of working against the music—whether in *Aida* or the calypso craze—characterizes the ethos of many black fad performers as they found themselves swept up in the currents of a fad cascade. It is less a negation of the calypso craze's counterfeit gestures than the fashioning of new stances toward such performances through aesthetic conflict. As an attitude toward the inauthenticity of the calypso craze, working against the music is yet another way to understand how performers might momentarily steal time (back) for themselves and, as Kayden inadvertently perceived, "create the new."

Empty Gestures

Of course, in the context of black fad performance, everything new is old again. This was especially true in the calypso craze's attempt to invent a dance craze to accompany the sudden popularity of calypso music. In May 1957, the lifestyle and fashion magazine *Glamour* treated readers to a calypso-themed issue. Alongside articles about how to pack for a Caribbean vacation and reports from feature editor Evelyn Harvey's recent "island-hopping jaunt to Barbados, Trinidad, and Tobago" (where she was part of a press tour for the filming of Harry Belafonte's *Island in the Sun*), the magazine featured an eight-page photo spread spotlighting Holder as he instructed readers how to dance the "Limbo-Calypso" and posed with models in calypso party attire.[24] A striking instance of the middlebrow sublimation of interracial desire, this spread photographed Holder dancing across the pages with three pairs of white models in a layout framed by a musical score and narrated by rhyming calypso verse. He appears first in a white jumpsuit cinched under his ribs that accentuates the length of his legs and amplifies his height, then shirtless wearing just a necktie and fanning himself with a wide-brimmed hat, and finally shirtless again but in tighter black pants that end midcalf. In each instance, the models spin around him in their calypso dresses, reaching out to him with limbs fully extended as they twirl away from his body, literally keeping Holder at arm's length (fig. 24). Incidentally, fashion photographers Diane and Allan Arbus directed this pas de trois, and soon after the shoot Diane Arbus denounced fashion photography and went on to international acclaim for her provocative portraits of the socially marginal and uncanny—twins and triplets, circus performers, children, female impersonators, peo-

Figure 24. Geoffrey Holder and models in calypso fashion spread, *Glamour*, May 1957. Diane and Allan Arbus/Glamour © Condé Nast.

ple with disabilities, and others who would strain the aesthetic conformity of the postwar years.

This spread in *Glamour* was the latest attempt to codify a social dance for the middle-class consumers of the calypso craze. Taking their cue from other music-dance race crazes—the Charleston, the Jitterbug, the Lindy Hop; the mambo, the samba, the tango—various dance studios and record companies proposed possible contenders for a calypso dance. This instruction in popular dance reminds us that black fad performances were pedagogical projects. They did not offer an education in African American or Caribbean cultural history (at least not directly), but rather instructed consumers in how to enjoy, consume, and perpetuate the fad itself. A uniquely personal distribution channel and feedback loop, dance crazes allowed individuals to participate in a fad through their own embodied movements and become performers themselves. This was one significant way that the calypso craze moved: through the dispersal of gestures, steps, and spins. Recreational dance was the corporeal infrastructure of the fad, holding up the curated and produced performances we have seen in previous chapters. Teaching people how to dance to the calypso craze helped to promote the sale of records and increase the turnout at calypso dance floors and nightclub shows (fig. 25). By 1957, for example, New York City's Palladium Ballroom, the epicenter of the mambo dance craze, temporarily turned into a calypso ballroom. For a few months during the calypso craze, the Palladium set aside Wednesday nights for spectacular calypso dance routines and provided free lessons to patrons early in the evening.[25]

For those who could not make it to the Palladium, the Savoy, or other ballrooms like them, calypso marketers turned to the time-tested genre of the dance instruction manual. Dance instruction manuals were "how-to" guides that used various combinations of dance notation, narrative descriptions, drawings, and photography to help readers learn the newest dance moves. In addition to meticulously describing the steps of a specific dance, such guides often included musical extracts, information about the dance's origins, etiquette pointers, and fashion insight. A number of these choreographic treatises appeared during the calypso craze, often in lifestyle magazines such as *Glamour* or calypso fanzines, offering differ-

Figure 25. Calypso band performing for dancers in ballroom, 1957.
Photo by Yale Joel. LIFE Picture Collection/Getty Images.

ent instructions for how to dance to calypso music. In the absence of a clear candidate for calypso dance, several contenders appeared. Most routines were versions of what came to be known as "calypso ballroom," a partner-based form that borrowed from other dances and bore no direct relationship to Trinidadian carnival dance. Dance instructor Robert Luis, for instance, printed a heavily illustrated manual that offered his version of calypso ballroom, explaining that "at the time of this writing, the New York dance studios seem to be in a hopeless quandary as to what constitutes authentic calypso." For Luis, this muddle was largely a geographical issue: the confusion was "directly traceable to the fact that different studios have gone to different places for their sources of information. To go to Nassau or the Virgin Islands in search of the authentic calypso is just as irrational as going to Mexico to learn the rumba."[26] His geographic admonishment notwithstanding, Luis's own instruction for a calypso dance was a mix of various Latin and Caribbean steps drawing from the rumba, samba, merengue, and beguine as well as standard ballroom postures.

This was common throughout the calypso craze. Lacking a readily identifiable move that could be easily translated from Trinidad carnival to the dance floors of North America, instructors and performers recycled dances that were already familiar to middle-class Americans from earlier race crazes. Dance instructor and entrepreneur Arthur Murray, whose mail-order dance lessons and studio franchise brought dance education to millions of Americans, offered a patchwork of moves for his "ballroom variation of the impromptu Carib dances."[27] In a calypso fanzine, Murray gave detailed instructions for his calypso dance, though ultimately he conceded that "the dance depends on the ingenuity of the dancers, themselves. The Calypso is not limited by stylized steps—and gives free rein to interpretation and improvisation. At times, the partners dance close together—and, at their whim, break apart, to move separately and 'shine'" (a reference to the improvisational break in Cuban mambo).[28] For those looking for insight into how to dance calypso, Murray's instruction did not offer much assistance. By the end of his lesson, Murray essentially undid the genre of the dance instruction manual as he faltered under the incoherence of the calypso craze. He concluded that "the Calypso has no formalized steps" and "a person learning it must know how to dance" already.[29] His calypso dance, like Luis's, was a literal placeholder, a vacancy to be filled with whatever movements and gestures one already knows.

In his *Glamour* magazine dance instruction, Holder too proffers a mishmash of dance movements. "The rhythm of dance to Calypso," he writes, "is part Mambo, some Merengue, a little Cha-cha, some Bebop, and basic

African, all mixed up."[30] In other venues—a television appearance and *Dance Magazine*—Holder described calypso dance steps as a modified Charleston, "but not like the old Charleston. No kicks, no hands crossing from knee to knee. No bounce. Very dignified from the hips up. Smooth and gliding Charleston-like foot-twisting movements from the knees down."[31] His invocation of this earlier dance craze reminds us of how previous black fad performances return within subsequent ones. On one hand, these recycled choreographies acknowledge the deep intermixture of dance forms in the Caribbean archipelago and the impossibility of fixed lines of origin, as well as the redundancy of many popular dances emerging around the same period. On the other hand, the constant substitution of other dance styles for a calypso dance and the inevitable retreat to individual improvisation suggests that there is, in fact, no referent for it other than itself. It is an empty gesture that refers only back to the fad.

Yet within this mélange of recycled steps and empty gestures, Holder managed to distinguish his recreational calypso dance from the others by being the first to introduce the movements of the Limbo to mass media. In Trinidad, the Limbo is part of the larger funereal rites of Shango religious practice, a sacred dance in which participants bend backward at the waist to pass under a bamboo pole amid singing and drumming during syncretic wake ceremonies that combined Kongolese and Catholic cosmologies. The movement under the bar enacted a suspension between two worlds. Scholars such as dancer-anthropologist Molly Ahye, performance geographer Sonjah Stanley Niaah, and theater historian Geneviève Fabre have all followed the inscription of slave ship logs and the whisper of folklore to locate the emergence of Limbo not in Africa but in the Atlantic, a symbolic reenactment of movement through the tight space and stifling hold of the slave ship.[32] In the mourning ceremonies of Trinidad, this ritual contortion and elongation of the body—its backward reach—symbolized not only the passage of the spirit from this world to the next but also the Middle Passage and the collective transport from Africa to the New World. Guyanese writer Wilson Harris suggests that we think of this musical and embodied "limbo perspective" as a vantage point from which to conceptualize a relationship to Caribbean history and its erasure by colonialism. From such a vantage point, he writes, the Limbo embodies "the curious dislocation of a chain of miles reflected in the dance so that a re-trace of the Middle Passage from Africa to the Americas and the West Indies is not to be equated with a uniform sum."[33] The distance of diaspora, in other words, is not measurable on a standard map or quantifiable as an expanse of miles, but appears as a differential, discontinuous, and qualitative relationship to the past and the future. That chain of miles, moreover, is dislocated or located elsewhere, not on a geographic plane but a bodily and psychic one. As a response to this "complex situation of apparent 'historylessness,'" the movement of the Limbo and its ritual passage from death to rebirth reimagines the spatial possibilities of the body and Caribbean "interior space" in the torque of history.[34]

In mid-twentieth-century Trinidad, this limbo perspective came to inform aesthetic projects of cultural nationalism as well as their repackaging in emergent tourist productions. As Stanley Niaah argues, the Limbo "offers an intellectual context, a framework, literal and artistic, to unearth meaning and narratives in the cultures of entertainment in the New World."[35] Such cultures of entertainment included the development of Trinidad's midcentury concert dance, Hollywood films, and the nightclub acts that furthered the calypso craze. Beginning in the 1940s, a number of Trinidadian choreographers began to treat folk dance as national cultural material to be celebrated on more formal stages as an intrinsically aesthetic practice. The most prominent among them was Beryl McBurnie, whose Little Carib Theater was a central institution in the promotion of Trinidadian folk culture.[36] McBurnie traveled between Trinidad and New York City throughout the 1940s and taught Caribbean movement to young dancers Katherine Dunham, Pearl Primus, and others who went on to incorporate such movement into their repertoires. In Trinidad, she worked closely with Boscoe Holder, who often supervised her troupe while she was abroad, until they parted professionally around 1947 when Holder founded his own dance company. According to firsthand accounts, the late 1940s was a moment of deep cultural education as Boscoe Holder and McBurnie made forays not only to the library but also to more rural parts of Trinidad to learn about native folk dance directly; McBurnie made even further ethnographic excursions to Suriname, Guiana, and elsewhere in the Caribbean.[37]

It was after these journeys that McBurnie brought the Limbo from Shango ritual to concert stage and then to tourist production.[38] She began incorporating the Limbo into her theatrical dance at the Little Carib Theater as early as its founding in 1947, but it crossed over into popular culture in the second half of the 1950s when North Americans were caught up in the calypso craze. Julia Edwards, another local dancer who performed with both Holder dance companies, started her own dance company and found great success performing the Limbo for tourists at Port of Spain hotels and restaurants. As the fad picked up momentum in North America, the Limbo appeared with more frequency in nightclub revues and eventually on film. *Variety* magazine described one Port of Spain nightclub Limbo act by dancer Jean Coggins (a former member of Boscoe Holder's company) as especially popular among the "customers who flock ashore from the Alcoa cruise ships on their swing around the Indies and South America."[39] That same year, the Limbo featured prominently in Harry Belafonte's film *Island in the Sun* (1957) (performed by Dorothy Dandridge) and Columbia Pictures' *Fire Down Below* (1957), which was partially filmed in Trinidad and included a Limbo dance sequence choreographed by McBurnie and Edwards and performed by members of the Little Carib Company.[40] While not explicitly part of the calypso craze, both of these films exploited the sudden interest in Trinidadian culture and were released alongside calypso films such as *Calypso Heat Wave* and *Bop Girl Goes Calypso* (discussed in chapter 2).

It is in the context of these New World cultures of entertainment that Holder introduced the Limbo to *Glamour*'s readership (just months before *Fire Down Below* and *Island in the Sun* popularized it on film). Edwards recounted attending a rural Trinidadian wake with Geoffrey Holder as early as 1949, while she was a part of his dance company. There the two of them carefully observed the ritual performance of the Limbo by a relative of the deceased who repeatedly passed trancelike below the bar as the tempo of the drums increased and those gathered chanted prayers.[41] Holder incorporated this folk ritual into his calypso craze dance instruction. The social dancing known as ballroom calypso, he instructed in *Glamour*, "builds Limbo mood" as couples approach the makeshift Limbo pole (made from "2 large upside down flower pots" and "broom sticks"). Holder further directs that after "a few ad lib steps, man circles bar. Checking clearance he makes try at passing beneath, feet edging forward to music, girl coaxing . . . he makes it, staggering. His partner then staggers around the bar, expertly shows him how . . . full skirts are a must, low heeled shoes handier, partner's aid allowed when going gets tough" (fig. 26).[42] With detailed photographic notation and Trinidadian patois, Holder narrated the movement, mood, and clothing of this Limbo dance party.

He named his dance the Limbo-Calypso, the hyphen both linking and separating the tradition from the fad, and drew a sharp distinction between the fad dance he outlined and the religious ritual he witnessed in Trinidad: *this* is not *that*. "The *real* Limbo (a ritual danced at wakes in which 'the soul passes from one life to another' under the horizontal bar) is for experts only," he explained. "Nobody says you can't *try* the real Limbo. But there is an easier way—if you are fairly supple and ingenious. Give a Limbo-Calypso party."[43] *Glamour*'s editorial commentary made similar distinctions, praising Holder for translating the Limbo from "a highly acro-

Figure 26. Limbo-Calypso dance instruction. *Glamour,* May 1957. Glamour © Condé Nast.

batic dance from the lower Caribbean into a much-modified party dance" and acknowledging that "though the Limbo is certainly a thing unto itself, it might be an interesting successor to the bunny hop, charades, or even 'London Bridge'—in any case, worth bending over backwards to learn."[44] Holder's Limbo-Calypso avowed its inauthenticity and declared itself as a deracinated, kitsch party game. In the context of the calypso craze and the genre of the dance instruction manual, Holder's *Glamour* guide worked like those of Robert Luis and Arthur Murray to capture Caribbean movement in writing and fixed images in order to better commodify and market black fad performance.

From the vantage point of Wilson Harris's Limbo perspective, however, Holder also worked against the immobilization of Caribbean movement and extended the Limbo's mark of historical discontinuity and spatial dislocation. In addition to his printed dance instruction, Holder made a mail-order specialty record as a tie-in with his *Glamour* appearance that readers could purchase with fifty cents and a coupon from the magazine.[45] On one side of the 45-rpm record, Holder narrated instructions on how to dance the Limbo-Calypso. On the other, he and his Trinidadian Hummingbirds performed a song they titled "Limbo-Calypso" (which was a variation on a traditional folk song associated with the tourist Limbo dance).

This record is a surprisingly complex bit of ephemera from the calypso craze. Just as *Glamour* and other magazines adopted the form of the dance instruction manual, this record is in the tradition of the dance instruction song: a genre of popular song in which the steps of a dance are explained and modeled within the performance of the song itself. While the dance instruction song seems like the logical extension of the dance instruction manual, it is in fact its opposite. The written dance manual, as dance theorist André Lepecki argues, developed historically in Western choreography as one way to contend with the tension between permanence and ephemerality that defined dance as a fleeting "art of self-erasure."[46] The dance instruction manual, that is, seeks the "illumination and arrest of presence for the sake of History."[47] It is an effort to make the ephemeral textually legible, reproducible, and preservable. While forms of dance notation and their collation in manuals allowed choreographers to disseminate classical dance moves, performance and sound recordings were more common vehicles for the spread of social dance. This oral transmission developed from a different context than written dance notation, one that approached dance instruction as participatory, reciprocal, and communal rather than as a textually fixed sequence of steps to be mastered. Scholars have traced the dance instruction song to African American traditions of call-and-response, and it quickly shaped American popular music more broadly.[48] If the dance instruction manual developed from an ontological imperative concerned with "arrest[ing] presence for the sake of History," the dance instruction song developed from an imperative to incite dance toward ephemerality and its self-erasure. Holder's record, then, is less a complement to the *Glamour* spread than a subtle act of working against the calypso craze's efforts to codify the steps of a calypso dance.

Accordingly, I take Holder's Limbo-Calypso dance instruction record as a remarkable performance of the calypso craze that models black fad performance's ontology of stolen time. The record simultaneously makes the absent (black) body present in a middlebrow fantasy of interracial desire without any threat of social transgression and, by foregrounding Holder's bodily nonappearance, makes (black Caribbean) presence absent in the material and musical culture of black fad performance. Holder speaks directly to the record's ideal listener-dancer, as structured by the context of *Glamour*: a female reader eager to participate in the newest fashions (of course, the actual listeners of the record and the contexts in which it was played could never be limited to its implied scenario, and we have no way of knowing who Holder may have imagined dancing with as he spoke). *Glamour* promoted the Limbo-Calypso as a party dance, and the record combined with the magazine spread allows us to imagine the scene of listening as a social one, perhaps a room full of novice dancers. Yet Holder's address is deeply intimate and personal. To the strum of a calypso melody in the background, he greets the dancer-listener with a flirtatious invitation, as if she waits in a dance hall: "Are you doing anything in particular?" he asks. He then explains, "In Trinidad, that is what we say when we ask a girl to dance. So let's do the Limbo. This is a new party dance I adapted for *Glamour* magazine from a Caribbean ritual dance called the Limbo. The music, which is a fast match, is catchy and easy to dance to. You can work out your own steps as we go along."

His thrown voice animates not his own fad body but that of its consumer. Holder's instruction in the Limbo-Calypso is a scene of seduction. Through the play of direct address, he outlines the dancer-listener's body and places it in imagined intimate proximity to his own. "First, we stand close together," he says softly, pulling the listener close to him. The instruction is related in the continuous present tense. "My left arm stretched out, holding your right hand. I lead off with my left foot. My left leg bending naturally as I step sideways. Do you follow? Good. You follow with your right, then I move my right foot to close with my left foot. My right leg, quite straight, you follow with your left. We pause an instant for the beat, both feet together. Then we repeat. We use the same step to move sideways, forward, backward, and to break away. There is really nothing to it."

Following this lesson in ballroom calypso, Holder as virtual dance partner proceeds to describe the Limbo portion of the dance ("as in real limbo, two standing poles are moved out on the floor. You can find out how to set them up in the May issue of *Glamour* magazine") and concludes his instruction by directing, "now let's turn over the record and let's dance the limbo." Unlike the dance instruction guide and fashion spread that freezes Holder's gestures in photography and notation, his voice on the record is a ghostly presence without a body that animates the fad body of the dancer-listener. Elaborating the aesthetic and folkloric elements of the Limbo perspective, Wilson Harris suggests that "it is legitimate, I feel, to pun on *limbo* as a kind of shared phantom *limb* which has become a subconscious variable in West Indian theater."[49] Holder's recorded instruction recalls and performs this notion of a phantom limb, extending it into a phantom body. We can take Holder's reassuring encouragement—"there is really nothing to it"—at face value. Holder choreographs a dance that inscribes his bodily and historical absence from the scene and works against the magazine's fashion spread.

Holder's recording performs a spacing or gap between body and presence that Lepecki describes as the condition of dance itself, adding that "dance as a critical social praxis may draw its force precisely by a creative, if not altogether subversive, occupation of this gap."[50] Holder's recording is one instance of creatively and subversively occupying this gap. The distance between Harris's Trinidadian Limbo and Holder's Limbo-Calypso is not the measure of miles or a uniform sum but a quality that marks the discontinuous routes of diaspora and disrupts the fixing of blackness by mass culture in this sonic supplement. Holder's performance on this record constitutes a reverse disappearing act, like his reverse strip tease, that uses vocal and rhetorical strategies to simulate presence. At the end of this appearing act, the dancer-listener is left with empty arms, holding only a piece of mass-produced plastic as she turns it over to play side B. The record once again becomes an effigy and substitute for the fad performer's body, as it did for Harry Belafonte (as we saw in chapter 1). Holder's voice limns his body even as it announces that body's absence from the scene. Rather than providing something that can be fixed in a receding fad time, Holder's record provides only a trace of his body. In the context of the calypso craze, Holder inscribes this absence on vinyl disk, and as the ideal dancer-listener plays the record on her phonograph it continually performs Holder's dematerialization. As we will see in the next section, Holder thus removed himself *from* the fad and re-moved himself *within* the fad in order to be somewhere and somewhen else.

Holder's brief turn as a popular dance instructor concludes with a curious epilogue. In 1961, with the calypso craze already a distant memory, Holder again took to the pages of the *New York Times* and repeated his earlier disavowal of the fad. In an article ostensibly about the new craze for the Twist (a dance he found wanting), Holder took the opportunity to revisit the failed dance steps of the calypso craze. Turning to the Limbo, he reminded readers of the unbridgeable gap between the sacred ritual from the villages of Trinidad and the vulgar scene of tourists from the north who "removed their hats and mink stoles, pulled their dresses above their knees and snaked under curtain rods to show folks back home at parties the marvelous native dance they had picked up in the Caribbean."[51] In the mood of mock-outrage, Holder describes his shock at the mass marketing of the Limbo:

> A short time ago my eyes popped when I caught a picture spread in a big magazine. The Limbo had been packaged into a do-it-yourself party kit by the Wham-O Manufacturing Co., one of the pioneers of the hula hoop. The Limbo kit comes complete with posts, crossbar, a calypso record and detailed instructions on how to be the first one on your block to do the upside down high jump to a calypso accompaniment. Exactly! Nothing is missing but the corpse and the coffin.[52]

At once a feint and a confession, a forfeit and an atonement, Holder's mock-outrage at this appropriation of Trinidadian culture marks his passage out of fad culture and fad consciousness. Reminding readers of the origins of Limbo as a funeral rite, he scoffs at the commercialization of the calypso craze while imagining postwar suburbia as an empty cemetery, missing only "the corpse and the coffin." Holder thus removed himself from the fad twice: once on the *Glamour* recording and again in this article, where he rhetorically removes that very recording by attributing it to someone else. On the *Glamour* recording he is a trace, a phantom body troubling the productive, performative negation—the not-real, the disavowal—that structures black fad performance. In the pages of the *New York Times* a few years later, he disappears even this disappeared body.

Elsewhen: *Belé*, *Banda*, and *Dougla*

At the same time as he was offering his phantom body as a dance partner for the readers of *Glamour*, Holder was beginning a decades-long project that comprises one of his signal contributions to black modern dance in the Americas. In a triptych of dance pieces that have their origins at the time of the calypso craze—*Belé* (1981), *Banda* (1982), and *Dougla* (1974)—Holder drew on Caribbean themes and movements as material for the concert stage. Taken together, these three pieces enact a mythic elsewhen, a temporal spacing that is neither the Trinidadian or Caribbean historical past nor the fading now of the calypso craze. This elsewhen is a disavowal of the calypso craze's disavowal and an instance of working against the music and movements of the fad. It is a formal experiment with the conditions of stolen time. As we will see, these three dances are not authentic Caribbean folk performances to be found behind the calypso craze. Rather, they exist alongside it—coextensive with the calypso craze and its acts of African American–Afro-Caribbean (dis)connection and (in)authenticity.

Following World War II, black choreographers worked against the forced frame of vaudeville and jazz dance that overdetermined the reception of black movement on stage.[53] Katherine Dunham spoke for many when she famously declared that one aim of this new movement in black modernist concert dance was to "take *our* dance out of the burlesque to make it a more dignified art."[54] Making this distinction was an important intervention that disrupted spectatorial common sense and expanded professional opportunities for black dancers. But there were just as often continuities as discontinuities between modernist black dance and jazz dance. Black dancers often used the latter to make space and opportunity for the former, and the nightclub stage was repeatedly revealed to have always been just as modernist as the concert stage (as Dunham's own work continually demonstrated). Even as Holder was making his name in popular culture, he was experimenting with ways that the choreographic abstraction of folk movement might create new aesthetic horizons. As one early review of his company at the White Barn Theatre in the African American *Pittsburgh Courier* put it, "Mr. Holder's group has taken Trinidad folk themes and worked them into dance pattern in such a way as to create an entirely new dance movement which gives a remarkable insight into the actual emotions, conflicts, superstitions, and loves of the people of Trinidad."[55] This project imagined Caribbean culture against the aesthetic and commercial constraints of the calypso craze.

Holder achieved such "remarkable insight" in his choreography by approaching Caribbean feeling through the idiom of myth, while at the same time departing from white modern dance's midcentury turn toward archetype and mythic abstraction. In doing so, he anticipated the calls of writers like Wilson Harris and Édouard Glissant for new forms in Caribbean arts. Harris, as we have seen, held that the ghostly ache of historical dismemberment aroused by the Limbo perspective required nothing less than "the renascence of a new corpus of sensibility."[56] Similarly, Glissant appealed to new methods to conceptualize Caribbean historical consciousness in the face of the ruptures and erasures of New World colonization. For Glissant, European historiography is unable to contend with the conditions of discontinuity and absence that shape the Antilles, a condition that he calls nonhistory.[57] In response to this "imposed nonhistory," Glissant proposes a wholesale reconceptualization of History and Literature as they were inherited in the New World from Europe as separate modes of apprehending the world.[58] Glissant seeks to break down the categorical divisions between Literature and History in order to create new forms for Caribbean consciousness. He locates their shared relationship to myth—as "the first state of a still naïve historical consciousness" and as "the raw material for the project of a literature"—as the genesis of their impulse to narrate the world.[59] At their origins, as first state or raw material, history and literature coincide in myth.

Glissant describes this coincidence in a richly paradoxical temporal formulation. In myth, he writes, history appears as "a premonition of the past" and literature appears as "a memory of the future."[60] Part of what I understand Glissant to voice in this formulation is that myth unsettles the linear temporality and transparent meaning of Western rationality. Myth retemporalizes temporality, and time is rendered pliable. Where literature and history touch in the realm of myth, the linear sequence of past-present-future has not yet been fixed. In myth, time is at once recursive and prophetic; effect does not always follow causality; origins are continually arrived at again; simultaneity and multiplicity replace binary logic; the world is depicted allegorically rather than realistically; and (Glissant writes) "the methodological and fundamental distinction between diachrony and synchrony could also be seen as a *trick*."[61] In its suspended doubling of the world, myth offers a formal touchstone for the Caribbean artist as she works within the condition of nonhistory.

Here I supplement Glissant's rich formulation of mythic temporality and his retemporalization of literature and history with dance. In the same spirit as Glissant and Harris, Jamaican choreographer Rex Nettleford describes a Caribbean existential condition of historical, psychic, and linguistic "severance" and the capacity for dance to assemble new modes of being in the postcolonial world.[62] For Nettleford, as for Holder, dance is another method for engaging the Caribbean past and another form through which Caribbean existence emplots its relationship to nonhistory. As we saw with the Limbo, dance serves as a point of continuity and discontinuity across the Middle Passage, slavery, colonization, and independence. Indeed, dance preexists both written histories and literature as a methodology of memory and futurity. If, as Glissant maintains, myth is a form in which history first appears as a premonition of the past and literature as a memory of the future, I propose that dance appears as an elsewhen of the present, a stolen time and shell game of presence that the dancing body plays with confidence. In Holder's modernist dance and his negotiation of the calypso craze, myth comes to Caribbean dance as just such a doubled present, a now that is not *this* now—an elsewhen. Holder's myth-based projects perform the phantom limb of the calypso craze—that which is not a part of the craze but nonetheless tingles with its sensation. The timelessness of the fad (its being-without-time) becomes in Holder's dance the timelessness of myth (an allegorical elsewhen that comments on and even alters the tempos of the present, but not in any direct way). Through such choreographic projects, Holder works against the craze and works the craze against itself.

To demonstrate this, let us return to Holder's Trinidadian dance triptych *Belé, Banda,* and *Dougla*. The dates I gave at the beginning of this section for these pieces identify the definitive versions as Holder set their choreography in the 1970s and 1980s, but he began working on them as early as his arrival in New York City (if not earlier), and they were choreographically in embryonic form at the time of the calypso craze—evolving in length, sophistication, and movement over the decades. De Lavallade remembers that *Belé* began as a solo for her that was performed at the 92nd Street YMHA in the mid-1950s and eventually expanded to a duet and then a dance for the entire company.[63] The earliest event that I have found in which these three pieces were staged together was at the Jacob's Pillow Dance Festival in July 1956, where Holder performed in all three of them (and with de Lavallade in both *Belé* and *Banda*).[64] Describing this early performance, dance critic Margaret Lloyd praised their distinctly Trinidadian hybridity and creolization. "Interesting was the blend of resident cultures in two of his choreographies, based on Trinidadian forms," she wrote. "The 'Doogla Suite' combined the East Indian head motions and characteristic leg extensions with the basic muscularity of West Indian dance. The 'Belé Suite' drew on the cabrioles and other brisk footwork of ballet, the high kicks of the Can-Can, and other elements of European infiltration, to mingle with the primitive movement. The costumes, designed by Mr. Holder, were lavish in expression of the native love of dressing up."[65]

Holder and de Lavallade danced this same program again at a concert in Central Park in 1957, where a review praised Holder's "half-freakish, half obscene dance of death, the 'Banda,' and an interesting combination of African and East Indian movement called 'Doogla Dance'" and observed that "Miss de Lavallade, magnificently costumed was an eyeful also in the 'Bele,' with William Millie."[66] He and de Lavallade also offered shorter excerpts from both *Belé* and *Banda*—alongside his instruction in the Limbo-Calypso—on a 1959 episode of the public television arts program *A Time to Dance*.[67] Thus at the same time that Holder appeared on stage and on recordings for the calypso craze, he was simultaneously staging the dance pieces that would become *Belé, Banda,* and *Dougla,* and I view them as intimately related to Holder's general negotiation of black fad performance through his choreographic transport to a different temporality that I describe as a mythic elsewhen.

Holder himself located this choreographic project in the domain of myth. As he explained in an interview, "Martha Graham made dances about Greek gods, and I do it with African gods. Everyone knows the Greek pantheon. No one knows the African pantheon."[68] At the same time that white modern dancers turned to myth and its temporal possibilities in their choreography, Holder and other black modern dancers made a similar turn. Dance scholar Susan Manning makes the persuasive argument that just as black dancers began to make inroads onto the concert stage, white modern dance, which had previously appropriated freely from Eastern, Native American, and African American cultures, began to turn away from such primitivist approaches and toward what she calls "mythic abstraction." This mythic abstraction "staged universal subjects without the mediation of bodies marked as culturally other. . . . At one end of the continuum, choreographers represented dancers as actors in mythic drama. At the other end of the continuum choreographers represented dancers as inhabitants of abstract worlds." In this way, she adds, "the culturally marked body became the province of Negro dance, as modern dance deployed the newly privileged unmarked body" within a mythic continuum.[69]

If mythic abstraction characterizes the postwar work of choreographers such as Martha Graham, Doris Humphrey, and Merce Cunningham, Holder's choreography could be described by contrast as the development of a *mythic particularity* that uses Caribbean nonhistory and racial distinction as the positive condition for aesthetic invention. Holder, too, represents dancers in mythic scenes and abstract worlds, but these scenes and worlds are marked by racial and geographic particularity. He takes inspiration form a mythic continuum not to abstract a universal subject but to mark various, specific forms and movements of intercultural exchange in the New World. Let us turn, now, to these dances: *Belé*, a work engaging with themes and movements of Trinidadian-Creole culture; *Banda* with that of Haitian-African culture; and *Dougla* with that of Trinidadian Hindu-African culture. Taken collectively, these three pieces address the unity-in-fragmentation (Nettleford) and the new corpus of sensibility (Harris) that Holder's midcentury Caribbean modern dance achieved.[70]

A woman in a bright yellow dress steps away from her partner and glides to the front of the stage. Her right hand rests on her hip, and her left hand extends outward from her body, spreading open a paper fan. Keeping her back straight, she steps a leg to the left from under her full skirt. Her carriage is upright and her eyes look just over the heads of the men and women admiring her. All the while her hand flutters the fan teasingly, extending her body like a blade into space, now the blunt side, now the cutting edge. On one television documentary of this dance, Dance Theatre of Harlem founding director Arthur Mitchell instructs the company at rehearsal: "Ladies, make the fans talk. Know how beautiful you are!" The woman in yellow spent hours preparing for the fete. Her briskly twirling wrist is the only outward sign of a tempestuous energy that is belied by her stately poise as the fan cuts through the humid, still air around her; were you near enough, you would feel its slightest breath against your skin. She smiles flirtatiously as she skates to the left, whipping the folds of her petticoat and drawing the eyes of possible suitors to the flash of color under her skirt. The dance is a both a preparation and a promise: a dropped ribbon. Even before she completely exits, another woman in a red skirt has already moved into her space, her fan talking loudly. She will be followed by another in pink, as other dancers line the stage behind them—men in fine white suits, women in brightly colored gowns—clapping and cheering at the display of beauty (fig. 27).[71]

A fifteen-minute piece that draws on the creole "fancy dance" of colonial society, *Belé* is a nonnarrative work that foregrounds movement and costume as the company occupies the dance space in various formations and configurations. Although without a narrative, the movement and costume itself tells the story of colonization and hybridity through form. As Holder succinctly explained, belé is the name for the "creole fete at which various European and African dances are executed."[72] It is a version of the Caribbean *quadrille* (or reel), a creolized version of courtly dance that emphasizes partner work, minuet, waltz, high kicks, processions, and other forms of display.[73] While the movement is an adaptation of European forms that advance and retreat across the stage in a series of parades, promenades, and figure eights, a polyrhythmic drumming punctuates the music and works against the stately character of the dance. In Holder's vision, it is a dance wherein the pleasure of the dancer is drawn from the appreciation and attention she derives from the spectator. It is a display of color and beauty. A review of its 1981 premiere described the female dancers wearing "flouncy white dresses set off by outlandish headdresses and knee socks in stinging vermillion," though found the overall effect given by "the basic pattern of Holder's dances—repeated horizontal stage crosses by small groups of figures in stylized postures—is nothing more than a fashion parade."[74] The critic's dismissive take on the dancers' sartorial display misunderstands the individual and collective Caribbean self-fashioning that *Belé* stages through the spatial and visual occupation of the stage. Thus there is no

Figure 27. Dancers Karen Brown and Donald Williams in Geoffrey Holder's *Belé*, performed by Dance Theatre of Harlem, 1981. Photo by Anne Knudsen. Herald-Examiner Collection/Los Angeles Public Library.

narrative other than form; on the bare stage, sound, movement, and costume are the cultural shape of the violence of conquest, the daily life of the plantation, and the reinhabitation of the colonizers' movement by the colonized. Holder elevates this fete to the realm of mythic particularity, both an abstraction of history and an allegory for history, outside time and place. It could be 1821, 1956, 1981, or 2018. It is a temporal elsewhen to whenever it is performed. Through all that, it is a celebration of beauty and the beauty of celebration—a new kind of beauty that emerges from the aesthetic, social, and sexual encounter between African and European. *Belé* is itself a performance of the performance of stolen time that exemplifies the Africanist aesthetic of working against the music.

Alone on stage, the grief-stricken mother crumples over the three-foot coffin containing her young child. The village mourners and priest were helpless in soothing her anguish and have retreated from her sorrow. In the stillness, Baron Samedi enters from stage left. After dancing provocatively around the pathetic tableaux, he reveals himself to the mother. He taps his cane on the coffin and then dances on and over and around it. He takes up a cross from the coffin lid and rubs it rudely against his crotch and over his body. Suddenly a long red bolt of fabric appears from his sleeve. He pulls the fabric back and forth between his legs, leering. He throws the scarf on the sacred ground before the mother and then reaches out his long leg. He picks the scarf off the ground with his toes and extends his leg toward her, coquettishly offering her the fabric. She snatches it away from him and twists it wildly around her. She covers herself with it from head to toe and struggles from beneath it, stretching outward. Now she is fully possessed, emerging from the cloth and mirroring his movements.

Unlike the suspended time and place of *Belé*'s and *Dougla*'s nonsettings and their abstracted figures, Holder's *Banda* is a folkloric narrative of grief and possession based on the Haitian funeral *banda* dance. As we saw previously, this piece was shaped by Holder's encounter with the Haitian dancer Jean-Léon Destiné in 1952, a meeting that would have a lasting effect on his choreographic vision. Holder's *Banda* finds a young mother grieving her infant. Inconsolable and heartbroken, villagers and the Catholic priest leave the mother at the gravesite where she is visited by Baron Samedi, vodou deity of both death and bacchanal. His irreverence and sexual precocity overcome her despair as he animates and then possesses her. Carrying the mother beyond her grief to intense sensual pleasure, his bodily movements spiral outward until she too is dancing with a sexual abandon that finally culminates in her suicide. Holder's dance struck critics as "macabre" and scandalously sexual, though it exemplifies the choreographer's deep study of vodou and his own exploration of Caribbean erotics.[75] Katherine Dunham, for one, proposed that the explicit sexual element often found in such Caribbean funeral dances "is an aid to a quicker, more complete externalization and re-direction of energy" and "a re-affirmation of community solidarity." Of the Haitian *banda* in particular she suggested that "most of the movements are extremely sexual and no doubt attest the need to stimulate procreation of a new life to replace death."[76] Holder stages this ritual encounter between the mother and Baron Samedi in an ecstatic time that, like the Trinidadian Limbo, explores the passage from life to death.

This is not the death-bound subjectivity of black fad performance that we saw in chapter 1 but its antithesis, a vodou vision of death and fertility that marks an alternative to the social and representational death of Jim Crow.

Finally, a wedding. This wedding, like all weddings, is a ceremony for the community as much as it is for the bride and groom—here the community formed by the social mixing of Afro-Trinidadians and Trinidadians of South Asian descent forged in the Caribbean crucible of forced and indentured labor. The groom enters first, carried on the shoulders of two shirtless men wearing crimson dhoti that visually echo the enormous blood moon projected above them. They set the groom down and remove the red scarf wound around his arms, which extend straight out from his sides. His biceps are bound with red tassels that dangle and bounce as he leaps across the stage. Behind him sit six women in a triangular arrangement draped in white saris, heads covered, left arms concealed beneath the fabric. Their right arms rise up and fall down in turn as each hand rotates around its wrist in precision. A formation of six men in red dhoti and bearing tall bamboo sticks cross before them, leaning backward from the waist as they move forward. The women each bring their right arm into their sari and conceal it momentarily as the formation passes, and then extend it out again, reaching high above their head with bent elbow and precise finger patterns of Hindu mudras. The bride enters next, carried like the groom on the shoulders of two men. They deliver her to the groom and the couple circle each other as African drums intensify the rhythm beneath the Indian bansuri (bamboo flute). The groom, bent ninety degrees at the waist, shuffles backward quickly and circles his bride, who grasps her lace veil between two fingers, waving the fabric before her in a graceful flow of fabric, flashing her face and just as quickly concealing it again, coyly. Bride and groom meet and are raised back to the shoulders of the men who carried them.

If *Belé* stylized movements that developed out of the encounter of European and African dance, *Dougla* similarly staged an allegory of the social mixture of East Indian populations brought to Trinidad in the eighteenth century as indentured laborers and the island's African descendants. Holder described the essence of this dance: "the children of their union are called Doogla [*sic*]. They took from both parents, both cultures, to produce their dances, the force of the African and such of the delicate 'finger words' of the Hindu that suited best the power of the African. The control of the body, so insistent in Hindu dances, is carried over; the inevitable coloring of the African is never quite freed, and this struggle between them gives this dance a drama that neither parent culture can boast."[77] The word *dougla* can carry pejorative connotations when it is delivered against this multiracial population, but is also used as a sign of self-identity and pride. In recent decades scholars have explored the elements of what Shalini Puri theorizes as a "dougla poetics" rooted not in a biological identity but a political and cultural one.[78] Holder's dance contributes to a dougla poetics, though he did not himself identify as such. The work stages the wedding celebration between two Afro-Indian Trinidadians who are less characters than formalist expressions of the hybridity and mixture of Asian and African cultures. Holder combines the gestural vocabularies of both Indian and African movement—the "finger words" and vertical hip circles of Classical Indian dance with the bent-knee movement and horizontal pelvic thrusts of Africanist dance. Holder stages the dougla as a "new corpus of sensibility" created in the nonhistory of the New World colony.[79]

Taken together this choreographic triptych represents Holder's experiment with mythic particularity and the carving out of a temporal elsewhen that is neither the fleeting now of the fad nor the ethnographic denial of temporal coevalness.[80] With these pieces—and also his significant choreographic work *The Prodigal Prince* (1967)—Holder should be viewed alongside modern black dancers who engaged with Caribbean culture such as Pearl Primus and Katherine Dunham. His contributions are well regarded within the dance world (*Belé, Banda,* and *Dougla* are all part of the Dance Theatre of Harlem's repertory, continuing Holder's elsewhen into new eras for new audiences), but a wider recognition has been hampered, I suspect, by his repeated forays into commercial culture and the realms of entertainment. Like many modern black dancers (Dunham most prominently), Holder performed on both popular stages and concert stages. While black dancers in the postwar years struggled with the expectation that black dance could only be entertainment, rarely achieving the technical and intellectual accomplishment of modern dance, Holder especially suffered from this bias.

More to the point, throughout his long career Holder continually refused to observe the boundaries between high and popular art (as his easy movement from the pages of *Glamour* to Jacob's Pillow indicates), and his choreography more often than not fell between the aesthetic cracks. It was either disparaged as too vaudeville and colorful for high art or deemed too conceptual for commercial theater. Reviews for his star turn in *Aida*, for example, praised his performance even as they found it out of place at the Metropolitan Opera House ("Adding to the nightclub act impression was Geoffrey Holder"; "Holder was a venture in off-norm ballet casting and resulted in a choreographic hodgepodge . . . more suitable for vaudeville than for opera.").[81] Yet when he toured on the nightclub circuit, critics routinely described his acts as "strictly 'art' entertainment that went over mildly" and "definitely not commercial enough for the bigger spots."[82] In between the cracks, however, would prove to be a deeply imaginative and creative, if sometimes lonely, space. Even as he was recording the "Limbo-Calypso" for *Glamour* magazine or staging calypso revues, he was developing complex dance pieces that would engage with Caribbean nonhistory by establishing a temporal elsewhen, a time that existed to the side of the black fad performance's death-bound time and continued into the future.

The Dancerly Text

This refusal to work within the boundaries between high and low extended to Holder's relationship to genre more broadly. Dance, painting, and costume design were his primary modes of creativity, but for him each of these forms blurred into one another. Holder described his own creative process as a generic cross-pollination: "When I'm dancing, I often get an idea for a painting, and when I'm painting, it often brings to mind something about dancing."[83] In 1959, shortly after the calypso craze's eclipse but still within its artistic orbit, he brought the sense of mythic particularity and temporal elsewhen developed in his choreography to literary culture in *Black Gods, Green Islands*, a collection of Trinidadian and Haitian folktales that he adapted (with writer Tom Harshman) into short stories. This collection of five stories was Holder's only foray into literature, and he announced it as a further disavowal of the calypso craze. He writes in an author's note to the text that he compiled the stories as a way "to say that the Caribbean islands are not all calypsoes [*sic*] or bongo drums," and I turn to this story collection in the context of Holder's dance because it remains an important instance of the new methodologies and experiments in form called for, by Glissant, as a response to Caribbean nonhistory and called for, by Holder, as a response to the calypso craze.[84]

Continuing the choreographic project of *Belé*, *Banda*, and *Dougla* in a literary medium, *Black Gods, Green Islands* breaks down categorical divisions between genres, mixing choreography with mythography and contributing to Caribbean literary history. The *New York Herald Tribune* announced that with this book Holder "takes an honored place with Samuel Selvon and the other brilliant re-creators of the Caribbean scene, as an exuberant fabulist."[85] Just as Selvon's *The Lonely Londoners* (1956) expanded modernist literary form to create a picaresque calypso novel, Holder's literary experiment similarly pushed the boundaries of form and theme to create what we should understand as a dancerly text.[86] By dancerly text, I do not mean to use dance as a simple metaphor to describe Holder's poetics. Nor do I mean something akin to the dance instruction manual previously discussed that seeks to fix dance in writing. Rather, in calling his collection of stories a dancerly text I draw on and distinguish it from what Henry Louis Gates Jr. influentially defined as the speakerly text in the African American tradition. The speakerly text, for Gates, is one "whose rhetorical strategy is designed to represent an oral literary tradition" and "in which all other structural elements seem to be devalued, as important as they remain to the telling of the tale, because the narrative strategy signals attention to its own importance, an importance which would seem to be the privileging of speech and its inherent linguistic features."[87]

With Gates's outline in view, I take *Black Gods, Green Islands* as a what I call a dancerly text, one whose patterns, imagery, pace, and transfers of energy are designed to be read foremost as moving, dancing bodies, with other narrative strategies subordinated to this goal. Unlike other literary representations of black folklore such as Charles Chesnutt's *The Conjure Woman* (1899) or Zora Neale Hurston's *Mules and Men* (1935), for example, Holder's adaptations do not seek to recreate an oral tradition. Although they are highly discursive, there is remarkably little direct speech in any of these stories, and virtually none in some of them. Rather, they approach folklore primarily not as oral tradition but as movement. The stories are not structured by speech but are generally dense narratives of impressionistic construction, color, and bodily transformation. *Black Gods, Green Islands* is a book that only a dancer and fashion designer such as Holder could have written.

Holder's collection announces itself as a dancerly text in several ways. The overall book is structured like a dance program, with the images, tempos, lengths, and rhythms of each of the five separate stories self-contained but collectively adding up to more than the sum of its parts. But unlike a conventional short story collection, plot and character are subordinated to the overall effect of mood and atmosphere. Pioneering historian J. Saunders Redding noted this element of the book and the way that bodies in space create a mythic, otherworldly realm. "The dissolution of character into background," he wrote, "is surprisingly successful in a rather odd direction. It does not produce the universality it aims at, but it does produce a magic suspension of disbelief in unreality. You accept the dreamlike scenes and episodes and quality of these five stories without questioning whether dream and reality are two things: you know, while you read, that they are one."[88] Holder brings to the literary the same mythic particularity he brought to *Belé*, *Banda*, and *Dougla*. The stories, like the dances, fail in establishing universality while still abstracting the world they create to a mythic elsewhen.

Moreover, dance thematics structure each of the stories in the collection. The stories are all organized around festivities, rituals, dances, ceremonies, flights, captures, movements, and stillnesses. The story "Soucouyan," for example, about the blood-sucking witches known as soucouyants who pass as old women in the daytime and shed their skin at night to hunt their victims, culminates in a detailed description of a belé dance after the protagonist escapes capture from the succubus. Weddings, funerals, and marketplace scenes that organize bodies in highly choreographic social formations similarly shape other stories. These thematic elements are skillfully furthered by formal and narrative strategies that bring into literature a dancerly transfer of energy. Dance scholar Ellen Goellner calls this a "dance understanding" of a novel, in which an "analogy of narrative dynamics to dance" can help us to better approach some works of literature that share affinities to dance by focusing our "attention on formal elements . . . which act as infusions of or drains on the energy that animates (and is) our understanding of the text."[89] The dancerly text brings together these formal and thematic elements in order to privilege dance and emphasize the importance of movement and the body to diasporic expressive traditions. Drawing on but subordinating other narrative elements to this project, the dancerly text transfigures literature into a form of dance.

For the sake of space, I will demonstrate the formal and thematic choreography of *Black Gods, Green Islands* by closely reading one of its stories, but the same effects can be found equally in the others. The collection's fourth story, "Congo Bara" narrates the wedding of fashionable Felicé and handsome Congo Bara, the island's social event of the year.[90] In the middle of the wedding celebration, the groom's jealous brother drunkenly appears and curses the couple. A year later, the curse is realized when their newborn son is taken by a dwenn, a baby spirit that steals the souls of unbaptized children. After a pursuit through the jungles of the island, the baby is returned to his parents unharmed, but only because the spirits took offense at the brother who issued the curse in the first place.

To approach this story as a dancerly text is to attend to its arrangement of bodies, to its physio-textual conservation and expenditure of energy, and to what Goellner describes as the formal and narrative strategies that develop the "work's underlying kinesthetic logic."[91] The kinesthetic logic of "Congo Bara," for example, is organized around two axial movements: a vertical climb upward and a horizontal rush forward. The story begins with townsfolk trekking up the steep hill of Maraval, a wealthy suburb of Port of Spain, to the small chapel at the mountaintop where the wedding is held. The opening sentences establish the direction of upward ascent and the sense of exertion as "broad-hatted women" in high heels, dresses, and ineffective hand-fans make their way up the stony path (143). We first see one guest leaning "on a big rock to catch her breath and after a moment of rest, in fear of being late, she rustled her pink taffeta dress and set off again on one heel three inches high, the other four and a half" (143). The ascent is marked by asymmetry and imbalance, describing an unsteadiness that will develop over the course of the wedding ceremony.

This hillside path then fills with bodies as "above and below her, on other paths from all directions, the villagers and those round about came. In new white suits the men swaggered along too" (144). A series of entrances are described as the church grounds fill with townsfolk who chat, gossip, and laugh. Finally, in a "calculated late entrance," the bride's sister Blanche catches the attention of the congregation, including the musicians who spontaneously provide a melody for her entrance. Their performance "tickled her to flesh-shaking giggles as she strutted against the impromptu song, the white-eyelet dress flashing its orange spots and switching taut over her full hips" (144). The movement of these opening passages brings together the village as a corps de ballet that fills the space and prepares for the formal wedding ceremony. If the speakerly text foregrounds the "communal speaking voice," the dancerly text foregrounds a community's kinesthetic sense: its collective breath, its shifts in gravity and force, its locomotive patterns, how it moves and when.[92]

In this case, the underlying kinesthetic logic of the story reflects the ill footing of the wedding and marriage to follow. After the ceremony, the festivities are repeatedly interrupted by a series of bad omens: a "sudden big-drop rain" that interrupts the procession to the cake (145); Congo's brother, who stumbles up the hillside spraying a sickening orange perfume from an atomizer and lays "a white baby's coffin among the wedding presents" (with shades of Holder's *Banda* dance) (148); and an unexpected funeral procession that makes its way past the wedding party and continues uphill to the church (149). The tossing of the bridal bouquet caps off the sense of imbalance and disharmony created by these events. When the bouquet is caught in the branches of a tree, Holder offers an image that encapsulates the wedding's vertical choreography of lurches and stumbles. One guest, he writes, "screaming like she had gone into fits, pulled at Alexander, shoved him in position, and scrambled up his back. Teetering wildly, she pulled down the bouquet and tumbled, skirts and screams, to the ground" (149). From bodies climbing hills to climbing each other, the choreography of rise/ascent and fall/collapse establishes the kinesthetic logic of the first half of Holder's tale and reflects its thematics of exertion and disequilibrium.

As everyday life returns to the village and Felicé becomes pregnant, the story rotates its axial alignment to the horizontal plane. Instead of the mountainside, the men return to work in the cacao plantation outside the village, where Congo is head cutter. To arrange and orchestrate the labor, he "divided the men into gangs and set their lanes of work" (150). He "improvised work chants, beating on a tree with a bamboo stick to set his pace . . . Congo's song was in the trees, spreading over the gangs with no need to use his eye or sharpen his tongue" (150–51). Everything moves outward rather than upward and the landscape shapes the movement and sound of the workingmen. Just as the vertical climb of the hill established a kinesthetic and thematic logic of instability, the horizon of the village plantation establishes the hope and apprehension that governs the arrival of Felicé's baby.

When in due course the curse is realized and the baby is discovered missing from its crib, Congo organizes the villagers to battle the evil spirits. With flambeaux torches, his small army "traveled on light, tense feet beyond the cries and shouts of the village and where the fast mountain stream was bridged they saw ahead in the light of their torches a boy come running, dressed as if for Sunday" (166). The unearthly child taunts the tense corps, telling them he saw the dwenns with Congo's child running through the forest. The story culminates with this pursuit of the spectral boy, who leads them on a protracted and dizzying chase through the forest after the crying infant. "The boy set a fast pace for his elders, keeping well out in front of them, always a little ahead" (168). Holder pays careful attention here to the breathless exertion of the chase as the villagers fan out across the forest after the spirit and his "grueling pace" as he "ran them wildly over the cacao estate and farther" (168). The imagery of forward-rushing movement increases as cries of the infant grow louder: "Congo began breathlessly chanting a hymn of his childhood. . . . The rest joined in, singing out as if the words were shot and arrow"; "over a rickety rope bridge spanning a ravine where the stream rushed they scrambled one by one, massing on the other side"; the child-spirit "had gone before, up the dark path and, shouting and singing, they followed" (169). The race of the villagers as they proceed across the valley, bottleneck across the bridge, and rush through the forest direct the textual energy of the story precipitously forward until it comes to a panting halt before a wiggling and squirming bundle.

Discovering the baby safe (the devil decided in the end not to satisfy the curse because of the liberties Congo's brother took with his orange perfume), Congo rushes to a mountain pool to baptize the baby to provide future protection from the dwenns. In this conclusion, the vertical and horizontal tensions of the story are visually, thematically, and kinesthetically resolved as the baptism takes place in a blue pool whose stillness is "ruffled" by the "narrow ribbon" of a waterfall that plunges downward, breaking its placid surface and jetting into its depths below (170). The story's routes of energy—stumbling upward, chasing outward—come together in its thematic resolution as the child is recovered and inoculated from further evil at the point where vertical and horizontal intersect. The terrain of the island's mountains, valleys, and plantations directs the kinesthetic expenditure of the story—its accumulation and discharge of energy—and the syncretic combination of vodou and Catholic lore sets its tempo. The interaction between this narrative dynamic, formal strategy, and thematic matter creates the dancerly system of Holder's story.

The story's play between vertical and horizontal axes thus suggests one way to read *Black Gods, Green Islands* as a dancerly—rather than a speakerly—approach to literary folklore. More: it allegorizes the very act of reading folklore. As anthropologist Claude Lévi-Strauss explained, written myth violates and reorganizes Western protocols of reading. "It is impossible," he suggests, "to understand a myth as a continuous sequence."[93] Compare this to Glissant, who similarly tells us that "myth *coils* meaning around the image itself: which means that it is as distant from pure realism as it is from scrupulous and in-depth analysis."[94] For both, the written myth requires a new way of reading, one that demands that "we have to read not only from left to right, but at the same time vertically, from top to bottom. We have to understand that each page is a totality."[95] The myth thus appears to us as a repetition of motifs more akin to a musical score or a dance sequence than a literary work. This intersection of horizontal and vertical reading axes is dramatized in "Congo Bara," and *Black Gods, Green Islands* overall is a dancerly text best apprehended as Glissant and Lévi-Strauss explain—in its totality, from all directions at once, as a moving body filling space on stage. This is also a reorganization of linear time. Rather than word following word, as in literature, the myth-as-dancerly-text asks us to read forward and backward, up and down, and to seize the totality in and as each page. Through this textual transformation and the demand it makes on its reader, we may recognize a literary performance of "the renascence of a new corpus of sensibility" that marks the Caribbean Limbo gateway.[96] This literary experiment was another instance of Holder's ongoing project of working against the sounds and movements of the calypso craze. Each page is the dancing body, and the author is both choreographer and premier danseur.

Curtain Call

Over the next five decades, Holder continued to develop a mythic elsewhen in dance, painting, photography, and costume design. The calypso craze, as we know, had a much shorter span, and Holder presided over one of the harbingers of its end. In addition to the scenes of social, theatrical, and textual dance we have seen in this chapter, Holder also brought his choreographic and directorial skills to vaudeville in one of the largest calypso revues of the 1950s: Geoffrey Holder's Caribbean Calypso Festival, a massive event held at the 3,625-seat Loew's Metropolitan Theater in Brooklyn in the spring of 1957. Collaborating with mambo bandleader Tito Puente and his orchestra, the bill included over sixty performers in a fast-paced, hour-long spectacle. Such a full-scale vaudeville revue was uncommon for the Metropolitan Theater, which had strictly screened films for the previous two decades.[97] The revue toured the Loew's circuit following its ten-day run in Brooklyn, playing theaters in Philadelphia and Washington, DC, before it fizzled out, and it ended as one of the early signs of the calypso craze's finish.[98]

Holder's Caribbean Calypso Festival was part of a larger marketing campaign and demographic experiment orchestrated by the Loew's corporation, which owned several hundred movie houses around the country, including several in New York City. Loew's turned Holder's carnival revue into a contest between calypso and rock and roll. At the same time as Holder's festival, Loew's programmed a nine-act rock 'n' roll show at their State Theater on Broadway hosted by disc jockey (and later an early pioneer of Philadelphia hip-hop) Douglas "Jocko" Henderson.[99] Counter-programming against itself, Loew's staged a contest and an experiment. According to sources, "executives of the theater chain feel the results of the two programs will give them some idea of the relative popularity of each of the current musical crazes. Thus, in a sense, the theater circuit will assemble some statistics which it can employ to determine its future live booking policy."[100]

Holder's revue featured a number of high-profile acts, including Boscoe Holder, Lord Flea, Lord Kitchener, Maya Angelou, Holder's company of sixteen Trinidadian Dancers, and others associated with the calypso craze such as dancer George Boreland (previously seen on stage in the chorus of *Jamaica*) and calypso dancer Helen Ferguson. Holder performed several numbers, including one that prompted a surprised critic to exclaim "he actually dips into the style of Hindu dance, including adaptations of the classic gesture language" (a likely sample of the movements that would become *Dougla*), and a closing ballet that staged a brightly costumed carnival that provided "passing opportunities for some vivacious turns, slides into split, lively torso rotations, prancing foot-beats and, of course, male-female incidents of an amorous, playful nature."[101] The rest of the acts were also highly kinesthetic and created an upbeat, sometimes frantic tempo. Lord Flea performed a set backed with "five happy calypso hooligans" who "desert[ed] their instruments from time to time to engage in an array of dance antics," and Kitchener sang three songs that likewise included some dancing, though he was "far more subtle, an almost reticent fellow."[102] Angelou and Ferguson both performed "sultry calypsongs." In contrast to her fixed choreography in the film *Calypso Heat Wave* discussed in chapter 2, this revue found Angelou incorporating "little dance excursions, skillfully traversed" in her numbers. On stage Angelou claimed more space to move, eluding the projection that fixed her on the cinematic screen. Even Tito Puente, from the orchestra pit, "turned his conducting duties into dance form."[103]

Critics praised the individual numbers, but most agreed that as a show the Caribbean Calypso Festival did not hold together. "Holder's efforts belong in a ballet house, Flea and Kitchener at small niteries and Puente is better served in the mambo halls of the Palladium Ballroom in Manhattan," according to one review that concluded it was "too lofty for vaudfilm consumption and b[ox] o[ffice] appreciation."[104] Another grumbled that "a good many (but not all, by any means) of its separate elements are fine; however, they are laxly put together and the show tends to amble along. Furthermore, there is too much material and a firm cutting job would help enormously. Individual acts could be tightened, waits between numbers avoided and deadwood removed."[105]

But it was not simply this lack of coherence that doomed Holder's undertaking. At the end of the run, the disappointing box-office earnings from the revue heralded calypso's rapid decline in popularity. *Variety*, which only six months earlier had declared rock and roll a fading fad, conceded that "the less-than-expected response to this show is likely to kill many future promotions of calypso on the road, unless some unforeseen development takes place."[106] While some industry watchers attributed the low turnout to other competing stage presentations that week, larger demographic trends were undeniable: "The kids failed to show up en masse and the small [calypso] trade is being brought in mainly by adults," noted one postmortem assessment; "Geoffrey Holder's terp artistry is grooved strictly for adult appreciation," pronounced another.[107] Without the youth market, there was no hope for prolonging the dwindling calypso fad.

This corporate and mass mediated Caribbeana shaped the nonhistory against which Holder choreographed his mythic elsewhen. In the days after his Caribbean Calypso Festival opened, *Time* magazine profiled Holder and found him already restlessly looking forward to whatever would come after the calypso craze:

> Although an enterprising publicity agent has stuck him with the label the Calypso King, Holder would like to forget commercial calypso as soon as his show closes next month after playing Philadelphia and Washington. Sitting last week in his dressing room, cluttered with the paintings he works on between shows, he tapped his shaven skull with nervous, spatulate fingers and speculated about what he would do next. In the fall he will present a concert show on Broadway starring himself and his wife and including no calypso at all. "Dancing," he says in his soft West Indian voice, "is something I have to do." He intends to continue choreography, perhaps attempt to compose to some U.S. jazz music. "But first I will have to knock all the Hollywood and Broadway out of the dancers' heads."[108]

The image of Holder backstage, rubbing his head with a nervous energy in search of a new form, working against the music, is a fitting one with which to bring this chapter, and this book, to an end. In this scene, I am most struck not by Holder's restless look toward what may come next, or by his frustrated desire for something other than middlebrow culture industries (Hollywood and Broadway) and their aesthetic demands. Rather, what captures my attention is the notable detail of the backstage dressing room "cluttered with the paintings" that he "works on between shows."

While Holder painted a variety of subjects, he was especially drawn to portraiture, and his gallery was made up of still, dark-brown faces against tropical greens and reds and oranges, most often looking directly at the viewer (fig. 28). We can imagine the scene *Time* describes as a dressing room peopled with a multiplicity of singular Trinidadian countenances. Holder's backstage sanctuary, then, is simultaneously crowded yet solitary, bustling yet quiet. Even as he was curating the kinetic energy of the revue on stage, he was also creating this other cast of characters behind the scenes. The canvases that the journalist sees as clutter might also be seen as a barricade against the commercial pressures and distortions of Caribbean

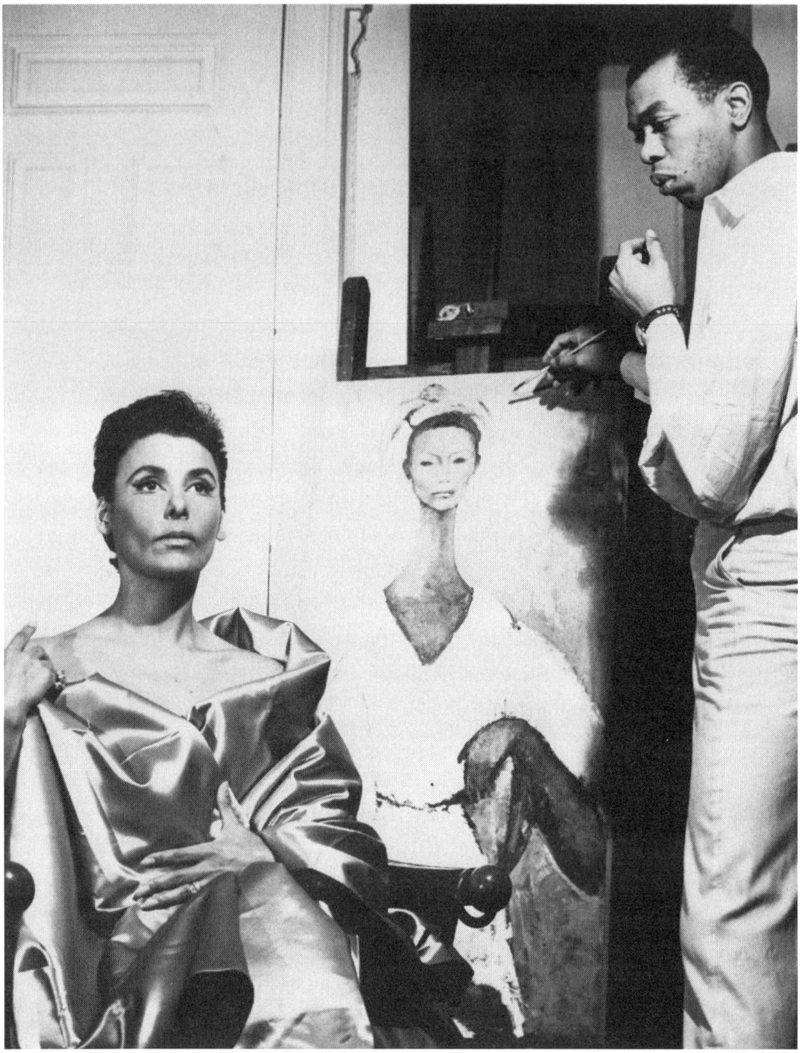

Figure 28. Lena Horne sits for a painting by Geoffrey Holder, 1959. Photo by Bettmann. Getty Images.

types that appear on stage. Or maybe the portraits within which Holder bunkers himself are a stand-in for a different audience before which he can place himself, rather than the overwhelmingly white faces looking at him in the Loew's Metropolitan: an army, maybe, or a pantheon of gods and goddesses. Or, given his later disavowals of the calypso craze, perhaps they are more hauntingly a form given to conscience, a silent jury of his peers.

Nested within the "clutter" of these canvases, Holder creates a time and space backstage that is very different from the one before the Loew's theater stage lights. Like the dancers in *Jamaica* we saw in chapter 4, he builds this world in the spare time he can steal away between shows. This world is an ongoing project, one that he continues working on when he comes off stage, and for decades longer. The paintings are both the "other work" that he would rather be doing while he is caught up in the machinery of the calypso craze and the time stolen (back) from the fad that allows him to do it. Notably, it is at this same time that he was developing *Belé, Banda,* and *Dougla*—another set of ongoing projects that work against the calypso craze and its legacy of commodified Caribbeana. In the backstage of the calypso craze we find these paintings and these dances. This other work stows away within the calypso craze, a pocket of another, authentic time: an elsewhen. Holder stands in for the black fad performer as such, looking searchingly beyond the necessary finitude of popular music, Hollywood, and Broadway. Like the performers we have seen throughout *Stolen Time*—Josephine Premice, Maya Angelou, Carmen de Lavallade, Lovey Gilman, Beryl McBurnie, Lena Horne, Ossie Davis, Lord Invader, Duke of Iron, Macbeth the Great, Duke Ellington, Billy Strayhorn, and others who appeared within the performative system of the calypso craze—Holder resolutely reaches toward an even further horizon, swimming steadfast out of the deep water of fad culture to more creative shores.

CONCLUSION

Don't Stop the Carnival

About a dozen years later, Harry Belafonte revisited the calypso craze in a remarkable performance of protest. On September 29, 1968, Belafonte appeared on CBS's *Smothers Brothers Comedy Hour* and performed the traditional calypso "Don't Stop the Carnival." A celebration of defiance, the song demands that carnival continue in the face of state repression and voices the long history of resistance to governmental attempts to regulate carnival festivities in Trinidad from the nineteenth century on. Belafonte's performance on the broadcast occurred exactly one month after the antiwar protests at the Democratic National Convention in Chicago and their violent suppression, and within months of the still-reverberating political assassinations of Martin Luther King Jr. and Robert F. Kennedy. In this context, Belafonte performed the song in proper calypso fashion. He improvised and updated the lyrics to comment on the topical events of the day:

> Oh Lord I feel so low
> About that town—Chicago.
>
> Humphrey, Muskie, McGovern, Eugene McCarthy
> Split the party, now nobody happy.
> Tell the whole population
> We're having a confrontation.
> Let it be known:
> Freedom's gone and the country is not our own.
>
> Lord, don't stop the Carnival!
> Carnival's an American bacchanal!

Belafonte sang in front of a green screen that was keyed to a montage of raw video footage of dancing Democratic Party delegates, antiwar protesters marching in the street, National Guard forces amassing in riot gear, Chicago police officers brandishing assault rifles and dragging protesters into police vans, and crowds lost in clouds of tear gas. With these images as his backdrop, Belafonte stretched "Don't Stop the Carnival" into a seven-minute medley of calypso craze staples that he and others recorded during the fad, including "Mama Look a Boo Boo," "Jump in the Line," "Marianne," "Sly Mongoose," "Zombie Jamboree," and Belafonte's own 1953 hit "Matilda," which helped launch his recording career. The visual and musical juxtapositions of this performance drew on the calypso tradition and Belafonte's founding disavowal of the calypso craze. In this tangle of leftist and antiracist politics, middlebrow television programming, and song, Belafonte direct wired the subterranean currents that have always connected carnival to political uprising; surfaced the fad's deep calypso tradition of improvised lyrics, topical commentary, and oppositional ethos; and reminded audiences that *this* and *that* are always shifting and unstable descriptors.

In the end, though, nobody in the United States saw this performance of protest. CBS censors cut it from the show and it never aired (adding insult to injury, fuming executives at CBS sold the segment's time to the Republican Party, which broadcast a five-minute campaign commercial for Richard Nixon). Belafonte's performance went unseen until portions of it ran on an E! Entertainment network documentary in 1993. It was later released on DVD in 2008 (*Smother Brothers Comedy Hour Best of Season 3* box set DVD) and is currently viewable on YouTube.[1] Yet though this performance was not broadcast, it would be a mistake to describe it as unsuccessful. In a 1930 article, philosopher W. E. B. Du Bois described two ways to measure the success of a protest: "first for its effect on your political enemies, and secondly, for its effect upon yourself."[2] He elaborated on this second purpose, suggesting that "even if the offending politician does not hear of your opposition; does not feel your lone vote, you know and you feel, and it is an awful thing to have to be ashamed of one's self."[3] For Du Bois, protest emerges in this formulation as an ontological question as much as a political one. Its purpose, he explains, is twofold: to protest not only against someone but also primarily for oneself, to see oneself in the first person rather than the third. In this sense, I understand Du Bois's formulation as part of the ongoing response to the question he identified in *The Souls of Black Folk* (1903) faced by people of color in the United States: "how does it feel to be a problem?"[4] This question is not only one of affect—how does it *feel*—but also of ontology—*to be* a problem. And what is black fad performance if not a problem: for blackness, for whiteness, for history, for performance? Belafonte's topical rendition of "Don't Stop the Carnival" and its nonbroadcast is as much a personal protest—protest for himself—as it is against the US government. It announces the drive to imagine ever-new acts of authentic emancipation and the imperative to keep the carnival and masquerade going. In its singing and its silencing, the song discloses a being-in-protest and a protest-in-being.

This unseen and unheard performance comments on and continues the stolen time or time stolen (back) that I have described in this book. In the black calypso craze, it was not Trinidadian culture that was stolen, but the culture industry and the temporality of the fad. This stolen time was not an imperial appropriation but a form of exchange across black difference within the idiom of fad culture. *Stolen Time* examined the constrained possibilities of this exchange as it occurred in the short-lived North American fad for calypso. By taking seriously these counterfeit performances of Afro-Caribbean cultures and histories, I argued that the black calypso craze provides insight into the development of diasporic consciousness in the mid-twentieth century as African American performers self-reflexively and circuitously engaged with Caribbean performance traditions. This exchange was not one way; it went in multiple directions, including back to Trinidad. Boscoe and Geoffrey Holder, for example, incorporated movement borrowed from US films into their Trinidadian choreography and learned much from African American dancers traveling through Port of Spain. Trinidadian calypsonians similarly borrowed from US popular music and Tin Pan Alley in developing the calypso tradition in the twentieth century. Even in its inauthenticity, the North American production of ersatz calypso not only took from Trinidadian culture but returned to it as well, further shaping the continual metamorphoses of the calypso ethos.

I located the calypso craze not only in relation to Trinidadian calypso and Latin jazz but also within a deep tradition of popular performance across the color line at a time of de jure and de facto segregation and mass cultural expansion: black fad performance. This longer trajectory of black fad performance in the Jim Crow era places the calypso craze beside similar moments of critical intensity such as the ragtime craze of the 1890s and the Negro vogue of the 1920s. While numerous scholarly studies have excavated those earlier moments of black creativity-in-constraint, the calypso craze has rarely been accorded such sustained attention. I hope to have helped remedy that here. In doing so, I approached the calypso craze not solely as a musical fad or a recording phenomenon, as most accounts have it, but within a larger field of transmediated performance that includes dance, theater, film, television, and nightlife. Taking these performances together, *Stolen Time* proposes a new framework for understanding the cycles of repetition and difference that shaped race, performance, and mass culture during the Jim Crow era.

To describe this framework, I have looked not only to black popular culture's semiotic manipulations, representational politics, and parodic responses but also to the historical-ontological situation that black fad performance discloses: stolen time. I focused on how, by modifying their stance toward the fad and staging a confrontation with its circumscribed temporality, performers could grasp a provisional sense of authenticity through the performance of the inauthentic. Closely studying specific performances, *Stolen Time* identifies a number of strategies—including critical solipsism, radical counterprogramming, mock transnational performance, and the choreographies of elsewhen—developed by performers as they negotiated mass public spheres. Across sound recordings, nightclub acts, film, television broadcasts, musical theater, and modern dance, the fad's relations of performance forged artistic networks and provided creative opportunities to slip away from or transcend the vulgar time of fad culture and the noise of mass mediated race crazes. Through such modifications, strategies, and relationships, performers made the calypso craze their own and claimed a time of creativity and selfhood. Some of these performers or their performances endured beyond the circumscribed time of the fad, staying ahead of the fad cascade or leaving an archival mark. But these exceptions serve to remind us of the much more common unhistoric figures and diffuse acts of black fad performance: the musicians, the dancers, the songs, and the shows not remembered; the scripts not produced in time; the auditions uncast; the gestures abandoned.

Black fad performance developed as a particular temporal formation that depended on the material conditions governing black entertainment and racialized spectatorship in the Jim Crow era. How might we understand black performance in mass culture before and after this period? It would be productive to situate black fad performance as I delimited it here within even deeper genealogies of race, performance, and mass culture, attending to its continuities as well as discontinuities. Provisionally, we might begin by noting that aspects of black fad performance persist in mass culture in the decades following the civil rights movement, but usually without the tight coherence it had as a historical formation during the Jim Crow era. Reggae, disco, and rap, for example, were all at various times described in the language of black fads by entertainment trade magazines in the 1970s and 1980s, and Latin American music crazes continued throughout the twentieth century.[5] In 1980, *Billboard* reported that many viewed rap music as "a passing novelty that will soon go the way of all fads," though producer Russell Simmons dismissed such charges.[6] In an unknowing but attuned echo of Belafonte's untelevised calypso protest, Simmons explained that "people have been telling me [rap's] going to dry up, that it's just a fad, for *10 years* now, and it only keeps getting stronger. And the point is, we didn't push rap on the people, the people pushed it on us. . . . The record business didn't make this music up, they tried to repress it. But rap is the peoples' choice."[7] Indeed, it is possible to see much of hip-hop itself as a musical, technological, and philosophical engagement with and response to the long history of black performance in mass culture and its historical-ontological condition of stolen time that I have detailed throughout this book.

Elements of black fad performance stubbornly continue to appear after the civil rights era, in ways that often manifest as a trace or haunting of segregated performance that endures within the material ideologies of integration. The historical consciousness of Jim Crowism, coherence of media distribution, corporate pursuit of nonwhite consumers, racialized spectatorial relations, and various structures of racial feeling all transformed in the latter half of the twentieth century in ways that altered the historical formation of black fad performance, rendering it less cohesive than it previously appeared but still obdurately adhesive. The ontological conditions of death-bound subjectivity and stolen time that characterize black fad performance found expression in new cultural forms and social formations in the decades following the US civil rights movement and worldwide decolonization movements. Nevertheless, the strategies developed in response to black fad performance also persist, remaining available to black performers as resources now as then to be adopted and adapted in their encounters with mass culture.

Near the end of his censored performance on the *Smothers Brothers Comedy Hour*, Belafonte interrupted his calypso medley with a refusal that musically announced the outmodedness of black fad performance as a coherent cultural formation for the post–civil rights movement era. One of his earliest and best-known hits was "Matilda," a calypso about a man whose unfaithful girlfriend takes all his money and leaves Trinidad for Venezuela. But instead of sounding its familiar notes in his medley, Belafonte withheld "Matilda" from performance and delivered an improvised explanation of its absence:

I can't even sing "Matilda."
I can't even sing "Matilda."
I tell you why I can't sing "Matilda":
These ain't the times to sing "Matilda."
Times like these would have almost killed her.
If she comes here, they'll probably jail her.
I keep Matilda down in Venezuela.

Lord, don't stop the Carnival!
Carnival is an American bacchanal!
People should not live under the big gun.
You know, there's another song we can all hum:

Because we shall overcome.
(Lord, Don't Stop the Carnival!)
We shall overcome.
(Lord, Don't Stop the Carnival!)

Belafonte invokes "Matilda" in order to mark its absence from the performance. The refusal to sing this song (and in doing so, figuratively protect Matilda from the police) rhetorically and musically observes a substitution of the politics of charismatic representation with a politics of organic democracy as Belafonte overlays the sound of black fad performance with "We Shall Overcome," the anthem of the civil rights movement and a song then-recently sung by tens of thousands of mourners at the funeral for Martin Luther King Jr. This nonperformance of "Matilda" displaces the displacements of the calypso craze with a call for emancipation that was distorted by the fad. In his refusal to sing "Matilda," he did not mark the end of the calypso craze—that ended a decade earlier, shortly after it began. Rather, he cleared space within the calypso program for a sound and a song that is different from that of black fad performance. As he explains, "these ain't the times" to sing such songs.

But rather than understand it as a corrective reproach to the performances of the calypso craze, this characteristically Belafontian disavowal allows us to recognize that an emancipatory aesthetics and historical consciousness were always present in black fad performance's avowals of inauthenticity and stolen time. Even as he sings the melody of "We Shall Overcome," the band responds in counterpoint with the Caribbean sound and lyrics of "Don't Stop the Carnival" and other calypso craze standards. Fad song and protest song sound through each other across the musical line and Belafonte's voice, which is simultaneously singular and collective. This banned performance and being-in-protest proclaims the Belafonte imperative: to press the difference between *this* and *that* while simultaneously questioning the distinction; to modify one's stance toward the fad and in doing so modify the fad itself; to hear in one's ownmost voice a chorus; to not stop the carnival.

NOTES

INTRODUCTION

1. For the definitive scholarly account of Belafonte's life and career, including his ambivalent role in the calypso craze and his long engagement with radical politics, see Judith E. Smith, *Becoming Belafonte: Black Artist, Public Radical* (Austin: University of Texas Press, 2014).
2. "Belafonte Says Calypso Craze Is 'Synthetic,'" *St. Petersburg Times*, June 20, 1957, 34.
3. Harry Belafonte, as told to Dick Kleiner, "Belafonte Says, 'I Want No Part of Calypso Craze,'" *Warsaw* (IN) *Times-Union*, February 26, 1957, 5.
4. See, for example, the fanzine *Calypso!* (New York: Modern Music Publications, 1957), 30, and "That Fad from Trinidad," *Ebony*, June 1, 1957, 48.
5. Belafonte, "Belafonte Says, 'I Want No Part of Calypso Craze,'" 5.
6. Michael S. Eldridge, "Bop Girl Goes Calypso: Containing Race and Youth Culture in Cold War America," in *Music, Memory, Resistance: Calypso and the Caribbean Literary Imagination*, ed. Sandra Pouchet Paquet, Patricia J. Saunders, and Stephen Stuempfle (Kingston and Miami: Ian Randle, 2007), 271; emphasis in original.
7. Cf. Hortense Spillers, "Interstices: A Small Drama of Words," in *Black, White, and in Color: Essays in American Literature and Culture* (Chicago: University of Chicago Press, 2003), 165, and Martin Heidegger, *Being and Time*, trans. Joan Stambaugh (Albany: State University of New York Press, 2010), 328. See also Catherine Malabou, *The Heidegger Change: On the Fantastic in Philosophy*, trans. Peter Skafish (Albany: State University of New York Press, 2011).
8. J. L. Austin, *Sense and Sensibilia*, ed. G. J. Warnock (Oxford: Clarendon Press, 1962), 71.
9. Austin, *Sense and Sensibilia*, 76; all emphasis in original. According to Stanley Cavell, Austin raised pigs as a hobby; see Cavell's foreword to Shoshana Felman's *The Scandal of the Speaking Body: Don Juan with J. L. Austin, or Seduction in Two Languages* (Stanford, CA: Stanford University Press, 2002), xii.
10. Austin, *Sense and Sensibilia*, 70; emphasis in original.
11. Austin, *Sense and Sensibilia*, 70; emphasis in original.
12. Ann Elliot, "Real, Real Calypso: How It Is Sung and Danced in Trinidad (Part 1)," *Dance Magazine*, July 1957, 30–33, 90–93.
13. Austin, *Sense and Sensibilia*, 76; emphasis in original.
14. Donald Hill, *Calypso Callaloo: Early Carnival Music in Trinidad* (Gainesville: Univer-

sity Press of Florida, 1993); Ray Funk and Michael Eldridge, *Calypso Craze* (Hamburg, Germany: Bear Family Productions, 2014). See also Ray Funk and Donald R. Hill, "'Will Calypso Doom Rock'n'Roll?' The U.S. Calypso Craze of 1957," in *Trinidad Carnival: The Cultural Politics of a Transnational Festival*, ed. Garth L. Green and Philip W. Scher (Bloomington: Indiana University Press, 2007), 178–97.

15. See, among others, *Caribbean Quarterly* 4 (1956), special issue on the Carnival of Trinidad; *TDR: The Drama Review* 42 (1998), special issue on Trinidad and Tobago Carnival; John Cowley, *Carnival, Canboulay, and Calypso: Traditions in the Making* (Cambridge: Cambridge University Press, 1996); Charles S. Espinet and Harry Pitts, *Land of Calypso: The Origin and Development of Trinidad's Folk Song* (Port of Spain, Trinidad: Guardian Commercial Printery, 1944); Garth L. Green and Philip W. Scher, eds., *Trinidad Carnival: The Cultural Politics of a Transnational Festival* (Bloomington: Indiana University Press, 2007); Jocelyne Guilbault, *Governing Sound: The Cultural Politics of Trinidad's Carnival Musics* (Chicago: University of Chicago Press, 2007); Errol Hill, *The Trinidad Carnival: Mandate for a National Theatre* (Austin: University of Texas Press, 1972); Raphael de Leon, *Calypso from France to Trinidad: 800 Years of History* (Port of Spain, Trinidad: Imprint Books, 1988); Hollis Liverpool, *Kaiso and Society* (Charlotte Amalie, Saint Thomas: Virgin Islands Commission on Youth, 1986); Peter Manuel, with Kenneth Bilby and Michael Largey, *Caribbean Currents: Caribbean Music from Rumba to Reggae* (Philadelphia: Temple University Press, 1995), 183–211; Sandra Pouchet Paquet, Patricia J. Saunders, and Stephen Stuempfle, eds., *Music, Memory, Resistance: Calypso and the Caribbean Literary Tradition* (Kingston and Miami: Ian Randle, 2007); Louis Regis, *The Political Calypso: True Opposition in Trinidad and Tobago, 1962–1987* (Kingston: Press University of the West Indies; Gainesville: University Press of Florida, 1999); Gordon Rohlehr, *Calypso and Society in Pre-Independence Trinidad* (Port of Spain, Trinidad: Gordon Rohlehr, 1990) and *A Scuffling of Islands: Essays on Calypso* (San Juan, Trinidad: Lexicon Trinidad, 2004); Philip W. Scher, *Carnival and the Formation of a Caribbean Transnation* (Gainesville: University Press of Florida, 2003); and Keith Q. Warner, *Kaiso! The Trinidad Calypso: A Study of the Calypso as Oral Literature* (Washington, DC: Three Continents Press, 1982).
16. See Ashley Dawson, *Mongrel Nation: Diasporic Culture and the Making of Postcolonial Britain* (Ann Arbor: University of Michigan Press, 2007); Trevor Phillips and Mike Phillips, *Windrush: The Irresistible Rise of Multi-Racial Britain* (New York: Harper Collins, 2009); Stuart Hall, "Calypso Kings," in *The Auditory Culture Reader*, ed. Michael Bull and Les Back (Oxford: Berg, 2003), 419–25; Kenetta Hammond Perry, *London Is the Place for Me* (New York: Oxford University Press, 2016); and the 2002 CD *London Is the Place for Me: Trinidadian Calypso in London, 1950–1956* (Honest John Records), which contains twenty recorded calypsos from and about this first wave of migration.
17. Rohlehr, *Scuffling of Islands*, 265.
18. C. L. R. James, "The Mighty Sparrow," in *The Future in the Present: Selected Writings* (London: Allison and Busby), 199. See also James, "Artist in the Caribbean," in *Future in the Present*, 183–90.
19. See Edward Kamau Brathwaite, *A History of the Voice: The Development of Nation Language in Anglophone Caribbean Poetry* (London: New Beacon Books, 1984); Derek Walcott, "What the Twilight Says: An Overture," in *Dream on Monkey Mountain and Other Plays* (New York: Farrar, Straus, and Giroux, 1970), 3–40; Gordon Rohlehr, "The Problem of the Problem of Form: The Idea of an Aesthetic Continuum and

Aesthetic Code-Switching in West Indian Literature," *Caribbean Quarterly* 31 (1985): 1–52, and *A Scuffling of Islands: Essays on Calypso* (San Juan, Trinidad: Lexicon Trinidad, 2004); and Errol Hill, *The Trinidad Carnival: Mandate for a National Theatre* (Austin: University of Texas Press, 1972).

20. Stephanie Leigh Batiste, *Darkening Mirrors: Imperial Representation in Depression-Era African American Performance* (Durham, NC: Duke University Press, 2011), 5.

21. Nadia Ellis, *Territories of the Soul: Queered Belonging in the Black Diaspora* (Durham, NC: Duke University Press, 2015), 6; Brent Hayes Edwards, *The Practice of Diaspora: Literature, Translation, and the Rise of Black Internationalism* (Cambridge, MA: Harvard University Press, 2003), 14.

22. Ellis, *Territories of the Soul,* 6, emphasis in original; Edwards, *Practice of Diaspora,* 14.

23. The progress of the case was carefully tracked across the entertainment industry press and the African American press. See Dolores Calvin, "Who Wrote Rum and Coca Cola Is Newest Gag," *Chicago Defender,* March 3, 1945, 13; E. B Rea, "Encores and Echoes," *Baltimore Afro-American,* March 10, 1945, 8; Carolyn Dixon, "Files Suit Over 'Rum and Coca Cola,'" *New York Amsterdam News,* March 10, 1945, 11A; "'Rum' Writers and Feist Sued by Calypso Pub in Infringement Action" *Variety,* March 14, 1945, 40; "Maurice Baron Sues Feist over 'Rum and Coke,'" *Billboard,* March 17, 1945, 12; "Surprise Charge Latest for 'Rum and Coca Cola,'" *Chicago Defender,* March 24, 1945, 17; Ramona Lowe, "Rum and Coke Author Sings Woes of Trinidad after Invasion by GIs," *Chicago Defender,* March 31, 1945, 11; "Grant Awarded Title to 'Rum,'" *Baltimore Afro-American,* July 28, 1945, 8; "Judge Clears Up Plagiarism Point; Holds Tune Must Be All New for Lifting Claim," *Billboard,* October 6, 1945, 16; "Feist and Writers of 'Rum & Coke' Ask That 2 Suits Be Dismissed," *Variety,* October 10, 1945, 44; "'Rum and Coke' in Two Legal Actions," *Billboard,* November 2, 1946, 15; "Rum and Coke Decish Pending," *Billboard,* December 21, 1946, 14; "Novel Folk-Song (Calypso) Defense in $150,000 'Rum and Coca-Cola' Suit," *Variety,* December 25, 1946, 35–36; "No More Rum and Cola," *New York Times,* February 28, 1947, 12; "Feist, Writers of 'Rum and Coke' Lose Infringement Rap in N.Y.," *Variety,* March 5, 1947, 45; "Court Enjoins 'Rum & Coke' Writers & Pub," *Billboard,* March 8, 1947, 4, 15; "'Rum and Coca Cola' Settled: Song Goes to Famed Calypso Singer," *Chicago Defender,* April 12, 1947, 22; "'Rum' Defendants Get Stay on Inj," *Variety,* April 16, 1947, 37; "'Rum & Coke' Writers, Feist, Face Revived Action Over Melody," *Variety,* June 4, 1947, 39; "Feist, Writers Face Second Suit; 'Rum' Ruling Is Reserved," *Billboard,* November 1, 1947, 37; "'Rum & Coke' in 2d Trial over Melody," *Variety,* November 19, 1947, 42; "Feist Loses 2d Appeal of 'Rum' Verdict in N.Y.," *Variety,* December 24, 1947, 42; "Novel Legal Ruling May Cut 'Rum' Damages Down to a Nominal $100," *Variety,* May 26, 1948, 40, 42; "Khan's Counsel, Ellis, Seeks 'Coke' Reversal," *Variety,* June 2, 1948, 43; "Injunction vs. Feist Writers on 'Rum,'" *Variety,* July 14, 1948, 42; "Feist, Abeles Lose Key Ground as Judge Reverses 'Rum' Acc'tg," *Billboard,* July 24, 1948, 17; "'Rum' Suit Nod Stayed by N.Y. Judge Pending Circuit Court Appeal," *Variety,* August 11, 1948, 39; "'Rum, Coca-Cola' Infringe Defense Get Stay in Suit," *Billboard,* August 14, 1948, 39; "'Rum and Coca-Cola' Defenders Obtain 2-Mo. Court Delay," *Billboard,* September 4, 1948, 36; "Deny Motion to Reopen 'Rum' Infringement Case," *Variety,* October 20, 1948, 42; "U.S. Court Spikes 'Rum & Coca-Cola' Suit's Reopening," *Billboard,* October 23, 1948, 22; "'Rum and Coke' Suit—Round 99," *Billboard,* April 2, 1949, 50; "'Rum and Coca Cola' Profits Awarded to Lord Invader after Five Years in Court," *Baltimore Afro-American,* March 11, 1950, 8. See also the exhaustive recounting of the trial on Kevin Burke's

website, "The Rum and Coca-Cola Reader," http://www.rumandcocacolareader.com/RumAndCocaCola/main.html; accessed March 18, 2016.

24. Ramona Lowe, "Rum and Coke Author Sings Woes of Trinidad after Invasion by GIs," *Chicago Defender*, March 31, 1945, 11.
25. E. B. Rea, "Encores and Echoes," *Baltimore Afro-American*, March 10, 1945, 8.
26. "Novel Folk-Song (Calypso) Defense in $150,000 'Rum and Coca-Cola' Suit," *Variety*, December 25, 1946, 35–36.
27. Langston Hughes, "The Whites Make the Money but Negroes Are Still Funny," *Chicago Defender*, July 9, 1955, 9.
28. "Calypso Here I Come—Maybe," *Variety*, January 23, 1957, 48.
29. Edward Kamau Brathwaite, "World Order Models—A Caribbean Perspective," *Caribbean Quarterly* 31 (1985): 62–63.
30. Ellis, *Territories of the Soul*, 80.
31. Sigmund Freud, "Fetishism," in *The Complete Psychological Works of Sigmund Freud*, vol. 21, trans. James Strachey (London: Hogarth and the Institute of Psychoanalysis), 147–57.
32. For more on calypso as feeling, see Fred Moten, "The New International of Rhythmic Feeling(s)," in *Sonic Interventions*, ed. Sylvia Mieszkowski, Joy Smith, and Marijke de Valck (Amsterdam: Rodopi, 2007), 31–56; and Shannon Dudley, "Judging 'By the Beat': Calypso versus Soca," *Ethnomusicology* 40 (1996): 269–98.
33. Espinet and Pitts, *Land of Calypso*, 15.
34. Brathwaite, *History of the Voice*, 5.
35. See George Lamming, "The Legacy of Eric Williams," *Callaloo* 20 (1997): 731–36.
36. See Espinet and Pitts, *Land of Calypso*, 39–49; Daniel Crowley, "Toward a Definition of Calypso (Part 1)," *Ethnomusicology* 3 (1959): 59–60; and Hill, *Calypso Callaloo*, 283n1. For context about the stakes of calypso's African, indigenous, or creole origins in the project of cultural nationalism, see Harvey R. Neptune, *Caliban and the Yankees: Trinidad and the United States Occupation* (Chapel Hill: University of North Carolina Press, 2007), 129–57.
37. Espinet and Pitts, *Land of Calypso*, 48.
38. Gordon Rohlehr, "The Problem of the Problem of Form: The Idea of an Aesthetic Continuum and Aesthetic Code-Switching in West Indian Literature," *Caribbean Quarterly* 31 (1985).
39. Funk and Eldridge, *Calypso Craze*, 28.
40. "N.Y. Palladium Goes Terping A La Trinidad," *Variety*, February 6, 1957, 56.
41. Arnold Shaw, "Puerto Rico, Virgin Islands Use Native Bands, Singers but Look to U.S. Talent," *Variety*, September 12, 1951, 43.
42. "Voodoo," *Melody Maker*, May 8, 1954, 2.
43. Dick Joseph, "A Work on the Lam: 1950 Points to Peak Tourism," *Variety*, January 4, 1950, 53.
44. "Caribbean Circuit in the Making; Dominicans Go After Yanqui Show Biz," *Variety*, March 30, 1955, 56.
45. Robert Reinhart, "Caribe's Coconut Circuit," *Variety*, May 28, 1958, 63.
46. Paul Pimsleur, "Caribbean Islands' Concert 'Boomlet,'" *Variety*, August 22, 1956, 60; Joe Cohen, "Hoisted by Bootstraps, Puerto Rico Lively All Over, Including Cafes," *Variety*, February 2, 1955, 1, 67.
47. Morton defined this term in his 1938 Library of Congress recordings with Alan Lomax to describe the influence of Afro-Cuban and Latin American rhythms, sounds, and instruments in the development of jazz; see Morton, *The Complete Library of*

Congress Recordings (Rounder Records, 2005). See also John Storm Roberts, *The Latin Tinge: The Impact of Latin American Music on the United States*, 2nd ed. (New York: Oxford University Press, 1999).

48. Martin Esslin, *The Field of Drama: How the Signs of Drama Create Meaning on Stage and Screen* (New York: Methuen, 1987), 10.
49. Alexandra Vazquez, *Listening in Detail: Performances of Cuban Music* (Durham, NC: Duke University Press, 2013), 68.
50. Vazquez, *Listening in Detail*, 73.
51. Vazquez, 68.
52. Fred Moten, *In the Break: The Aesthetics of the Black Radical Tradition* (Minneapolis: University of Minnesota Press, 2003), 172–73.
53. For histories of postwar cool, see Joel Dinerstein, *The Origins of Cool in Postwar America* (Chicago: University of Chicago Press, 2017), and Lewis MacAdams, *Birth of the Cool: Beat, Bebop, and the American Avant-Garde* (New York: Free Press, 2001).
54. Farah Jasmine Griffin, *Harlem Nocturne: Women Artists and Progressive Politics during World War II* (New York: Basic Civitas, 2013); Lawrence P. Jackson, *The Indignant Generation: A Narrative History of African American Writers and Critics, 1934–1960* (Princeton, NJ: Princeton University Press, 2011); Mary Helen Washington, *The Other Blacklist: The African American Literary and Cultural Left of the 1950s* (New York: Columbia University Press, 2014); and William J. Maxwell, *F. B. Eyes: How J. Edgar Hoover's Ghostreaders Framed African American Literature* (Princeton, NJ: Princeton University Press, 2015).
55. Christina Klein, *Cold War Orientalism: Asia in the Middlebrow Imagination, 1945–1961* (Berkeley: University of California Press, 2003); Anna McCarthy, *The Citizen Machine: Governing by Television in 1950s America* (New York: New Press, 2010).
56. Hazel Rowley, *Richard Wright: The Life and Times* (Chicago: University of Chicago Press, 2008), 286–91. See also Michel Fabre, *The Unfinished Quest of Richard Wright* (New York: William Morrow, 1973), 178–79, 254–55.
57. Janice Radway, *A Feeling for Books: The Book-of-the-Month Club, Literary Taste, and Middle-Class Desire* (Chapel Hill: University of North Carolina Press, 1997), 315.
58. Harry Belafonte, with Michael Shnayerson, *My Song: A Memoir* (New York: Knopf, 2011), 146; ellipsis and emphasis in original. This liberal attitude toward the easy consumption of race was lampooned several years later by folk singer Phil Ochs in his mordant "Love Me, I'm a Liberal": "I love Harry and Sidney and Sammy / Hope every colored boy becomes a star."
59. Belafonte, *My Song*, 146; emphasis in original.
60. "Hot Trend: Trinidado Tunes," *Variety*, December 26, 1956, 1. See also Abel Green, "Tin Pan Alley on a Turntable," *Variety*, January 9, 1957, 242.
61. Lisa McGill, *Constructing Black Selves: Caribbean American Narratives and the Second Generation* (New York: New York University Press, 2005), 33.
62. James Baldwin, "Unnameable Objects, Unspeakable Crimes," BlackState.com, http://www.blackstate.com/baldwin1.html, accessed May 7, 2016.
63. An especially vivid example of such sublimated interracial sexual erotics is on display in an episode of *The Nat King Cole Show* with special guest Harry Belafonte that aired August 6, 1957. In a medley at the center of the broadcast, the two men reenact Belafonte's career arc from his time in the US Navy to his study of theater with Erwin Piscator to his first national success in the calypso craze. Throughout the medley, Belafonte poses with a number of prominently featured phallic props, including a mop and a rolled-up diploma. These props draw attention to the sexual-

ized presentation of black masculinity, homoeroticism (at one point, Belafonte admonishes Cole not to "fondle my mop"), and their sublimation and displacement through humor, song, and middlebrow cultural forms.

64. McGill, *Constructing Black Selves*, 49.
65. Clement Greenberg, "Avant-Garde and Kitsch," *Partisan Review* 6 (Fall 1939): 39.
66. Greenberg, "Avant-Garde and Kitsch," 40.
67. Tavia Nyong'o, "Racial Kitsch and Black Performance," *Yale Journal of Criticism* 15 (2002): 383.
68. See Noliwe M. Rooks, *Ladies' Pages: African American Women's Magazines and the Culture That Made Them* (New Brunswick, NJ: Rutgers University Press, 2004), 113–39.
69. Belinda Edmondson, *Caribbean Middlebrow: Leisure Culture and the Middle Class* (Ithaca, NY: Cornell University Press, 2009), 23.
70. Edmondson, *Caribbean Middlebrow*, 8.
71. Batiste, *Darkening Mirrors*, xi.
72. Batiste, xii.
73. Batiste, xv.
74. Frantz Fanon, *Black Skin, White Masks*, trans. Charles Lam Markmann (New York: Grove, 1967), 111–12.
75. Fanon, *Black Skin, White Masks*, 111.
76. Fanon, 8.
77. See Ashley Dawson's reading of *The Lonely Londoners* as a calypso novel in *Mongrel Nation*, 27–48, as well as Jennifer Rahim, "(Not) Knowing the Difference: Calypso Overseas and the Sound of Belonging in Selected Narratives of Migration," in *Music, Memory, and Resistance: Calypso and the Caribbean Literary Imagination*, ed. Sandra Pouchet Paquet, Patricia J. Saunders, and Stephen Stuempfle (Kingston and Miami: Ian Randle, 2007), 283–305.
78. Samuel Selvon, *The Lonely Londoners* (New York: St. Martin's Press, 1956), 95, 94.
79. Selvon, *Lonely Londoners*, 96.
80. See, among others, "On Being 'White' . . . and Other Lies" and "An Open Letter to My Sister, Angela Y. Davis," in James Baldwin, *The Cross of Redemption: Uncollected Writings*, ed. Randall Kenan (New York: Vintage, 2011), 166–70, 254–60, and "Stranger in the Village" in Baldwin, *Collected Essays*, ed. Toni Morrison (New York: Library of America, 1998), 117–29.
81. Selvon, *Lonely Londoners*, 96.
82. Like Fanon, Selvon goes on to imagine blackness as a kind of lamination, a personified entity that covers his body but is distinct from him, though his response to this epidermalization (to use Fanon's word) is again pitched in a calypso tone of playful curiosity, irony, and absurdity. Selvon, *Lonely Londoners*, 97–98.

CHAPTER 1

1. R. W. Thompson, "The Mirror Up to Nature," *Indianapolis Freeman*, December 19, 1896, 5. For a different discussion of Thompson's article, see David Krasner, *Resistance, Parody, and Double Consciousness in African-American Theater, 1895–1910* (New York: St. Martin's Press, 1997), 21–22.
2. On the fad as a sign of temporality and the limits of historicism, see Jennifer L. Fleissner, *Women, Compulsion, Modernity: The Moment of American Naturalism* (Chicago: University of Chicago Press, 2004), 138.
3. Emory Bogardus, *Fundamentals of Social Psychology* (New York: Century, 1924), 152,

154. See also Bogardus, "Social Psychology of Fads," *Journal of Applied Sociology* 8 (1924): 239–43.

4. Bogardus, *Fundamentals of Social Psychology*, 153.
5. Bogardus, 161.
6. Bogardus, 161.
7. Bogardus, 161.
8. James A. Snead, "On Repetition in Black Culture," *Black American Literature Forum* 15 (1981): 149.
9. Joel Best, *Flavor of the Month: Why Smart People Fall for Fads* (Berkeley: University of California Press, 2006), 80.
10. Snead, "On Repetition in Black Culture," 146.
11. This argument builds on discussions in the field of performance studies about the ontology of performance and the relationship between performance's disappearance (theorized most elegantly by Peggy Phelan as "performance's being . . . becomes itself through disappearance") and its persistence (elaborated most extensively by Rebecca Schneider's inquiry into how performance can be the very "*act* of remaining and a means of re-appearance"). I begin from the assumption that there is not an ontology of performance but ontologies of performances that must be considered in their particularity. While Phelan developed her theory about performance's disappearance within a psychoanalytic register, she reminds us that it was also intended to be a critique of commodity culture and performance's ability to resist capital's quick incorporation of everything before it. Consequently, this influential theory does not consider the ontology of the performances of commodity culture itself. See Peggy Phelan, *Unmarked: The Politics of Performance* (New York: Routledge, 1993), 146; "Performance, Live Culture, and Things of the Heart," interview with Peggy Phelan, *Journal of Visual Culture* 2 (2003): 291–302; Rebecca Schneider, *Performing Remains: Art and War in Times of Theatrical Reenactment* (New York: Routledge, 2011), 101.
12. Alain Locke, *The Negro and His Music* (Port Washington, NY: Kenikat Press, 1936), 59.
13. See Thomas Riis, *Just before Jazz: Black Musical Theater in New York, 1890 to 1915* (Washington, DC: Smithsonian Institution Press, 1989), 38; Paul Oliver, *Songsters and Saints: Vocal Traditions on Race Records* (Cambridge: Cambridge University Press, 1984), 49; Karen Sotiropoulos, *Staging Race: Black Performers in Turn of the Century America* (Cambridge, MA: Harvard University Press, 2008), 90; and James Dorman, "Shaping the Popular Image of Post-Reconstruction American Blacks: The 'Coon Song' Phenomenon of the Gilded Age," *American Quarterly* 40 (1988): 453.
14. For an overview of the dance crazes associated with blackness in the 1890s, see Nadine George Graves, "'Just Like Being at the Zoo': Primitivity and Ragtime Dance," in *Ballroom, Boogie, Shimmy Sham, Shake: A Social and Popular Dance Reader*, ed. Julie Malnig (Champaign: University of Illinois Press, 2009), 55–71. On the cakewalk, see Daphne Brooks, *Bodies in Dissent: Spectacular Performances of Race and Freedom, 1850–1910* (Durham, NC: Duke University Press, 2006), 269–80; Sam Dennison, *Scandalize My Name: Black Imagery in Popular Culture* (New York: Garland, 1982), 352; Jayna Brown, *Babylon Girls: Black Women Performers and the Shaping of the Modern* (Durham, NC: Duke University Press, 2008), 128–55; and Eric Sundquist, *To Wake the Nations: Race in the Making of American Literature* (Cambridge, MA: Belknap Press of Harvard University Press, 1998), 271–322. On the Pas Ma Las, see Marshall

Stearns and Jean Stearns, *Jazz Dance: The Story of American Vernacular Dance* (New York: Da Capo Press, 1968), 100–102. On the Rag, see Lynn Abbott and Doug Seroff, *Out of Sight: The Rise of African American Popular Music, 1889–1895* (Jackson: University Press of Mississippi, 2002), 443–45.

15. Quoted in Brooks, *Bodies in Dissent*, 277.
16. Brooks, *Bodies in Dissent*, 274.
17. Fleissner, *Women, Compulsion, Modernity*, 138.
18. Isidore Witmark and Isaac Goldberg, *From Ragtime to Swingtime: The Story of the House of Witmark* (New York: Lee Furman, 1939), 113–14.
19. As historian Sam Dennison notes, these illustration "became more colorful and more insulting to blacks than at any other time in the history of American popular song." Dennison, *Scandalize My Name*, 354.
20. See Krasner, *Resistance, Parody, and Double Consciousness in African-American Theater*, 33–38, and Sotiropoulos, *Staging Race*, 95–96.
21. Quoted in Abbott and Seroff, *Ragged but Right*, 35.
22. Nathan Irvin Huggins, interview with Eubie Blake, in *Voices from the Harlem Renaissance*, ed. Nathan Irvin Huggins (New York: Oxford University Press, 1976), 339.
23. Langston Hughes, *The Big Sea* (New York: Hill and Wang, 1940), 224.
24. See Samuel Charters and Leonard Kunstadt, *Jazz: A History of the New York Scene* (Garden City, NY: Doubleday, 1962), 85, 91, and Günther Schuller, *Early Jazz: Its Roots and Musical Development* (New York: Oxford University Press, 1968), 226n34.
25. See David Krasner, *A Beautiful Pageant: African American Theater, Drama, and Performance in the Harlem Renaissance, 1910–1927* (New York: Palgrave, 2003), 270–80, and Brown, *Babylon Girls*.
26. William Shack, *Harlem in Montmartre: A Paris Jazz Story between the Great Wars* (Berkeley: University of California Press, 2001), 36. For more on the *vogue nègre*, see Brett Berliner, *Ambivalent Desire: The Exotic Other in Jazz-Age France* (Amherst: University of Massachusetts Press, 2002); Brent Hayes Edwards, *The Practice of Diaspora: Literature, Translation, and the Rise of Black Internationalism* (Cambridge, MA: Harvard University Press, 2004); Michel Fabre, *From Harlem to Paris: Black American Writers in France, 1840–1980* (Urbana: University of Illinois Press, 1991) and "The Harlem Renaissance Abroad: French Critics and the New Negro Literary Movement," in *Temples for Tomorrow: Looking Back at the Harlem Renaissance*, ed. Genevieve Fabre and Michel Feith (Bloomington: Indiana University Press, 2001), 314–32; Tyler Stovall, *Paris Noir: African Americans in the City of Lights* (New York: Houghton Mifflin, 1996); and Barbara L. Tischler, "Europa Jazz in the 1920s and the Musical Discovery of Harlem," in *The Harlem Renaissance: Revaluations*, ed. Armritjit Singh, William S. Shiver, and Stanley Brodwin (New York: Garland, 1989), 185–93.
27. Alain Locke, "The Legacy of the Ancestral Arts," in *The New Negro*, ed. Alain Locke (New York: Albert and Charles Boni, 1925), 262.
28. See Helen Armstead Johnson, "*Shuffle Along*: Keynote of the Harlem Renaissance," *Speech Journal* 8 (1970): 25–29. Reprinted in *The Theater of Black Americans: A Collection of Critical Essays*, ed. Errol Hill (New York: Applause, 1980), 126–35.
29. For more on the Caribbean presence in the ragtime craze, see Louis Chude-Sokei, *The Last "Darky": Bert Williams, Black-on-Black Minstrelsy, and the African Diaspora* (Durham, NC: Duke University Press, 2006).
30. Nightclub review, *Variety*, June 5, 1957, 57; "Basie-Vaughan's Boff Biz Atop Posh Waldorf; also 'Mixed' Dancing," *Variety*, June 19, 1957, 1.

31. George Rosen, "Ten Frantic Years of Television," *Variety*, January 4, 1956, 146, 145–48.
32. "Will It Soon Be TV Pan Alley?" *Variety*, September 28, 1955, 55.
33. Ray Funk and Donald R. Hill, "'Will Calypso Doom Rock'n'Roll?' The U.S. Calypso Craze of 1957," in *Trinidad Carnival: The Cultural Politics of a Transnational Festival*, ed. Garth L. Green and Philip W. Scher (Bloomington: Indiana University Press, 2007), 185.
34. "Calypso Films to Flood the Market?" *Variety*, March 13, 1957, 1; "Race for Market with Calypso Films," *Variety*, May 1, 1957, 3. For an extensive analysis of *Island in the Sun* and the relationship between racialization and new film technologies, see Michelle Ann Stephens, *Skin Acts: Race, Psychoanalysis, and Black Male Performance* (Durham, NC: Duke University Press, 2014), 111–51.
35. "Boston Gets New Accent as Pat Matthews Teaches 'Em to Talk Trinidado," *Variety*, March 27, 1957, 60.
36. "BBC-TV's 'Calypso News,'" *Variety*, March 20, 1957, 50.
37. "Belafonte as Bert Williams," *Variety*, July 2, 1958, 1.
38. Cf. philosopher Kojin Karatani, who argues that "repetition in history does not signify the recurrence of the same events, for repetition is possible only in terms of *form* (structure) and not *event* (content)." *History and Repetition*, trans. Seiji M. Lippit (New York: Columbia University Press, 2012), 2.
39. E. Patrick Johnson, *Appropriating Blackness: Performance and the Politics of Authenticity* (Durham, NC: Duke University Press, 2003), 2.
40. Sushil Bikhchandani, David Hirshleifer, and Ivo Welch, "A Theory of Fads, Fashion, Custom, and Cultural Change as Informational Cascades," *Journal of Political Economy* 100 (1992): 1016; emphasis in original.
41. Bikhchandani, Hirshleifer, and Welch, "Theory of Fads, Fashion, Custom, and Cultural Change as Informational Cascades," 992.
42. Sushil Bikhchandani, David Hirshleifer, and Ivo Welch, "Learning from the Behavior of Others: Conformity, Fads, and Informational Cascades," *Journal of Economic Perspectives* 12 (1998): 161.
43. Erica Edwards, *Charisma and the Fictions of Black Leadership* (Minneapolis: University of Minnesota Press, 2012).
44. Of course, many performers recognized the inherent instability of the fad cascade and were alert to these conditions that would consign them to obsolescence. Some managed to outlast the temporal conditions of the cascade regime to inhabit new public roles and performance personas. Belafonte, for one, recognized this danger. Writing in his 2011 autobiography, he explains, "Fortunately, I'd kept my repertoire varied, and so managed not to peter out with it. In my act, I never performed more than a handful of calypso songs, even when the trend was at its peak, and my follow up album, *An Evening with Belafonte*, had folk songs from around the world—from 'Hava Nagila' to 'Danny Boy.' I was deeply aware of the consequences of being pigeonholed." Harry Belafonte, with Michael Shnayerson, *My Song: A Memoir* (New York: Knopf, 2011), 159. In some cases, the initial popularity afforded by the fad could be transformed into more long-lasting and continually inventive careers.
45. Bikhchandani, Hirshleifer, and Welch, "Learning from the Behavior of Others," 163.
46. "Disk Industry Growing Pains," *Variety*, September 7, 1955, 49, 56.
47. "Disk Industry Growing Pains," 49, 56.
48. "Disks' Supermarket Gravy," *Variety*, September 14, 1955, 49.

49. "Victor Sprees on Belafonte Singles," *Variety*, February 6, 1957, 51.
50. Merchandiser display ad by RCA Victor, *Variety*, February 13, 1957, 81. See also coverage of this promotion in "Victor Maps Belafonte Disc Drive," *Washington Afro-American*, February 10, 1957, 6.
51. Bikhchandani, Hirshleifer, and Welch, "Theory of Fads, Fashion, Custom, and Cultural Change as Informational Cascades," 1015.
52. Bikhchandani, Hirshleifer, and Welch, "Theory of Fads, Fashion, Custom, and Cultural Change as Informational Cascades," 1015.
53. Bikhchandani, Hirshleifer, and Welch, "Learning from the Behavior of Others," 157–58; emphasis in original.
54. "Calypso Is Stone Cold Dead," *Variety*, May 22, 1957, 41, 48; "Calypso's Slip Is Showing—In NY," *Variety*, June 19, 1957, 2.
55. "Natural Death or Murder?" *Variety*, June 12, 1957, 61.
56. "Calypso's Slip Is Showing—In NY," *Variety*, June 19, 1957, 2.
57. Abdul R. JanMohamed, *The Death-Bound-Subject: Richard Wright's Archaeology of Death* (Durham, NC: Duke University Press, 2005), 2.
58. JanMohamed, *The Death-Bound-Subject*, 2, 6; emphasis in original.
59. Bogardus, *Fundamentals of Social Psychology*, 158.
60. See James Weldon Johnson, *Black Manhattan* (New York: Atheneum, 1977 [1930]), 126–27; Sotiropoulos, *Staging Race*, 42–44, and Krasner, *Resistance, Parody, and Double Consciousness in African-American Theater*, 49–50.
61. Nathan Huggins, *Harlem Renaissance* (New York: Oxford University Press, 1971), 260.
62. Geoffrey Holder, "The Awful Afro Trend," *Show* (March 1962): 95.
63. Thompson, "The Mirror Up to Nature," 5.
64. See, for example, Friedrich Nietzsche, *The Gay Science: With a Prelude in Rhymes and an Appendix of Songs*, trans. Walter Kaufman (New York: Vintage 1974), 273–74; *The Will to Power*, trans. Walter Kaufman and R. J. Hollingdale (New York: Vintage 1968), 544–50; and *Thus Spoke Zarathustra: A Book for Everyone and No One*, trans. R. J. Hollingdale (New York: Penguin, 1961), 178–80, from which the epigraph to this section is taken.
65. Bernd Magnus, *Nietzsche's Existential Imperative* (Bloomington: Indiana University Press, 1978), 71.
66. Robert Gooding-Williams, "Foreword: Supposing Nietzsche to Be Black—What Then?," in *Critical Affinities: Nietzsche and African American Thought*, ed. Jacqueline Scott and A. Todd Franklin (Albany: State University of New York Press, 2006), vii–xviii. See also Snead, "On Repetition in Black Culture," 146, 153n11.
67. "A new collection of fashionable gowns enhance[s] her lithe figure and general timing is sharper with added comedy bits for additional impact." Nightclub review, *Variety*, April 17, 1957, 53.
68. *Variety* on *Caribe*: "She fools around with the island material but seems to prefer to transfer the tempo to such unlikely material as 'The Man I Love' and 'Taking a Chance on Love.'" Nightclub review, *Variety*, June 26, 1957, 44.
69. "Josephine Premice Set for Broadway Musical," *Jet*, November 20, 1952, 58. For more on Premice's biography, see the family memoir written by her daughter, Susan Fales-Hill, *Always Wear Joy: My Mother Bold and Beautiful* (New York: Harper Collins, 2003).
70. Nightclub review, *Variety*, November 14, 1956, 68.
71. Liner notes, *Caribe* (Verve 1957).

72. See Cynthia Mahabir, "The Rise of Calypso Feminism: Gender and Musical Politics in the Calypso," *Popular Music* 20 (2001): 409–30, and Rudolph Ottley, *Women in Calypso*, Part 1 (Arima, Trinidad: Rudolph Ottley, 1992), and Part 2 (Arima, Trinidad: Rudolph Ottley, 2007).
73. Gordon Rohlehr, *Calypso and Society in Pre-Independence Trinidad* (Port of Spain, Trinidad: Gordon Rohlehr, 1990), 412.
74. Harvey R. Neptune, *Caliban and the Yankees: Trinidad and the Unites States Occupation* (Philadelphia: Temple University Press, 2007), 122.
75. Nightclub review, *Variety*, November 14, 1956, 68.
76. The omitted verse reads:

    The matron hit on an idea
    That she could find the watch around somewhere.
    She said she had an incentive,
    She could find the watch if given privilege
    To divest Melda entirely
    And search her as if she was crazy.
    The search was such, so they decide
    That the matron turned Melda's inside outside
    I'm hearing . . . [chorus]

77. Micol Seigel, *Uneven Encounters: Making Race and Nation in Brazil and the United States* (Durham, NC: Duke University Press, 2009), 136–78.
78. Seigel, *Uneven Encounters*, 157.
79. Susan Fales-Hill, quoted in Norman Darwen, review of *Caribe* and *Calypso*, *Blues and Rhythm Magazine* (January 2013), at http://www.freshsoundrecords.com/josephine-premice-albums/5731-caribe-sings-calypso-2-lps-on-1-cd.html, accessed June 30, 2017.

CHAPTER 2

1. See Ray Funk and Michael Eldridge, *Calypso Craze* (Hamburg, Germany: Bear Family Productions, 2014), 19.
2. "Mid-Summer Calypso Concert, Dance, Features Stars in Super Battle 'War,'" *Chicago Defender*, July 12, 1947, 19.
3. Donald R. Hill, *Calypso Callaloo: Early Carnival Music in Trinidad* (Gainesville: University Press of Florida, 1993), 165.
4. "King of 'Calypso' to Stage Huge Carnival in Harlem; Import Stars," *Chicago Defender*, January 25, 1947, 10.
5. "Trinidad Steps into Picture at 'Dame Lorainne' Fete," *New York Amsterdam Star-News*, February 14, 1942, 17.
6. "Calypso Aces at Carnegie," *Chicago Defender*, May 3, 1947, 19. See also "Carnegie Hall Bills Calypso," *Chicago Defender*, June 7, 1947, 18; "Carnegie Hall Likes Calypso," *Chicago Defender*, June 14, 1947, 18; "Calypso Tunes Invade Famous Carnegie Hall," *Chicago Defender*, May 10, 1947, 18; "Calypso Songs at Carnegie Hall," *New York Times*, October 13, 1947, 31; "Carnegie Hall Gets Calypso Carnival," *Baltimore Afro-American*, May 3, 1947, 6; "Calypso Carnival in N.Y. May 8," *Pittsburgh Courier*, May 3, 1947, 17.
7. Cf. Mae G. Henderson, "Josephine Baker and *La Revue Nègre*: From Ethnography to Performance," *Text and Performance Quarterly* 23 (2003): 107–33.
8. Vilém Flusser, *Towards a Philosophy of Photography*, trans. Anthony Matthews (London: Reaktion Books, 2000 [1983]), 30. Flusser develops his concept of the pro-

gram and the apparatus across a number of books. I rely in this discussion on (and admittedly take liberties with) *Towards a Philosophy of Photography*; *Post-History*, trans. Rodrigo Maltez Novaes (Minneapolis: Univocal, 2013 [1983]); and *Into the Universe of Technical Images*, trans. Nancy Ann Roth (Minneapolis: University of Minnesota Press, 2011 [1985]). Although Flusser was primarily concerned with the technical reproduction of images, I enlarge his theorization to include the apparatuses of sound reproduction as well. For more exploratory inquiries into Flusser's contributions to musical reproduction, see the special issue "Music and Sound in Vilém Flusser's Work," *Flusser Studies* 17 http://www.flusserstudies.net/archive/flusser-studies-17-double-issue.

9. Flusser, *Towards a Philosophy of Photography*, 29.
10. Flusser, *Post-History*, 5.
11. Flusser, *Post-History*, 163.
12. "Calypsomania," *Time*, March 25, 1957, 55; "Hollywood Bounces to Calypso Beat; 30 Titles Added," *Reading* (PA) *Eagle*, March 26, 1957, 20; Lucy Kavaler, "Where Go Calypso," *New York Herald Tribune*, May 26, 1957, F4.
13. Flusser, *Into the Universe of Technical Images*, 127.
14. Eric J. Hobsbawm, "The Machine-Breakers," *Past and Present* 1 (1952): 57–70.
15. Alexandra Vazquez, *Listening in Detail: Performances of Cuban Music* (Durham, NC: Duke University Press, 2013), 54. To note that all performance is deferred performance is just another way of restating one of the central tenets of deconstruction. See, for example, Jacques Derrida, *Limited Inc.*, trans Jeffrey Mehlman and Samuel Weber (Evanston, IL: Northwestern University Press, 1988); *Margins of Philosophy*, trans. Alan Bass (Chicago: University of Chicago Press, 1982); and *Positions*, trans. Alan Bass (Chicago: University of Chicago Press, 1982).
16. In this I am influenced by and follow pathbreaking scholars in performance studies who continually worry the line between race, performance, and mediation, including Vazquez, *Listening in Detail*; Fred Moten, *In the Break: The Aesthetics of the Black Radical Tradition* (Minneapolis: University of Minnesota Press, 2003); Alexander G. Weheliye, *Phonographies: Grooves in Sonic Afro-Modernity* (Durham, NC: Duke University Press, 2005); Michael Awkward, *Soul Covers: Rhythm and Blues Remakes and the Struggle for Artistic Identity* (Durham, NC: Duke University Press, 2007); Nicole Fleetwood, *Troubling Vision: Performance, Visuality, and Blackness* (Chicago: University of Chicago Press, 2011); Gayle Wald, *Shout Sister, Shout! The Untold Story of Rock and Roll Trailblazer Sister Rosetta Tharpe* (Boston: Beacon, 2007), and *It's Been Beautiful: "Soul!" and Black Power Television* (Durham, NC: Duke University Press, 2015); David Marriott, *Haunted Life: Visual Culture and Black Modernity* (New Brunswick, NJ: Rutgers University Press, 2007); and Brian Hochman, *Savage Preservation: The Ethnographic Origins of Modern Media Technology* (Minneapolis: University of Minnesota Press, 2014).
17. Vazquez, *Listening in Detail*, 105.
18. Aside from the brief discussion of calypso recounted here, the Herskovitses refer readers to an important Trinidadian publication on the history of calypso—Charles S. Espinet and Harry Pitts, *Land of Calypso: The Origin and Development of Trinidad's Folk Song* (Port of Spain, Trinidad: Guardian Commercial Printery, 1944)—though it is highly unlikely that most North American readers would have had any access to this volume.
19. Melville J. Herskovits and Frances S. Herskovits, *Trinidad Village* (New York: Knopf, 1947), 284, 285.

20. Herskovits and Herskovits, *Trinidad Village*, 277.
21. Herskovits and Herskovits, 285.
22. Herskovits and Herskovits, 286.
23. Herskovits and Herskovits, 24.
24. Bryan Wagner, *Disturbing the Peace: Black Culture and the Police Power after Slavery* (Cambridge, MA: Harvard University Press, 2009), 186.
25. Wagner, *Disturbing the Peace*, 192.
26. Wagner, 193.
27. José Esteban Muñoz, *Disidentifications: Queers of Color and the Performance of Politics* (Minneapolis: University of Minnesota Press, 1999), 188.
28. Wagner, *Disturbing the Peace*, 194.
29. Invoice from the Sound Specialties Company, Stamford, Connecticut, Trinidad Field Trip Preparations, box 15, folder 84, Melville and Frances Herskovits Papers, Schomburg Center for Research in Black Culture, New York Public Library.
30. Donald R. Hill, Maureen Warner-Lewis, John Cowley, and Lise Weiner, liner notes, *Peter Was a Fisherman: The 1939 Trinidad Field Recordings of Melville and Frances Herskovits*, vol. 1 (Rounder Records Corp., 1998), n.p.
31. Melville Herskovits, Trinidad Field Trip Diary (June 9–September 11, 1939), p. 23, box 15, file 82, Melville and Frances Herskovits Papers, Schomburg Center for Research in Black Culture, New York Public Library. See also a discussion of this session in Hill et al., liner notes, *Peter Was a Fisherman*. There they explain that "the Gilmans and the Saunders appear to have been friends. Lovey Gilman, who told Melville that her father was a 'Congo,' worked clearing coconut fields. Nothing is known about Louisa Neptune. Martha Saunders was the mother of Venice Talbott."
32. Melville Herskovits, Letter to Lincoln Thompson, Trinidad Field Trip Preparations, box 15, folder 84, Melville and Frances Herskovits Papers, Schomburg Center for Research in Black Culture, New York Public Library.
33. Melville Herskovits, Trinidad Field Trip Diary (June 9–September 11, 1939), p. 65, 75, 101, box 15, file 82, Melville and Frances Herskovits Papers, Schomburg Center for Research in Black Culture, New York Public Library.
34. For a representative sample of the study's favorable, if sometimes skeptical, reception, see Alfred Métraux, review of *Trinidad Village* in *American Anthropologist* 50 (1948): 116–19; Carter G. Woodson, review of *Trinidad Village* in *Journal of Negro History* 32 (1947): 247–49; Eric Williams, "In the Land of Rum and Coca-Cola," *Journal of Negro Education* 16 (1947): 548–50; and Zora Neale Hurston, "The Transplanted Negro," *New York Herald Tribune*, March 9, 1947, E20. See also Jerry Gershonhorn, *Melville Herskovits and the Racial Politics of Knowledge* (Lincoln: University of Nebraska Press, 2007), 80–86.
35. Hill et al., liner notes, *Peter Was a Fisherman*. The originals and copies made in the field are held at Indiana University's Archive of Traditional Music and the Library of Congress's Archive of Folk Culture, where folklorist Alan Lomax heard them and later incorporated at least one song into the calypso craze of the 1940s.
36. Hill et al., liner notes, *Peter Was a Fisherman*.
37. Melville Herskovits, Trinidad Field Trip Diary (June 9–September 11, 1939), p. 28, box 15, file 82, Melville and Frances Herskovits Papers, Schomburg Center for Research in Black Culture, New York Public Library; Hill et al., liner notes, *Peter Was a Fisherman*.
38. For the theorization of the resistance of the object, See Moten, *In the Break*.
39. For more on People's Songs, Inc., see Ronald D. Cohen, *Rainbow Quest: The Folk*

Music Revival and American Society, 1940–1970 (Amherst: University of Massachusetts Press, 2002), 39–66; John Szwed, *Alan Lomax: The Man Who Recorded the World* (New York: Penguin, 2010), 224–28; and Alan Lomax, foreword to *The People's Songbook*, ed. Waldemar Hille (New York: Boni and Gaer, 1947).

40. "Calypso at Midnight" is the only one of Lomax's Town Hall concerts for which a recording exists. The twelve ten-minute discs were discovered in the late 1990s in the closet of Lomax's sister, Bess Hawes, and issued on CD in 1999 in two parts: *Calypso at Midnight* (act 1) and *Calypso after Midnight* (act 2) (Rounder Records Corp., 1999).
41. *Calypso at Midnight* (Rounder Records Corp., 1999), Donald R. Hill and John H. Cowley, liner notes, n.p.
42. Hill and Cowley, liner notes, *Calypso at Midnight*, n.p.
43. Hill and Cowley, liner notes, *Calypso at Midnight*, n.p.
44. Wagner, *Disturbing the Peace*, 217.
45. Hill and Cowley, liner notes, *Calypso at Midnight*, n.p.
46. Hill and Cowley, liner notes, *Calypso at Midnight*, n.p.
47. Flusser, *Post-History*, 22. Those familiar with the philosophy of J. L. Austin will recognize this necessary fact of failure as a constitutive element not only of the performance of technology but also the performativity of language. See *How to Do Things with Words* (Cambridge, MA: Harvard University Press, 1962) and "A Plea for Excuses," in *Philosophical Papers* (Oxford: Clarendon Press, 1961), 175–204.
48. See "Big Hi-Fi Promotions Up Disks, Equipment," *Billboard*, July 17, 1954, 30; Frank Folsom, "Hi-Fi, Color TV New Billion $ Babies," *Variety*, October 19, 1955, 45; "Hi-Fi's Price Package Payoff," *Variety*, October 19, 1955, 61; Emory Cook, "High Fidelity—Does It Exist?" *New York Times*, March 9, 1952, X37; Keir Keightley, "'Turn It Down!' She Shrieked: Gender, Domestic Space, and High Fidelity, 1948–1959," *Popular Music* 15 (1996): 149–77; Joshua Jelly-Schapiro, "Sounds of Our Times," *The Believer* (July/August 2013): 43–54; and Greg Milner, "Presence," in *Perfecting Sound Forever: An Aural History of Recorded Music* (New York: Faber and Faber, 2009), 129–82.
49. Wagner, *Disturbing the Peace*, 235.
50. For more on the nightclub revue, see Vazquez, *Listening in Detail*; Jayna Brown, *Babylon Girls: Black Women Performers and the Shaping of the Modern* (Durham, NC: Duke University Press, 2008); and my own *The Scene of Harlem Cabaret: Race, Sexuality, Performance* (Chicago: University of Chicago Press, 2009). See also "Rise of Intimeries in N.Y. Night Life; Star Making Potential Is Marked," *Variety*, January 18, 1956, 1, 60.
51. See, for example, "'Trinidad Time' Up in N.Y.; Hub's 1st," *Variety*, February 6, 1957, 53.
52. Nightclub review, *Variety*, November 21, 1956, 55; Nightclub review, *Variety*, February 8, 1956, 54; Nightclub review, *Variety*, December 14, 1955, 62; Nightclub review, *Variety*, August 17, 1955, 60.
53. Nightclub review, *Variety*, February 8, 1956, 54; see also Nightclub review, *Variety*, October 12, 1955, 69.
54. Nightclub review, *Variety*, April 24, 1957, 54; Nightclub review, *Variety*, August 17, 1955, 60. "Niteries" is show-business lingo for "nightclubs." Sometimes calypso-themed nightclubs would be referred to as "calypseries." See Nightclub review, *Variety*, June 1, 1955, 52.
55. Nightclub review, *Variety*, June 5, 1957, 55.

56. See "Calypsomania," *Time*, March 25, 1957, 55; "Calypso Films to Flood Market?" *Variety*, March 13, 1957, 1; "Hollywood Bounces to Calypso Beat; 30 Titles Added," *Reading* (PA) *Eagle*, March 26, 1957, 20; "Race for Market with Calypso Films," *Variety*, May 1, 1957, 3; and Edwin Schallert, "Calypso Craze Inspires Tide of New Films," *Los Angeles Times*, April 14, 1957, E1, 3; "Jeffries Flick Shares Record," *Baltimore Afro-American*, June 4, 1957, 6; "Calypso Trends in New Films," *The Age* (Melbourne, Australia), July 11, 1957, 4; "'First Run' Films of the Week in Review," *Baltimore Afro-American*, October 19, 1957, 18.
57. On the cinema of attraction, see Tom Gunning, "The Cinema of Attraction: Early Film, It's Spectator, and the Avant-Garde," *Wide Angle* 8 (1986): 63–70, and Miriam Hansen, "The Mass Production of the Senses: Classical Cinema as Vernacular Modernism," *Modernism/Modernity* 6 (1999): 59–77. For more on soundies, see Anthony Slide, *New Historical Dictionary of the American Film Industry* (Chicago: Fitzroy Dearborn, 1998), 191, and Scott MacGillivray and Ted Okuda, *The Soundies Book: A Revised and Expanded Guide* (Lincoln, NE: iUniverse, 2007). Eldridge and Funk include two calypso soundies from the 1940s in their *Calypso Craze: 1956–57 and Beyond* box set of CDs and DVD.
58. Michael S. Eldridge, "Bop Girl Goes Calypso: Containing Race and Youth Culture in Cold War America," in *Music, Memory, Resistance: Calypso and the Caribbean Literary Imagination*, ed. Sandra Pouchet Paquet, Patricia J. Saunders, and Stephen Stuempfle (Kingston and Miami: Ian Randle, 2007), 273.
59. "Hollywood Bounces to Calypso Beat; 30 Titles Added," *Reading* (PA) *Eagle*, March 26, 1957, 20.
60. For an analysis of how the serial production of musical teen films in the 1950s was shaped by this feedback loop, see Peter Stanfield, "Crossover: Sam Katzman's 'Switchblade Calypso Bop Reefer Madness Swamp Girl' or 'Bad Jazz,' Calypso, Beatniks and Rock 'n' Roll in 1950s Teenpix," *Popular Music* 29 (2010): 437–55.
61. Martin Esslin, *The Field of Drama: How the Signs of Drama Create Meaning on Stage and Screen* (New York: Methuen, 1987), 92.
62. Erika Fischer-Lichte, *The Transformative Power of Performance: A New Aesthetics*, trans. Saskya Iris Jain (New York: Routledge, 2008), 38.
63. Diana Taylor, *The Archive and the Repertoire: Performing Cultural Memory in the Americas* (Durham, NC: Duke University Press, 2003), 20.
64. Esslin, *Field of Drama*, 26, 27.
65. Esslin, 29–35.
66. André Bazin, "Theater and Cinema—Part Two," in *What Is Cinema?*, vol. 1, trans. Hugh Gray (Berkeley: University of California Press, 1967), 97.
67. Flusser, *Into the Universe of Technical Images*, 53.
68. Flusser, *Into the Universe of Technical Images*, 53–54. Flusser goes on to argue that in a mass mediated society, "the circuit can't actually be closed, however, for then the images would fall into entropic decay. To get better (to always give the receiver something new, to be able to program innovatively), the image must get feedback from somewhere other than the receiver" (55).
69. Rebecca Schneider, *Performing Remains: Art and War in Times of Theatrical Reenactment* (New York: Routledge, 2011), 210n30.
70. "Hollywood Bounces to Calypso Beat; 30 Titles Added," *Reading* (PA) *Eagle*, March 26, 1957, 20.
71. James Baldwin, *Collected Essays*, ed. Toni Morrison (New York: Library of America, 1998), 533.

72. "Run Joe" was written by Dr. Walter E. Merrick and Trinidadian Joseph Willoughby. Merrick was a successful Harlem physician who wrote calypso music on the side, often sharing the music with his performer patients, including Jordan and Dinah Washington. Merrick also testified as an expert in the copyright trial over the origins of the song "Rum and Coca-Cola" in the mid-1940s. See "Louis Jordan Disc 'Run Joe' Written by New York Doctor," *Los Angeles Sentinel*, July 29, 1948, 21, and "Jordan's 'Run Joe' Most Nickel-Fed Disc; Doctor Composer Has Another 'Sleeper,'" *Baltimore Afro-American*, July 31, 1948, 6.
73. Maya Angelou, *Singin' and Swingin' and Gettin' Merry Like Christmas* (New York: Random House: 1976), 96.
74. W. J. T. Mitchell, *Seeing through Race* (Cambridge, MA: Harvard University Press, 2012), 13.
75. Frantz Fanon, *Black Skin, White Masks*, trans. Charles Lam Markmann (New York: Grove, 1967), 140. The Richard Philcox translation renders this passage as: "I can't go to the movies without encountering myself. I wait for myself. Just before the film starts, I wait for myself. Those in front of me look at me, spy on me, wait for me. A black bellhop is going to appear. My aching heart makes my head spin," in *Black Skin, White Masks*, trans. Richard Philcox (New York: Grove, 2008), 119.
76. Kaja Silverman, *The Threshold of the Visible World* (New York: Routledge, 1996), 27.
77. Kara Keeling, *The Witch's Flight: The Cinematic, the Black Femme, and the Image of Common Sense* (Durham, NC: Duke University Press, 2007), 36.
78. Keeling, *The Witch's Flight*, 36.
79. Keeling, 38.
80. Keeling, 38–39.
81. Keeling, 39.
82. Hiroshi Sugimoto, "Theaters," http://www.sugimotohiroshi.com/theater.html, accessed on October 26, 2014; emphasis in original.
83. Sugimoto, "Theaters."
84. Sugimoto.
85. Keeling, *Witch's Flight*, 27.
86. Mitchell, *Seeing through Race*, 13.
87. Angelou, *Singin' and Swingin' and Gettin' Merry Like Christmas*, 112.
88. Flusser, *Post-History*, 25; emphasis in original.
89. Flusser, *Into the Universe of Technical Images*, 163.

CHAPTER 3

1. David Sarnoff, "Our Next Frontier . . . Transoceanic TV," in *Mass Communication and American Social Thought: Key Texts: 1919–1968*, ed. John Durham Peters and Peter Simonson (Oxford: Rowman and Littlefield, 2004), 309.
2. Duke Ellington, interview by Ted Allen, January 1961. Quoted in David Hajdu, *Lush Life: A Biography of Billy Strayhorn* (New York: Farrar, Straus and Giroux, 1996), 157.
3. Susan Murray, *Hitch Your Antenna to the Stars: Early Television and Broadcast Stardom* (New York: Routledge, 2005), xv.
4. "Television Chatter," *Variety*, September 14, 1955, 44; "Variety Hour, Climbing, Aims for Half of Sunday Viewers," *Variety*, October 29, 1955, 2.
5. William Ewald, "Belafonte Series to Start Sunday," *Racine* (WI) *Journal Times*, October 1, 1955, 8. The other songs in the segment were "The Jack-Ass Song," "Come Back, Liza," and "Hosanna," all of which were included on *Calypso*. For more on Belafonte's *Colgate Variety Hour* appearance, see also Judith E. Smith, *Becoming Be-*

lafonte: Black Artist, Public Radical (Austin: University of Texas Press, 2014), 125–26, and Richard Yarborough, "William Attaway," in *Writers of the Black Chicago Renaissance*, ed. Steven C. Tracy (Champaign: University of Illinois Press, 2011), 45.

6. In 1973, *Billboard* magazine commented on the significance of television—and *A Drum Is a Woman* in particular—to Ellington's career: "For too many years, Ellington's TV work was devoted largely to guest appearances of the Ed Sullivan type in which he appeared with or without orchestra playing one or two of his popular songs. But he was not content to let the medium be lost to him, and in May of 1957, 'A Drum Is a Woman,' a CBS spectacular (color was very rare on CBS in those days) was built around him, with Ellington's music and lyrics (in collaboration with the late Billy Strayhorn) in a highly visual fantasy, based on a story roughly paralleling the history of jazz. Ellington's sacred concert was seen on educational television; he has been off and on the tube frequently during the 16 years since 'A Drum Is a Woman,' but that event remains unique." "The Ten Worlds of Duke Ellington," *Billboard*, February 10, 1973, 24.
7. See "Biggest Col[umbia] Beat for Ellington LP," *Billboard*, April 27, 1957, 17, and "Summary of Station Promotion for U.S. Steel Hour Presentation of 'A Drum Is a Woman,'" series 4B, box 4, folder 13, Duke Ellington Collection, Archives Center, National Museum of American History, Smithsonian Institution.
8. Important exceptions include Harvey G. Cohen, *Duke Ellington's America* (Chicago: University of Chicago Press, 2010), 329–31, and Graham Locke, *Blutopia: Visions of the Future and Revisions of the Past in the Work of Sun Ra, Duke Ellington, and Anthony Braxton* (Durham, NC: Duke University Press: 1999), 137–41.
9. Duke Ellington, *Music Is My Mistress* (New York: Doubleday, 1973), 191.
10. See Mary L. Dudziak's pioneering analysis of the relationship between the cold war and the civil rights movement, *Cold War Civil Rights: Race and the Image of American Democracy* (Princeton, NJ: Princeton University Press, 2000).
11. Penny Von Eschen, *Satchmo Blows Up the World: Jazz Ambassadors Play the Cold War* (Cambridge, MA: Harvard University Press, 2004), 1–26.
12. Anna McCarthy, *The Citizen Machine: Governing by Television in 1950s America* (New York: New Press, 2010).
13. See, for example, "Even Institutional U.S. Steel Going after Teenage Market," *Variety*, March 13, 1957, 22.
14. "La Conga Samba Rhumba Chica Chica Bomba," series 4B, box 4, folder 11, Duke Ellington Collection, Archives Center, National Museum of American History, Smithsonian Institution.
15. For more on Ellington as a writer and his literary style, see Brent Hayes Edwards's *Epistrophies: Jazz and the Literary Imagination* (Cambridge, MA: Harvard University Press, 2017), 86–119.
16. Dallas Smythe, "The Consumer's Stake in Radio and Television," in *Mass Communication and American Social Thought: Key Texts, 1919–1968*, ed. John Durham Peters and Peter Simonson (Oxford: Rowman and Littlefield, 2004), 319.
17. Smythe, "Consumer's Stake in Radio and Television," 320.
18. George Rosen, "Ten Frantic Years of Television," *Variety*, January 4, 1956, 145.
19. "Pat's Credo," *Variety*, January 4, 1956, 147.
20. Michel Foucault, *Security, Territory, Population: Lectures at the Collège de France, 1977–78*, trans. Graham Burchell (New York: Palgrave, 2007), 366.
21. See Michel Foucault, *The Birth of Biopolitics: Lectures at the Collège de France, 1978–79*, trans. Graham Burchell (New York: Palgrave, 2008), 21–22.

22. Foucault, *Security, Territory, Population*, 366.
23. George F. Brown, "Echoes from Duke's 'Drum,'" *Pittsburgh Courier*, May 25, 1957, A22.
24. Ellington Scrapbooks, roll 2, Duke Ellington Collection, Archives Center, National Museum of American History, Smithsonian Institution.
25. Foucault, *Security, Territory, Population*, 43–44.
26. See Harvey G. Cohen, "Duke Ellington and *Black, Brown, and Beige*: The Composer as Historian at Carnegie Hall," *American Quarterly* 56 (2004): 1003–34, for a detailed analysis of the conceptualization of this suite, which bears many similarities to his later vision in *A Drum Is a Woman*.
27. Barry Ulanov, *Duke Ellington* (New York: Da Capo, 1975 [1946]), 259.
28. Ulanov, *Duke Ellington*, 261.
29. Ellington's elaboration of the people stands in counterpoint to two other midcentury conceptualizations of the people. On one hand, "the people" as a rhetorical device described a sentimental unity that sought to surpass racial, ethnic, regional, and class differences and was quickly co-opted into the figure of an average American and the material for "public opinion"—what Warren Susman calls "the people-as-consumer." On the other hand, for the artists and intellectuals of the 1930s Cultural Front, the people was understood primarily as what Michael Denning describes as a "formal and aesthetic problem" that was as much about its absence and the difficulty of representation than its sentimental affirmation or populist mythology. *A Drum Is a Woman* reflects and exceeds both of these aspects of the people. It is at once a co-opted unity-turned-consumer (from the point of view of the calypso craze and the *US Steel Hour*) and an aesthetic problem (from the point of view of auteurs such as Ellington and Strayhorn). See Susman, *Culture as History: The Transformation of American Society in the Twentieth Century* (New York: Pantheon, 1984), 212, 215, and Denning, *The Cultural Front: The Laboring of American Culture in the Twentieth Century* (New York: Verso, 1996), 123–36, 309–19.
30. Philosopher Réal Fillion defines speculative philosophy of history as the "*explicit* consideration of the importance of distinguishing how the present both arises out of, and in doing so differs from, the past *that then* suggests reconsidering how to conceive of what the future holds. . . . It is speculative because it attempts to grasp history as a whole, that is, to treat it as an intelligible whole, and in doing so distinguishes itself from those activities that seek to establish facts." See Réal Fillion, "Moving Beyond Biopower: Hardt and Negri's Post-Foucauldian Speculative Philosophy of History," *History and Theory* 44 (2005): 52; emphasis in original.
31. Gordon Rohlehr, "The Problem of the Problem of Form: The Idea of an Aesthetic Continuum and Aesthetic Code-Switching in West Indian Literature," *Caribbean Quarterly* 31 (1985): 48.
32. "A Drum Is a Woman" script, series 4B, box 4, folder 9, Duke Ellington Collection, Archives Center, National Museum of American History, Smithsonian Institution.
33. Nat Shapiro and Nat Hentoff, eds., *Hear Me Talkin' to Ya: The Story of Jazz as Told by the Men Who Made It* (Toronto: Rinehart, 1955); Marshall W. Stearns, *The Story of Jazz* (New York: Oxford University Press, 1956); Studs Terkel, *Giants of Jazz* (New York: Thomas Crowell, 1957); Shapiro and Hentoff, eds., *The Jazz Makers: Essays on the Greats of Jazz* (New York: Rinehart, 1957).
34. Quoted in Donald Freeman, "Duke Cites TV's 'Fear' of Jazz," *Joliet* (IL) *Herald-News*, March 23, 1958. Ellington Scrapbooks, roll 2, Duke Ellington Collection, Archives Center, National Museum of American History, Smithsonian Institution.

35. Bill Ladd, "Is Duke a Musician—A Playwright—or Both?" *Louisville Courier Journal*, May 2, 1957. Ellington Scrapbooks, roll 3, Duke Ellington Collection, Archives Center, National Museum of American History, Smithsonian Institution.
36. Dan Burley, "Dan Burley's Back Door Stuff," *New York Amsterdam News*, May 18, 1957, 13.
37. Edward Towler, "Reflections on Hearing 'A Drum Is a Woman,'" *Jazz Monthly* (September 1957): 30, 31.
38. Errol Hill, *The Trinidad Carnival: Mandate for a National Theatre* (Austin: University of Texas Press, 1972), 80.
39. Hill, *Trinidad Carnival*, 76. Although I am not arguing that Ellington studied the tradition of calypso theater in any comprehensive way, he was familiar with the history and trends of calypso music as it made significant inroads into US recording studios and nightclubs throughout the 1930s and 1940s, as well as with the various styles of Latin jazz at the time, as Candido's presence on *A Drum Is a Woman* indicates. In 1946, folklorist Alan Lomax curated *Calypso at Midnight*, a concert at New York City's Town Hall that featured Trinidadian performers and showcased aspects of Trinidadian folk culture, including what might have been the first live performance of a calypso drama in the United States: a skit titled *The GI and the Lady* performed by calypsonians Macbeth the Great, Duke of Iron, and Lord Invader (who also composed, directed, and produced the skit), as I discuss in chapter 2.
40. Jocelyne Guilbault, *Governing Sound: The Cultural Politics of Trinidad's Carnival Musics* (Chicago: University of Chicago Press, 2007), 3.
41. Guilbault, *Governing Sound*, 41.
42. Donald Hill, *Calypso Callaloo: Early Carnival Music in Trinidad* (Gainesville: University Press of Florida, 1993), 203.
43. Unless otherwise noted, descriptions and transcriptions of the CBS broadcast of *A Drum Is a Woman* are based on my viewing of the kinescope recording of the show at the Paley Center for Media archives.
44. Robert Tracy, "Celebrating Carmen de Lavallade's Fifty-Year Career," *Dance Magazine* (August 1999): 37.
45. Carmen de Lavallade, personal interview, August 18, 2016.
46. "A Drum Is a Woman" script, series 4B, box 4, folder 11, Duke Ellington Collection, Archives Center, National Museum of American History, Smithsonian Institution.
47. "A Drum Is a Woman" script, series 4B, box 4, folder 9, Duke Ellington Collection, Archives Center, National Museum of American History, Smithsonian Institution.
48. Rawle Gibbons, "Room to Pass: Carnival and Caribbean Aesthetics," in *Enterprise of the Indies*, ed. George Lamming (Port of Spain, Trinidad: Trinidad and Tobago Institute of the West Indies, 1999), 153.
49. Carmen de Lavallade, personal interview, August 18, 2016.
50. See Lynn Spigel, *TV by Design: Modern Art and the Rise of Network Television* (Chicago: University of Chicago Press, 2008), 52–55.
51. Rob Roy, "Duke's 'A Drum Is a Woman' Has TV Merit—But: Scribe Quarrels with Scriptors over Letdown," *Chicago Defender*, May 18, 1957, 8.
52. Vic Miller, "The 'Duke Swings and the Kremlin Is Seen Again," *People's World* (San Francisco), May 25, 1957. Ellington Scrapbooks, roll 2, Duke Ellington Collection, Archives Center, National Museum of American History, Smithsonian Institution.
53. John Crosby, "'Flesh and Blood' Fumbles Storyline," *St. Petersburg Times*, May 14, 1957, 49.
54. Roger Abrahams, afterword in *Trinidad Carnival: The Cultural Politics of a Transna-*

tional Festival, ed. Garth L. Green and Philip W. Scher (Bloomington: Indiana University Press, 2007), 220; emphasis in original.

55. Abrahams, afterword in *Trinidad Carnival*, 223.
56. Anthony LaCamera, "Ellington Explains Show Title," *Boston American*, May 3, 1957. Ellington Scrapbooks, roll 3, Duke Ellington Collection, Archives Center, National Museum of American History, Smithsonian Institution.
57. Jayne Cortez, *Coagulations: New and Selected Poems* (New York: Thunder's Mouth Press, 1984), 57. The recording of the piece can be heard on *There It Is* (Bola Press, 1982).
58. Aldon Lynn Nielsen, *Black Chant: Languages of African American Postmodernism* (New York: Cambridge University Press, 1997), 227.
59. Duke Ellington, interview by Ted Allen, January 1961. Quoted in Hajdu, *Lush Life*, 158.
60. "Duke Turns a Drum into a Woman," *Hue* (June 1957): 26.
61. See Eve Kosofsky Sedgwick, *Between Men: English Literature and Male Homosocial Desire* (New York: Columbia University Press, 1985), for the classic account of this phenomenon.
62. Quoted in Hajdu, *Lush Life*, 95.
63. Irving Townsend, "Ellington in Private," *Atlantic Monthly* (May 1975): 80.

CHAPTER 4

1. "Belafonte Leaves Musical," *New York Times*, February 5, 1957, 27.
2. For more on the struggle over creative control of *Jamaica* and its revisions in the wake of Horne's casting, see James Gavin, *Stormy Weather: The Life of Lena Horne* (New York: Atria Books, 2009), 269–80; Edward Jablonski, *Harold Arlen: Rhythm, Rainbows, and Blues* (Boston: Northeastern University Press, 1996), 279–89; Howard Kissel, *David Merrick, the Abominable Showman: The Unauthorized Biography* (New York: Applause, 1993), 130–238; Robert Lewis, *Slings and Arrows: Theatre in My Life* (New York: Stein and Day, 1984), 247–51; and Harold Meyerson and Ernie Harburg, with Arthur Perlman, *Who Put the Rainbow in "The Wizard of Oz"?: Yip Harburg, Lyricist* (Ann Arbor: University of Michigan Press, 1993), 308–11. Harburg and Arlen's Pigeon Island is probably unrelated to Saint Lucia's Pigeon Island National Park, which was occupied by the French and British throughout the eighteenth and nineteenth centuries.
3. Errol G. Hill, "The Caribbean Connection," in *A History of African American Theatre*, ed. Errol G. Hill and James V. Hatch (New York: Cambridge University Press, 2003), 274; see also Allen Woll, *Black Musical Theatre: From "Coontown" to "Dreamgirls"* (Baton Rouge: Louisiana State University Press, 1989), 205.
4. In addition to the works cited in this chapter, see also James Weldon Johnson, *Black Manhattan* (New York: Atheneum, 1977); Susan Curtis, *The First Black Actors on the Great White Way* (Columbia: University of Missouri Press, 1998); and Paula Marie Seniors, *Beyond Lift Every Voice and Sing: The Culture of Uplift, Identity, and Politics in Black Musical Theatre* (Columbus: Ohio State University Press, 2009).
5. For further approaches to thinking about US and diasporic racial formations through island geographies and imaginaries, see Michelle Ann Stephens and Brian Russell Roberts, *Archipelagic American Studies* (Durham, NC: Duke University Press, 2017).
6. Stuart Hall, "What Is This 'Black' in Black Popular Culture?," in *Black Popular Culture*, ed. Gina Dent (Seattle: Bay Press, 1992), 27.
7. Hall, "What Is This 'Black' in Black Popular Culture?," 26, 27.

8. Hall, 25. Hall is quoting Antonio Gramsci in this passage.
9. Édouard Glissant, *Poetics of Relation*, trans. Betsy Wing (Ann Arbor: University of Michigan Press, 1997), 33.
10. *Jamaica* script (draft), T-Mss. 1990-002, box 15, folder 1, E. Y. Harburg Papers, Billy Rose Theatre Division, New York Public Library for the Performing Arts.
11. *Jamaica* script (draft), T-Mss. 1990-002, box 15, folder 1, E. Y. Harburg Papers, Billy Rose Theatre Division, New York Public Library for the Performing Arts.
12. Brent Hayes Edwards, *The Practice of Diaspora: Literature, Translation, and the Rise of Black Internationalism* (Cambridge, MA: Harvard University Press, 2003), 5.
13. Glissant, *Poetics of Relation*, 33.
14. For more on Baker's performance as a knowing parody that worked as "a recoding that radically called into question the originary and essentialist assumptions underlying the construction of the primitive," see Mae G. Henderson, "Josephine Baker and *La Revue Nègre*: From Ethnography to Performance," *Text and Performance Quarterly* 23 (2003): 107–33, especially page 124, where this quotation can be found.
15. Daphne A. Brooks, *Bodies in Dissent: Spectacular Performances of Race and Freedom, 1850–1910* (Durham, NC: Duke University Press, 2006), 211–12.
16. Brooks, *Bodies in Dissent*, 263.
17. Louis Chude-Sokei, *The Last "Darky": Bert Williams, Black-on-Black Minstrelsy, and the African Diaspora* (Durham, NC: Duke University Press, 2006), 173.
18. Brooks, *Bodies in Dissent*, 213; Chude-Sokei, *The Last "Darky,"* 174. See also David Krasner, *Resistance, Parody, and Double Consciousness in African American Theatre, 1895–1910* (New York: St. Martin's Press 1997), 41–74, which contextualizes *In Dahomey* within ideologies of Progressive-era racial uplift, the double consciousness of segregated spectatorship, and histories of African American migration.
19. For more on *Abyssinia*, which sent Williams and Walker's characters on a world tour after winning the lottery, see Krasner, *Resistance, Parody, and Double Consciousness*, 99–115. For more on *Rang Tang*, a follow-up to Miller and Lyle's earlier success, *Shuffle Along* (1920), see Woll, *Black Musical Theatre*, 121–22. Heywood's *Africana* had, according to Hill, "a strong plot in which an Oxford-educated prince of the Belgian Congo returns home resolved to reform and modernize the country against the wishes of its people. The prince also announces plans to marry the mulatto daughter of a missionary, prompting a threat from his father the king to disown him." This show is different from Heywood's 1927 revue *Africana* (written with Earl Dancer and featuring Ethel Waters), from which he recycled the title and that was itself a reworking of Dancer and Heywood's earlier revue, *Miss Calico* (1926). See Hill, "Caribbean Connection," 277, and Woll, *Black Musical Theatre*, 159.
20. Howard Barnes, "I Ain't Like," *New York Herald Tribune*, September 28, 1945, 16; see also Margaret Lloyd, *The Borzoi Book of Modern Dance* (New York: Knopf, 1949), 251–52.
21. See, for example, Barnes, "I Ain't Like": "Miss Dunham is a gifted artist, but she should know better than to substitute rhythmical convolutions for the variety and pace which define the best Negro musical shows."
22. Cyrus Durgin, "Musical 'House of Flowers' Full of Color, Naughty Fun," *Daily Boston Globe*, February 27, 1955, C41; Miles Jefferson, "The Negro on Broadway, 1954–1955: More Spice than Substance," *Phylon* 16 (1955): 304, quoted in Hill, "Caribbean Connection," 281.
23. Walter Terry, "The Dance World: 'House of Flowers'; Mr. Robbins," *New York Herald Tribune*, January 9, 1955, D5.

24. Celia Weiss Bambara, "Did You Say Banda?: Geoffrey Holder and How Stories Circulate," *Journal of Haitian Studies* 17 (2011): 186.
25. "Young Mr. Holder Is Jack-of-All-Arts," Holder Clippings File, Jerome Robbins Dance Division, New York Public Library for the Performing Arts.
26. The shifting field of *Jamaica*'s racial and national indeterminacy is further indexed by the dislocated internationalism of the cast, which featured Mexican-born Ricardo Montalbán (famous by the time of *Jamaica* for playing both Latin and Asian roles), second-generation Haitian actress Josephine Premice, and black expatriate Adelaide Hall (returned from England), in addition to Horne, a ghosting Belafonte, and an interracial chorus.
27. John Chapman, "'Jamaica' Has Horne, Needs Plot; Vivid New 'Don Giovanni' at Met," *Daily News*, November 1, 1957, 68.
28. Edward Jablonski, "The Unsung Songsmith of 'Jamaica,'" *Theatre Arts* 41 (1957): 74.
29. Harburg and Saidy are likely playing here on the Soviet-era Intourist agency, the state travel agency founded by Joseph Stalin in 1929 to arrange, manage, and monitor foreign visitors to the Soviet Union. The Soviet Intourist agency discouraged tourism, and *Jamaica*'s parodic invocation of it can be seen as a commentary on the indigenous management of North American tourists to the Caribbean.
30. *Jamaica* script (draft), T-Mss. 1990-002, box 15, folder 1, E. Y. Harburg Papers, Billy Rose Theatre Division, New York Public Library for the Performing Arts.
31. *Jamaica* script (draft), T-Mss. 1990-002, box 15, folder 2, E. Y. Harburg Papers, Billy Rose Theatre Division, New York Public Library for the Performing Arts.
32. David Timothy Duval, "Trends and Circumstances in Caribbean Tourism," in *Tourism in the Caribbean: Trends, Development, Prospects*, ed. David Timothy Duval (New York: Routledge, 2004), 10.
33. For more on the relationship between Trinidadian calypso and the US occupation of Trinidad, see Harvey R. Neptune, *Caliban and the Yankees: Trinidad and the United States Occupation* (Chapel Hill: University of North Carolina Press, 2007), 129–57.
34. *Jamaica* script (draft), T-Mss. 1990-002, box 15, folder 1, E. Y. Harburg Papers, Billy Rose Theatre Division, New York Public Library for the Performing Arts.
35. George Jean Nathan, "Expressing Gratitude for Some Small Favors," *New York Journal American*, May 28, 1951, 18.
36. Meyerson and Harburg, *Who Put the Rainbow in "The Wizard of Oz"?*, 305.
37. Oral History interview with E. Y. Harburg (1959), page 41 and 47, Columbia Center for Oral History Archives, Rare Book and Manuscript Library, Columbia University in the City of New York.
38. Cf. Joseph Roach, *Cities of the Dead: Circum-Atlantic Performance* (New York: Columbia University Press, 1996), and Marvin Carlson, *The Haunted Stage: Theatre as Memory Machine* (Ann Arbor: University of Michigan Press, 2002).
39. Michelle Stephens, "The First Negro Matinee Idol: Harry Belafonte and American Culture in the 1950s," in *Left of the Color Line: Race, Radicalism, and Twentieth-Century Literature of the United States*, ed. Bill V. Mullen and James Smethurst (Chapel Hill: University of North Carolina Press, 2003), 234.
40. Lisa D. McGill, *Constructing Black Selves: Caribbean American Narratives and the Second Generation* (New York: New York University Press, 2005), 25.
41. Stephens, "First Negro Matinee Idol," 223–37.
42. Brooks Atkinson, "One Yes; One No," *New York Times*, November 10, 1957, 143.
43. Brooks, *Bodies in Dissent*, 224.

44. Brooks, 4, 5–6.
45. Lewis Nichols, "'Carib Song,' with Katherine Dunham and Avon Long, Makes Its Bow at the Adelphi Theatre," *New York Times*, September 28, 1945, 17.
46. "Lena Lights Up 'Jamaica,'" *Life*, November 18, 1957, 112.
47. See Harry Belafonte, interview with Cornel West, in *Restoring Hope: Conversations on the Future of Black America*, ed. Kelvin Shawn Sealey (New York: Beacon, 1997), 4.
48. Oral history interview with E. Y. Harburg (1959), page 48, Columbia Center for Oral History Archives, Rare Book and Manuscript Library, Columbia University in the City of New York.
49. Oral history interview with E. Y. Harburg (1959), page 46.
50. Oral history interview with E. Y. Harburg (1959), page 47.
51. For Lewis's own account of his role in US theater history, see his *Method—or Madness?* (New York: Samuel French, 1958), and *Slings and Arrows: Theater in My Life* (New York: Applause Books, 1984).
52. Oral history interview with E. Y. Harburg (1959), page 48, Columbia Center for Oral History Archives, Rare Book and Manuscript Library, Columbia University in the City of New York.
53. Oral history interview with E. Y. Harburg (1959), pages 48–49.
54. Oral history interview with E. Y. Harburg (1959), pages 50–51.
55. Susan Sontag, "Notes on Camp," in *Against Interpretation and Other Essays* (New York: Picador, 2001), 280.
56. Oral History interview with E. Y. Harburg (1959), pages 49–50, Columbia Center for Oral History Archives, Rare Book and Manuscript Library, Columbia University in the City of New York.
57. Glissant, *Poetics of Relation*, 33.
58. Hall, "What Is This 'Black' in Black Popular Culture?," 27.
59. *Scandalize My Name: Stories from the Blacklist*, DVD, dir. Alexandra M. Isles (Urban Works Entertainment, 1999).
60. Thomas DeFrantz, *Dancing Revelations: Alvin Ailey's Embodiment of African American Culture* (New York: Oxford University Press, 2004), 55.
61. Gavin, *Stormy Weather*, 269. See also Louis Calta, "Merrick Thinking of Entering Film," *New York Times*, April 25, 1968, 52; and Kissel, *David Merrick*, 137–38. For more on the struggle to integrate Broadway in the 1950s, both front stage and back stage, see Woll, *Black Musical Theatre*, 210–28.
62. See Meyerson and Harburg, *Who Put the Rainbow in "The Wizard of Oz"?*, 311.
63. Glissant, *Poetics of Relation*, 21.
64. The reading of Horne's autobiography that follows is part of an ongoing engagement with Horne's writings that takes her autobiographies and essays as acts of black feminist performance theory, a body of thought that is elaborated through and inseparable from her singular performance history. For a further discussion of reading Horne's work in this way, see my *The Scene of Harlem Cabaret: Race, Sexuality, Performance* (Chicago: University of Chicago Press, 2009), 167–93.
65. Lena Horne, with Richard Schickel, *Lena* (Garden City, NY: Doubleday, 1965), 260–61.
66. Horne, with Schickel, *Lena*, 265–66.
67. Judith Butler and Gayatri Chakravorty Spivak, *Who Sings the Nation-State? Language, Politics, Belonging* (New York: Seagull, 2007), 63.
68. Hall, "What Is This 'Black' in Black Popular Culture?," 27.

CHAPTER 5

1. Jennifer Dunning, *Geoffrey Holder: A Life in Theater, Dance, and Art* (New York: Harry N. Abrams: 2001), 60.
2. Geoffrey Holder, "That Fad from Trinidad," *New York Times*, April 21, 1957, 14, 60.
3. Holder, "That Fad from Trinidad," 60.
4. Édouard Glissant, *Caribbean Discourse: Selected Essays*, trans. J. Michael Dash (Charlottesville: University Press of Virginia, 1989), 61–62, 64.
5. Wilson Harris, "History, Fable, and Myth in the Caribbean and the Guianas," in *Explorations: A Selection of Talks and Articles, 1966–81*, ed. Hena Maes-Jelinek (Mundelstrup, Denmark: Dangaroo Press, 1981), 35.
6. Quoted in Hyman Goldberg, "Holders of Endless Talent," *New York Mirror Magazine*, June 15, 1958. Holder Clippings file, Jerome Robbins Dance Division, New York Public Library for the Performing Arts.
7. Dunning, *Geoffrey Holder*, 24–26, 32.
8. Gilbert Millstein, "Man of Many Muses," *New York Times*, January 20, 1957, 212; "Geoffrey Holder," *Current Biography* (October 1957): 19–20. Holder Clippings File, Jerome Robbins Dance Division, New York Public Library for the Performing Arts.
9. Molly Ahye, *Cradle of Caribbean Dance: Beryl McBurnie and the Little Carib Theater* (Petit Valley, Trinidad and Tobago: Heritage Cultures, 1983), 42. McBurnie herself was working and performing in England that year and did not attend the festival. Her company went under the directorship of dancers Percival Borde and Barney Maurice. Although their performances were well received, according to Ahye many felt that McBurnie's absence "negatively affected the company," which had less success at the festival than Holder's company: "some members were of the opinion that, with Miss McBurnie's guidance, greater artistic heights could have been achieved" and further international performance opportunities gained. Ahye, *Cradle of Caribbean Dance*, 42.
10. Margalit Fox, "Jean-Léon Destiné, Dancer, Dies at 94," *New York Times*, January 30, 2013, A20.
11. Emory Lewis, "Talented Lad from Trinidad," *Cue* (January 1955). Holder Clippings file, Jerome Robbins Dance Division, New York Public Library for the Performing Arts.
12. "Trinidad Dance Group Impresses in U.S. Bow," *Variety*, July 8, 1953, 66.
13. Review, *Billboard*, November 6, 1954, 44.
14. Quoted in Dunning, *Geoffrey Holder*, 39.
15. Allyn Moss, "Who Is Geoffrey Holder?," *Dance Magazine* (August 1958): 37.
16. Walter Terry, "Holder's Trinidad Dance Features Lee Festival," *Daily Boston Globe*, July 17, 1954, 22.
17. John Martin, "Dance: Nice Work," *New York Times*, November 18, 1956, 143.
18. For more on the social, historical, and psychoanalytic dimensions of the modern (black) male dancer's performance, See Ramsay Burt, *The Male Dancer: Bodies, Spectacle, Sexualities*, 2nd ed. (New York: Routledge, 2007), and Thomas DeFrantz, *Dancing Revelations: Alvin Ailey's Embodiment of African American Culture* (New York: Oxford University Press, 2004).
19. Owen Dodson, "Josephine Baker Scores in National Appearance," *Baltimore Afro-American*, March 28, 1964, 11. See also Dunning, *Geoffrey Holder*, 82.
20. *Banda*, Dance Theatre of Harlem, artistic direction by Arthur Mitchell, choreography by Geoffrey Holder (1999), VHS. Jerome Robbins Dance Division, New York Public

Library for the Performing Arts. See also Anna Kisselgoff, "Dance: Harlem Troupe in Two Holder Premiers," *New York Times*, January 21, 1982, C16.

21. Geoffrey Holder, *Adam* (New York: Viking, 1986). See also Hedy Weiss, "Geoffrey Holder Truly Is an Un-Common Man," *Chicago Sun-Times*, October 12, 1986, 4.
22. Patricia T. Alleyne-Dettmers, "The Moko Jumbie: Elevating the Children," in *Caribbean Dance from Abakuá to Zouk*, ed. Susanna Sloat (Gainesville: University Press of Florida, 2002), 273.
23. Brenda Dixon Gottschild, *Digging the Africanist Presence in American Performance: Dance and Other Contexts* (Westport, CT: Greenwood Press, 1996), 13; revised and reprinted as "Crossroads, Continuities, and Contradictions: The Afro-Euro-Caribbean Triangle," in Sloat, *Caribbean Dance from Abakuá to Zouk*, 5.
24. *Glamour*, May 1957, 101, 8, 126–33.
25. See "New York's Calypso Center," *Calypso Album* (New York: Modern Music Publications, 1957), 63, and Lucy Kavaler, "Where Go Calypso," *New York Herald Tribune*, May 26, 1957, F4. For more on the opportunities for improvisation and instruction at the Palladium, see Danielle Goldman, *I Want to Be Ready: Improvised Dance as a Practice of Freedom* (Ann Arbor: University of Michigan Press, 2010), 28–54.
26. Robert Luis, *Authentic Calypso: The Song, the Music, the Dance* (New York: Aloha Printing, 1957), 5.
27. Arthur Murray, "How to Dance the Calypso," *Calypso Album* (New York: Modern Music Publications, 1957), 10.
28. Murray, "How to Dance the Calypso," 13.
29. Murray, 15.
30. Geoffrey Holder, "Do the Limbo-Calypso," *Glamour*, May 1957, 126.
31. Quoted in Dorothea Duryea Ohl, "Calypso Bandwagon," *Dance Magazine* (March 1957): 53–54.
32. Molly Ahye, "In Search of the Limbo," in Sloat, *Caribbean Dance from Abakuá to Zouk*, 247–61; Sonjah Stanley Niaah, *Dancehall: From Slave Ship to Ghetto* (Ottawa: University of Ottawa Press, 2010), 18–20, and "Mapping Black Atlantic Performance Geographies: From Slave Ship to Ghetto," in *Black Geographies and the Politics of Place*, ed. Katherine McKittrick and Clyde Woods (Cambridge, MA: South End Press, 2007), 193–96; and Geneviève Fabre, "The Slave Ship Dance," in *Black Imagination in the Middle Passage*, ed. Maria Diedrich, Henry Louis Gates Jr., and Carl Peterson (New York: Oxford University Press, 1999), 41–44.
33. Harris, "History, Fable, and Myth," 25.
34. Harris, "History, Fable, and Myth, 35, 28.
35. Stanley Niaah, *Dancehall*, 35.
36. See Molly Ahye, *Cradle of Caribbean Dance*, and Ray Funk, "Beryl McBurnie: The Flowering of LaBelle Rosette," *Caribbean Beat* 94 (November/December 2008), at http://caribbean-beat.com/issue-94/flowering-la-belle-rosette-beryl-mcburnie#axzz31Xan032w, accessed on February 10, 2017.
37. Ahye, *Cradle of Caribbean Dance*, 16–28.
38. Ahye, 35–69.
39. Nightclub review, *Variety*, July 24, 1957, 70.
40. See Ahye, *Cradle of Caribbean Dance*, 56–57.
41. Ahye relays this account from Edwards in "In Search of the Limbo," 254.
42. Holder, "Do the Limbo-Calypso," 127.
43. Holder, "Do the Limbo-Calypso," 126; emphasis in original.
44. *Glamour*, May 1957, 126, 8.

45. "How to Do the Calypso Limbo: A New Party Dance by Geoffrey Holder, Produced for Glamour Magazine" (Vik Records, 1957). See also coverage of this promotion in "Vik and Glamour Mag in Tieup on Calypso," *Variety*, April 17, 1957, 42, and "Vik-mag Calypso Tie In," *Billboard*, April 29, 1957, 21.
46. André Lepecki, "Inscribing Dance," in *Of the Presence of the Body: Essays on Dance and Performance Theory*, ed. André Lepecki (Middletown, CT: Wesleyan University Press, 2004), 125.
47. Lepecki, "Inscribing Dance," 130.
48. See Sally Banes and John Szwed, "From 'Messin' Around' to 'Funky Western Civilization': The Rise and Fall of Dance Instruction Songs," in *Dancing Many Drums: Excavations in African American Dance*, ed. Tommy DeFrantz (Madison: University of Wisconsin Press, 2002), 169–203.
49. Harris, "History, Fable, and Myth," 26.
50. Lepecki, "Inscribing Dance," 3.
51. Geoffrey Holder, "The Twist? 'It's Not a Dance,'" *New York Times*, December 3, 1961, 78.
52. Holder, "The Twist? 'It's Not a Dance,'" 78. The Wham-O Manufacturing Company, a toy manufacturer that continues to quickly produce cheap, mass-produced novelty objects that often have a short-lived market value, did in fact sell a Limbo party kit around the time of Holder's article. See www.wham-o.com/about-us/, accessed June 30, 2017, for a history of the company, including its marketing of the slingshot, the Frisbee, the Hula-Hoop, the Superball, the Slip 'N Slide, and other popular toys and fads it manufactured from its founding in 1948.
53. For histories of this movement, see Lynne Fauley Emery, *Black Dance from 1916 to Today* (Princeton, NJ: Dance Horizons, 1988), 241–338; John O. Perpener, *African-American Concert Dance: The Harlem Renaissance and Beyond* (Urbana: University of Illinois Press, 2001); Richard Long, *The Black Tradition in American Dance* (New York: Rizzoli, 1989); and Susan Manning, *Modern Dance, Negro Dance: Race in Motion* (Minneapolis: University of Minnesota Press, 2004).
54. Quoted in Frederick Orme, "The Negro in the Dance as Katherine Dunham Sees Him," *American Dancer* 11 (1938): 46.
55. "G. Holder Dancers in Conn.," *Pittsburgh Courier*, July 3, 1954, 18.
56. Harris, "History, Fable, and Myth," 26–27.
57. Glissant, *Caribbean Discourse*, 61–62.
58. Glissant, 65.
59. Glissant, 71.
60. Glissant, 71–72.
61. Glissant, 76; emphasis in original.
62. Rex Nettleford, "Cultural Resistance in Caribbean Society: Dance and Survival," in *Inward Stretch, Outward Reach: A Voice from the Caribbean* (London: Macmillan, 1993), 108–13.
63. Carmen de Lavallade, personal interview, August 18, 2016.
64. See Program [194], Jacob's Pillow Dance Festival (1956) at http://archives.jacobspillow.org/index.php/Detail/objects/4836, accessed on February 7, 2017. The music for these early performances was written by Japanese composer Toijo Ito, though the music to the set choreography for *Dougla* (1974) and *Belé* (1981) was written by Cuban composer Tania León.
65. Margaret Lloyd, "Dance from Native Folklore." Holder Clippings file, Jerome Robbins Dance Division, New York Public Library for the Performing Arts.

66. Frances Herridge, "Holder and Amaya in Central Park," *New York Post*, June 8, 1957. Holder Clippings file, Jerome Robbins Dance Division, New York Public Library for the Performing Arts. See also Dunning, *Geoffrey Holder*, 140.
67. Geoffrey Holder, *Ethnic Dance: Roundtrip to Trinidad*, directed by Greg Harney, performed by Geoffrey Holder and Company, with Carmen de Lavallade, National Education Television, 1959.
68. Quoted in Leslie Kandell, "A Revival and, as Ever, a Revelation," *New York Times*, April 11, 1999, NJ13.
69. Manning, *Modern Dance, Negro Dance*, 118.
70. Nettleford, "Cultural Resistance in Caribbean Society: Dance and Survival," 108–13; Harris, "History, Fable, and Myth," 26–27.
71. This and the following descriptions of *Belé*, *Banda*, and *Dougla* are collectively drawn from recorded performances available on Geoffrey Holder, *Ethnic Dance: Roundtrip to Trinidad*; *Dance Theatre of Harlem*, Danmarks Radio and WNET/13 New York, directed by Thomas Grimm, 1986, Jerome Robbins Dance Division, New York Public Library for the Performing Arts; *Dougla* video recording 1970?–1979?, Jerome Robbins Dance Division, New York Public Library for the Performing Arts; *Banda* video recording, Dance Theatre of Harlem, 1999, Jerome Robbins Dance Division, New York Public Library for the Performing Arts; and *Carmen and Geoffrey*, directed by Linda Atkinson and Nick Doob (New York: First Run Features, 2009). I am also grateful to Carmen de Lavallade for sharing her memories and impressions of these dances with me.
72. Program [194], Jacob's Pillow Dance Festival (1956), http://archives.jacobspillow.org/index.php/Detail/objects/4836, accessed on February 7, 2017.
73. See Hillary S. Carty's dance instruction guide, *Folk Dances of Jamaica: An Insight* (Alton, Hampshire: Dance Books, 1988), 48–55, for a discussion of the history of the Creole quadrille and detailed notation of its movements. There is a Trinidadian funeral dance that also goes by the name belé, and while the courtly dance Holder choreographs may have its origins in this mourning ritual, belé also serves as a dance of celebration for weddings, carnival, and other village functions.
74. Tobi Tobias, "Exotica Revisited," *New York*, January 26, 1981, 49.
75. See, for example, the close resemblance between reviews of performances as far apart as 1958 and 1982: Kevin Kelly, "Dancers Pristine and Trite: Geoffrey Holder and Company," *Daily Boston Globe*, December 6, 1958, 22, and Anna Kisselgoff, "Dance: Harlem Troupe in Two Holder Premiers," *New York Times*, January 21, 1982, C16.
76. Katherine Dunham, quoted in Emery, *Black Dance from 1916 to Today*, 45; Dunham, *Island Possessed* (Chicago: University of Chicago Press, 1969), 216.
77. Program [241], Jacob's Pillow Dance Festival (1960), http://archives.jacobspillow.org/index.php/Detail/occurrences/4883, accessed on February 7, 2017.
78. Shalini Puri, *The Caribbean Postcolonial: Social Equality, Postnationalism, and Cultural Hybridity* (New York: Palgrave, 2004), 189–222. See also Rhoda Reddock, "Jahaji Bhai: The Emergence of a Dougla Poetics in Trinidad and Tobago," *Identities* 5 (1999): 569–601; Sarah England, "Reading the Dougla Body: Mixed-Race, Post-Race, and Other Narratives of What It Means to Be Mixed in Trinidad," *Latin American and Caribbean Ethnic Studies* 3 (2008): 1–31; and Jennifer Rahim, "Dougla, Half-doogla, Travesao, and the Limits of Hybridity," *Anthurium: A Caribbean Studies Journal* 7 (2010), article 14.
79. Harris, "History, Fable, and Myth," 26–27.

80. See Johannes Fabian, *Time and the Other: How Anthropology Makes Its Object* (New York: Columbia University Press, 1983), 37–69.
81. Douglas Watt, "New Aida." Holder Clippings file, Jerome Robbins Dance Division, New York Public Library for the Performing Arts; Opera review, *Variety*, November 28, 1956, 60.
82. "Geoffrey Holder and Carmen," *Variety*, May 29, 1957, 62; Abel Green, "B'way and B'klyn R&R and Calypso New Test of Vaude-Film Potential," *Variety*, April 24, 1957, 55.
83. Quoted in Hyman Goldberg, "Holders of Endless Talent," *New York Mirror Magazine*, June 15, 1958. Holder Clippings file, Jerome Robbins Dance Division, New York Public Library for the Performing Arts. See also Moss, "Who Is Geoffrey Holder?," 41.
84. Geoffrey Holder, *Black Gods, Green Islands*, with Tom Harshman (New York: Doubleday, 1959), 7, further references will be made parenthetically in the text; Glissant, *Caribbean Discourse*, 61.
85. Selden Rodman, "Exuberant Fabulist of the Caribbean," *New York Herald Tribune*, December 27, 1959, E4.
86. See Ashley Dawson, *Mongrel Nation: Diasporic Culture and the Making of Postcolonial Britain* (Ann Arbor: University of Michigan Press, 2007), 27–48, for an analysis of *The Lonely Londoners* as a calypso novel.
87. Henry Louis Gates Jr., *The Signifying Monkey: A Theory of African American Literary Criticism* (New York: Oxford University Press, 1988), 181.
88. J. Saunders Redding, "Voodoo, Witchcraft Become Normal," *Baltimore Afro-American*, November 21, 1959, A2. See also Esther J. Piercy, "Caribbean Folk Tales," *Baltimore Sun*, November 22, 1959, A9.
89. Ellen W. Goellner, "Force and Form in Faulkner's *Light in August*," in *Bodies of the Text: Dance as Theory, Literature as Dance*, ed. Ellen W. Goellner and Jacqueline Shea Murphy (New Brunswick, NJ: Rutgers University Press, 1995), 184.
90. "Congo Bara" is also the title of a Trinidadian calypso recorded in French patois by the Keskidee Trio (Atilla the Hun, Lord Beginner, and Growling Tiger) with the Gerald Clark Orchestra on Decca Records in 1935. The calypso (about a prison warden named Congo Bara) bears no relationship to Holder's story about dwenns, though Congo Bara may be a mutable folk character who can appear in various situations. It is notable that Holder once said, "the earliest calypso I can recall is 'Congobara' and I heard my mother sing it." Holder, "That Fad from Trinidad," 59.
91. Goellner, "Force and Form in Faulkner's *Light in August*," 185.
92. Gates, *Signifying Monkey*, 199.
93. Claude Lévi-Strauss, *Myth and Meaning: Cracking the Code of Culture* (New York: Schocken Books, 1995 [1978]), 44.
94. Glissant, *Caribbean Discourse*, 71; emphasis in original.
95. Lévi-Strauss, *Myth and Meaning*, 45.
96. Harris, "History, Fable, and Myth," 26–27.
97. "Loew's Metropolitan Sets Calypso Show," *New York Amsterdam News*, April 13, 1957, 14.
98. "Calypso Festival to Make Tour," *Chicago Daily Tribune*, April 7, 1957, E12; "Calypso Fete Opens in East," *Chicago Defender*, May 11, 1957, 8; Richard L. Coe, "Coe Digs That Calypso Beat," *Washington Post*, May 17, 1957, D8.
99. "Rock 'n' Roll vs. Calypso at Loew's," *New York Amsterdam News*, March 30, 1957, 11; Green, "B'way and B'klyn R&R and Calypso New Test of Vaude-Film Potential,"

55; Ren Grevatt, "On the Beat," *Billboard*, April 29, 1957, 61; "Young Mr. Holder is Jack-of-All-Arts." Holder Clippings file, Jerome Robbins Dance Division, New York Public Library for the Performing Arts.

100. "Pit Rock 'n' Roll vs. Calypso for Easter Week Teen Come-on," *Variety*, April 10, 1957, 69; "Rock 'n' Roll Versus Calypso," *Pittsburgh Courier*, April 20, 1957, A20.
101. Walter Terry, "Calypso Dance Festival," *New York Herald Tribune*, April 20, 1957, 10.
102. Terry, "Calypso Dance Festival," 10; Green, "B'way and B'klyn R&R and Calypso New Test of Vaude-Film Potential," 55; Coe, "Coe Digs That Calypso Beat," D8.
103. Terry, "Calypso Dance Festival," 10; Green, "B'way and B'klyn R&R and Calypso New Test of Vaude-Film Potential," 55.
104. Green, "B'way and B'klyn R&R and Calypso New Test of Vaude-Film Potential," 55.
105. Terry, "Calypso Dance Festival," 10.
106. "N.Y.'s Easter Specials; R&R Bklyn Par Ace 150G, State 85G; Satchmo-Roxy Fat HOG, Bklyn Met 50G, Liberace 35G," *Variety*, April 24, 1957, 51.
107. "N.Y.'s Easter Specials," 51; Green, "B'way and B'klyn R&R and Calypso New Test of Vaude-Film Potential," 55.
108. "Tornado from Trinidad," *Time*, May 6, 1957. Holder Clippings file, Jerome Robbins Dance Division, New York Public Library for the Performing Arts.

CONCLUSION

1. For more on Belafonte's censored performance of "Don't Stop the Carnival," see David Bianculli, *Dangerously Funny: The Uncensored Story of "The Smothers Brothers Comedy Hour"* (New York: Touchstone, 2010), 194–205, and Aniko Bodroghkozy, *Groove Tube: Sixties Television and the Youth Rebellion* (Durham, NC: Duke University Press, 2001), 143–45. The censored medley can be viewed at https://www.youtube.com/watch?v=FDDEGBv8Hgc, accessed on June 30, 2017.
2. W. E. B. Du Bois, "Protest," in *Writings: The Suppression of the African Slave-Trade, The Souls of Black Folk, Dusk of Dawn, Essays and Articles*, ed. Nathan Huggins (New York: Library of America, 1986), 1231.
3. Du Bois, "Protest," 1232.
4. Du Bois, *The Souls of Black Folk*, in *Writings*, 363.
5. For a sample, see Leroy Robinson, "Reggae Waits in Wings for Recognition," *Billboard*, November 17, 1973, 32; Ed Ochs, "Disco: Paradox or Paradise," *Billboard*, June 9, 1979, BM16, BM28; Nelson George, "Rapping Records Flooding Stores in N.Y. Market," *Billboard*, December 22, 1979, 37, 53; and David Nathan, "Major Labels Are Suddenly Singing a Different Tune While Indies Grow Stronger as Rap Emerges as the Most Popular and Vital New Music Form of the '80s," *Billboard*, December 24, 1988, R1+.
6. "Rap Records: Are They Fad or Permanent?" *Billboard*, February 16, 1980, 57.
7. Russell Simmons, "Rap Visionary Russell Simmons: 'It's More Than Making Records, It's Building Careers,'" *Billboard*, April 20, 1985, R8; original emphasis.

INDEX

Page numbers in italics indicate illustrations.